What the Hands Reveal about the Brain

The MIT Press Series on Issues in the Biology of Language and Cognition
John C. Marshall, editor

What the Hands Reveal about the Brain, by Howard Poizner, Edward S. Klima, and Ursula Bellugi, 1987

What the Hands Reveal about the Brain

Howard Poizner, Edward S. Klima, and
Ursula Bellugi

A Bradford Book
The MIT Press
Cambridge, Massachusetts
London, England

First MIT Press paperback edition, 1990

This book was set in Palatino by Achorn Graphic Services and printed and bound by Halliday Lithograph in the United States of America.

Library of Congress Cataloging-in-Publication Data

Poizner, Howard.
 What the hands reveal about the brain.

 (MIT Press series on issues in the biology of language and cognition)
 "A Bradford book."
 Bibliography: p.
 Includes index.
 1. Brain damage. 2. Sign language. 3. Deaf—Means of communication. 4. Psycholinguistics. I. Klima, Edward S., 1931–   . II. Bellugi, Ursula, 1931–   .
III. Title. IV. Series. [DNLM: 1. Brain—physiology.
2. Cerebrovascular Disorders—physiopathology.
3. Dominance, Cerebral. 4. Language. 5. Manual Communication. 6. Space Perception—physiology.
WL 355 P758w]
RC387.5.P65 1987   153.6   86-31056
ISBN 0-262-16105-2 (hb)
      0-262-66066-0 (pb)

Contents

Series Foreword

The MIT Press series on Issues in the Biology of Language and Cognition brings new approaches, concepts, techniques, and results to bear on our understanding of the biological foundations of human cognitive capacities. The series will include theoretical, experimental, and clinical work that ranges from the basic neurosciences, clinical neuropsychology, and neurolinguistics to formal modeling of biological systems. Studies in which the architecture of the mind is illuminated by both the fractionation of cognition after brain damage and formal theories of normal performance are specifically encouraged.

John C. Marshall

Preface and Acknowledgments

The long-range objective of our research program has been the study of the biological foundations of human language. At first glance, our studies may seem to take an unusual point of departure—the data come not from spoken language but from a language that has evolved outside of hearing and speech: American Sign Language, the visual-gestural language used by many deaf people in the United States. By investigating brain organization for sign language processing, we seek to illuminate spoken languages as well as signed languages and thus provide insight into brain organization for language in general.

Our view is that one window into brain functioning for language comes from examining its dissolution under conditions of brain damage. The subjects around whom this book centers are six deaf signers who have experienced strokes that impair the left or the right side of the brain. Such subjects, of course, are extremely rare—prelingually deaf signers are rare, and among those the few with unilateral brain damage even more scarce. When we began this study, it was unknown whether or not sign language disorders would follow from localized lesions to the brain, what forms these disorders might take, or what their underlying neural substrate might be.

We focus in this book on what we have learned from examining what are typically left- and right-hemisphere functions in hearing people, but we tailor this examination to the specific domain of deaf people who live in a silent world and communicate through a language of the hands expressed in space. We do not attempt to review the broader domain of studies of aphasia, although the field is now in a lively state of debate. The general issues are addressed by, for example, Arbib, Caplan, and Marshall (1982); Caplan, Lecours, and Smith (1984); Caramazza and Zurif (1978); Damasio and Geschwind (1984); Gardner et al. (1983); Kean (1985); and Marshall (1982). This book presents and elaborates on a specific set of case studies in the context of the interrelated disciplines of linguistics, cognitive psychology, and neuroscience. Our studies provide new perspectives for an understanding of brain organization for language and for visuospatial functions.

One of the most important features of our research has been the close collaboration between hearing and deaf people. Over the course of our studies of the structure, processing, acquisition, and breakdown of American Sign Language, hundreds of deaf people have taken part in many different capacities: researchers, subjects, and informants. Our research group always involved deaf and hearing researchers, in constant interactions in sign language. Among those involved in our studies of sign aphasia are Ben Behan, Amy Bihrle, David Corina, Karen van Hoek, Cheryl Fleck, Leslie Jamison, Shelly Marks, Diane Lillo-Martin, Lucinda O'Grady, Maureen O'Grady, Carol Padden, Laura Petitto, Patricia Richey, Dennis Schemenauer, and James Tucker. The insights and contributions of these researchers are important to the studies presented here.

We are most grateful to the people who were so ready and eager to share their experiences with us: the six special deaf signers represented in this book and their families and friends. We appreciate their sharing personal information. At the same time, we have been careful to preserve their privacy; we have given them pseudonyms, and sometimes changed places and identifying information in irrelevant details. Similarly, the drawings of the sign errors are reconstructions and not semblances of the subjects themselves. Because brain-damaged deaf signers are so rare, we had to travel to different parts of the country to do our testing. The subjects were willing and eager to work with us, and we saw them as often as we could but never as often as we wished; therefore there are occasional gaps in our data. We appreciate the six subjects' willingness to have their stories told, in the interests of contributing to an understanding of deeper issues.

In a book that spans several years of research in an interdisciplinary field of studies, the debt we owe others is great. Many colleagues have contributed in important ways, including Robbin Battison, Emilio Bizzi, Elizabeth Criswell, Antonio Damasio, Hanna Damasio, Dean Delis, Jennings Falcon, Howard Gardner, Norman Geschwind, Harold Goodglass, Nancy Helms-Estabrook, John Hollerbach, Vicente Iragui, Edith Kaplan, Robert Knight, Mark Kritchevsky, Harlan Lane, Arlene Lazerson, Helen Neville, Carol Padden, Frank Phillips, and Edgar Zurif.

Some of the content of three chapters has appeared in previous publications: (1) U. Bellugi, H. Poizner, and E. S. Klima, "Brain organization for language: Clues from sign aphasia," *Human Neurobiology* 2:155–170 (1983); (2) H. Poizner, U. Bellugi, and V. Iragui,

"Apraxia and aphasia in a visual-gestural language," *American Journal of Physiology: Regulatory, Integrative and Comparative Physiology* 246:R868–R883 (1984); (3) H. Poizner, E. Kaplan, U. Bellugi, and C. Padden, "Visual-spatial processing in deaf brain damaged signers," *Brain and Cognition* 3:281–306 (1984). All have been revised and rewritten for this book.

This work could certainly not have been carried out without the research-oriented atmosphere provided by the institutions with which we are affiliated: The Salk Institute for Biological Studies and the University of California at San Diego. The research reported in this book was supported primarily by the National Institutes of Health under grant NS 19096. We also draw on research supported by the NIH under grants HD 13249 and NS 15175, and by the National Science Foundation under grant BNS83-09860. We are grateful for this support.

Finally we thank Harry and Betty Stanton, who first encouraged us to bring together our results into a book and then patiently nurtured us through the process. Frank A. Paul made most of the sign illustrations; we are grateful to Michele Hand and Lisa Churchill for help in typing, proofing, editing and organizing.

Introduction

John C. Marshall

Sign Aphasia in the Context of Modern Neuropsychology

In an early discussion of the psychobiology of human cognition, Noam Chomsky referred to a language as "a specific sound-meaning correspondence." When asked if he thereby meant to exclude sign languages, he replied: "I mean 'signal.' I should have said 'signal-meaning correspondence.' It is an open question whether the sound part is crucial. It could be but certainly there is little evidence to suggest it is" (Chomsky 1967). At the time there was indeed little evidence on which to base an informed judgment about the linguistic status of sign. True, there had appeared, from Gallaudet College, some preliminary indications of the richness of vocabulary to be found in American Sign Language (Stokoe 1960; Stokoe, Casterline, and Croneberg 1965), but for the rest prejudice ran riot.

It was all too easy for the hearing world "to dismiss the manual communication of deaf people as a mishmash of pantomime and iconic signals, eked out by finger spelling" (Marshall 1986b). Communities of deaf people, accustomed through many generations to using ASL as their primary means of communication for everyday needs, intellectual discussion, and the expression of wit, poetry, and drama, knew better. Yet even there the hostility of the dominant culture sometimes led the deaf themselves to incorporate the hearing world's assessment of their language as a primitive pidgin, a gestural analogue of "You Tarzan, me Jane." The comparison with Yiddish is instructive; there, too, surrounding societies often regarded the language as a degenerate form of German baby talk, an assessment that was sometimes shared by those who wanted to "modernize" the culture of the *shtetl* from within. But deaf "speakers" of ASL suffered additional disadvantages. Communicating in a visual language, quite unrelated to spoken English and expressed in a transitory medium even more difficult to notate than classical ballet, a sign language poet could not hope that his or her work would be printed for posterity. Prior to widespread use of cinematography, the deaf literary artist was thus deprived of the permanent record of cultural tradition to which a new Peretz, Landau, or Ansky could further contribute.

Happily, ASL is now alive and well, thriving as the living language of a community and as the object of serious scientific investigation. For the latter we are indebted in large part to the work of the Salk Institute and the University of California, San Diego, where Ursula Bellugi, Edward Klima, and Howard Poizner have, with their colleagues and students, revolutionized our understanding of ASL (Klima and Bellugi 1979). We are beginning to see how universal grammatical categories and features are realized in a four-dimensional moving medium that places very different constraints on the overt expression of linguistic form from those found in spoken (or written) languages. ASL, then, is a language, albeit not just a language like any other (in the dismissive sense of that idiom).

Unhappily, deaf signers are no less likely than the hearing to suffer major brain damage, whether from stroke, tumor, or closed head injury. And it is to the important topic of how to describe and explain (and, in the long term, help to remediate) the cognitive deficits consequent on such trauma and disease that Poizner, Klima, and Bellugi have now turned their attention.

The first paradox presented by a natural language expressed in three dimensions of space and one of time goes back to the very foundations of modern neuropsychology. In 1865, Paul Broca convinced the neurological world that the material substrate for (spoken) language was the *left* cerebral hemisphere in the vast majority of right-handed people (see Berker, Berker, and Smith 1986); in 1876, John Hughlings Jackson first produced evidence to suggest that the *right* hemisphere may play a similarly "leading" role with respect to (many) visuospatial abilities (Jackson 1876). Subsequent discoveries have perhaps modified, but never fundamentally contradicted this picture of complementary hemispheric specialization that could be regarded as the central dogma of neuropsychology. But which hemisphere takes precedence when the communication system simultaneously qualifies as both a language and an extremely precise set of gestures executed in space and perceived visually? The clear and unambiguous answer that emerges from these studies by Poizner, Klima, and Bellugi is that language per se is committed to the left hemisphere, irrespective of the modality whereby language is made manifest. It would seem, then, that the biological foundations of grammatical structure are not to be found exclusively in some privileged interaction between cognitive capacity and the auditory-vocal system (Liberman and Mattingly 1985). Neither is the human brain intrinsically specialized for the "what and the where" of objects in general (Newcombe 1985). Rather, when the objects form part of a linguistic system, their representations are realized by the left hemisphere; when other objects enter into the topographical memory system for place and space, the right hemisphere assumes primary processing responsibility (Landis et al. 1986). In the geography of mind, domain-specific, cognitive computations take precedence over the representation of modality and (purely) physical form (Marshall 1984).

Still more surprisingly, there appear to be strong parallels between the different forms of aphasic impairment in sign and spoken languages, despite the superficial antithesis of the two systems. In spoken languages damage to anterior areas of the left hemisphere often results in a nonfluent aphasia (Grodzinsky 1986): Speech is slow and laborious, often misarticulated; markers of inflectional and derivational processes are simplified or left out; and, in the extreme case, expression may be restricted to major lexical classes (the base forms of nouns, adjectives, and verbs). By contrast, damage to more posterior regions provokes a variety of fluent aphasia: Speech may be fast and flowing until the patient is held up by an inability to retrieve specific lexical items; although mostly produced without apparent effort, speech is contaminated by phonological, morphological, and semantic paraphasias, by copious circumlocution, and by a tendency to "splice together" grammatically incompatible syntactic structures (Butterworth 1985). This basic contrast between two broad classes of aphasic impairment is upheld in the neuronal substrate for sign. Gail D., who suffered an extensive left frontal infarct, was found to have her signing reduced to the production of uninflected, referential open-class signs, stripped of the intricate morphological apparatus of ASL; Paul D., who sustained a subcortical lesion that extended posteriorly to the supramarginal and angular gyri, signed fluently in long, complex sentences, but with numerous inappropriate, even neologistic, jargonlike signs, much lexical and morphological substitution, and erroneous elaboration of sign/inflection combinations. The distinction between frontal "agrammatism" and posterior "paragrammatism" seems to hold good in both signed and spoken languages. Likewise, relatively pure disorders of lexical retrieval are found in both modalities. Karen L., with an infarct centered in the left parietal region, continued to produce a wide range of correct grammatical forms in ASL, but individual lexical items were often semantically underspecified or exhibited sublexical errors analogous to the phonological paraphasias of spoken language impairment.

Although it is far too early for us to have any precise ideas about the extent of neuronal overlap between the physical substrate for spoken and signed language, these findings do indicate broadly congruent cortical and subcortical areas committed to different aspects of modality-neutral language processing. Further advances will depend on the development of information-processing accounts of language disorder that go beyond the nineteenth-century clinical taxonomy of aphasic disorder (Marshall 1986a) and on more fine-grained architectonic analyses of language-committed cells and pathways (Galaburda 1984). Current in vivo imaging techniques show considerable biological variability in the neuronal representation of spoken languages and many counterexamples to the traditional syndrome/lesion correlations (Basso et al. 1985). Whether this variability is any greater in signed than in spoken languages and whether the new scanning technologies will resolve or further complicate the problems of functional localization are critical topics for the future.

And there are yet other classical controversies that the work of Poizner, Klima, and Bellugi enables us to reopen in new form. For example: In an early attack on the adequacy of the Wernicke-Lichtheim taxonomy of the aphasias, Pierre Marie (1906) suggested that the nonfluent (Broca's) aphasias were merely fluent (Wernicke's) aphasias aggravated by dysarthria. The hypothesis has not fared too well, although it still has its supporters. Studies of the sign aphasias allow us to rephrase the issue in terms of the question, Can nonfluent signing impairment be regarded as Wernicke's aphasia plus dyspraxia? And, more generally, What is the relationship between praxic impairment and linguistic impairment? Although the higher-level (ideational and ideomotor) apraxias are preferentially associated with left-hemisphere damage, current studies show that apraxias and (spoken language) aphasias can be doubly dissociated (Selnes et al. 1982; Basso and Capitani 1985). The results of Poizner, Klima, and Bellugi support this position in a strong form; aphasia and apraxia can dissociate even when both language and skilled action are overtly expressed by motor performance of the upper limbs. Modularity with a vengeance! The conclusion is further reinforced by the dissociations seen after right-hemisphere damage; here also a dramatic impairment in the cognition of spatial topography (objects in extrapersonal space) can coexist with a relatively intact execution of spatially encoded syntactic structures. Once again, the innate specialization of the right hemisphere for manipulating spatial relationships is constrained by the cognitive domain within which particular places, spaces, and movements fall (Bisiach et al. 1981). Space in the service of language falls within the competence of the left hemisphere.

These, then, are just a few of the intellectual treasures revealed in *What the Hands Reveal about the Brain.*

References

Basso, A., and Capitani, E. 1985. "Spared musical abilities in a conductor with global aphasia and ideomotor apraxia." *Journal of Neurology, Neurosurgery and Psychiatry* 48:407–412.

Basso, A., Lecours, A. R., Moraschini, S., and Vanier, M. 1985. "Anatomoclinical correlations of the aphasias as defined through computerized tomography: Exceptions." *Brain and Language* 26:201–229.

Berker, E. A., Berker, A. H., and Smith, A. 1986. "Translation of Broca's 1865 report: Localization of speech in the third left frontal convolution." *Archives of Neurology* 43:1065–1072.

Bisiach, E., Capitani, E., Luzzatti, C., and Perani, D. 1981. "Brain and conscious representation of outside reality." *Neuropsychologia* 19:543–551.

Butterworth, B. 1985. "Jargon aphasia: Processes and strategies," in *Current Perspectives in Dysphasia*, S. Newman and R. Epstein, eds. London: Churchill Livingstone.

Chomsky, N. 1967. "The general properties of language," in *Brain Mechanisms Underlying Speech and Lanuage*, C. H. Millikan and F. L. Darley, eds. New York: Grune and Stratton, 73–80.

Galaburda, A. M. 1984. "The anatomy of language: Lessons from comparative anatomy," in *Biological Perspectives on Language*, D. Caplan, A. R. Lecours, and A. Smith, eds. Cambridge, Mass.: The MIT Press, 290–302.

Grodzinsky, Y. 1986. "Language deficits and the theory of syntax." *Brain and Language* 27:135–159.

Jackson, J. H. 1876. "Case of large cerebral tumor without optic neuritis and with left hemiplegia and imperception." *Royal London Ophthalmic Hospital Reports* 8:434–440.

Klima, E. S., and Bellugi, U. 1979. *The Signs of Language*. Cambridge, Mass.: Harvard University Press.

Landis, T., Cummings, J. L., Benson, D. F., and Palmer, E. P. 1986. "Loss of topographic familiarity: An environmental agnosia." *Archives of Neurology* 43:132–136.

Liberman, A. M., and Mattingly, I. G. 1985. "The motor theory of speech perception revised." *Cognition* 21:1–36.

Marie, P. 1906. "Révision de la question de l'aphasie: La troisième circonvolution frontale gauche ne joue aucun rôle spécial dans la fonction du langage." *Semaine médicale* 26:241–266.

Marshall, J. C. 1984. "Multiple perspectives on modularity." *Cognition* 17:209–242.

Marshall, J. C. 1986a. "The description and interpretation of aphasic language disorder." *Neuropsychologia* 24:5–24.

Marshall, J. C. 1986b. "Signs of language in the brain." *Nature* 322:307–308.

Newcombe, F. 1985. "Neuropsychology *qua* interface." *Journal of Clinical and Experimental Neuropsychology* 7:663–681.

Selnes, O. A., Rubens, A. B., Risse, G. L., and Levy, R. S. 1982. "Transient aphasia with persistent apraxia: Uncommon sequela of massive left-hemisphere stroke." *Archives of Neurology* 39:122–126.

Stokoe, W. C. 1960. *Sign Language Structure*. Studies in Linguistics, Occasional Papers 8. Department of Anthropology and Linguistics, University of Buffalo, New York.

Stokoe, W. C., Casterline, D., and Croneberg, C. 1965. *A Dictionary of American Sign Language*. Washington, D.C.: Gallaudet College Press.

What the Hands Reveal about the Brain

Chapter 1

Preliminaries: Language in a Visual Modality

In all known societies of hearing people, language takes the form of speech. In the course of human evolution, the vocal tract, the breathing organs and muscles, and the brain have all developed in conjunction with spoken language. Until recently, nearly everything learned about the human capacity for language came from the study of spoken languages. It has been assumed that the organizational properties of language are inseparably connected with the sounds of speech. The fact that, normally, language is spoken and heard presumably determined in part the basic structural principles of grammar. There is good evidence that the structures involved in breathing, chewing, and the ingestion of food have evolved into a versatile and more efficient system for producing sound. Studies of brain organization for language indicate that the left cerebral hemisphere is specialized for linguistic material in the vocal-auditory mode and that the major language-mediating areas of the brain are intimately connected with the vocal-auditory channel. It has even been argued by some that hearing and speech are necessary prerequisites to the development of cerebral specialization for language in the individual (McKeever et al. 1976). Thus the link between biology and linguistic behavior has been identified with the auditory modality, the particular modality in which language has naturally developed.

Language, however, is not limited to the vocal tract and ears. There also exist systems of symbolic communication, passed down from one generation of deaf people to the next, that have become forged into autonomous languages not derived from spoken languages. These visual-gestural languages of the deaf, with deep roots in the visual modality, provide a testing ground for competing explanations of how the brain is organized for language, how the brain came to be so organized, and how modifiable that organization is.

One direct window into brain organization for language is language breakdown under conditions of brain damage. A century of investigating deficits in the spoken language of brain-damaged patients has revealed that the neural substrate for language is primarily in the left cerebral hemisphere. Moreover, localized damage to the left hemisphere produces differentiated patterns of language impairment, depending on the site of the lesion. Unlike spoken languages, however, sign languages make use of visuospatial distinctions. Although the left hemisphere has the dominant role in processing spoken languages it is the right hemisphere that is dominant for processing visuospatial relations. This specialization of the right hemisphere is particularly important because in sign language many grammatical processes crucially involve spatial relations and the manipulation of space by the signer.

Over the past years we have enjoyed a rare opportunity to delve into the biological foundations of language. The focus of our study has been the analysis of the breakdown of sign language following localized brain damage in deaf signers. The implications of brain organization for sign language reach far beyond issues in sign language processing per se. Indeed, the study of sign language breakdown promises to uncover the basic principles underlying both the specialization of the two cerebral hemispheres and their functional modifiability.

Let us begin with the nature of American Sign Language (ASL) itself. ASL is the visual-gestural language of the deaf community in the United States. Like other sign languages, ASL has developed its own linguistic mechanisms, independent of the spoken language of the surrounding community, American English. As we show, ASL is a fully developed natural language with a highly complex grammar; it serves everyday conversation, intellectual argumentation, wit, and poetry. Research on ASL allows us to raise some fundamental questions about the determinants of language form: What is language like when produced with the hands and perceived by the eyes? How is it different from simple gestural communication? So long as our knowledge of language structure is based solely on studies of language in a single modality, we cannot know whether that structure is merely the product of the transmission modality or of some more basic cognitive requirements, or both. Our findings about ASL—about the structure and organization of a language in a modality entirely different from that of speech—provide some fascinating clues to the resolution of this issue.

1.1 Modality and Language Form

The fact that signed languages use as articulators the hands, face, and body rather than the vocal tract suggests that spoken and signed languages might be vastly different from one another and that signed languages might lack some of the properties shared by grammars of spoken languages. It has long been thought that there is a highly privileged speech-language connection (Liberman 1982). However, despite the differences in resources provided by the two forms of communication, signed languages have been demonstrated to be highly constrained, following general restrictions on structure and organization comparable to those proposed for spoken languages. Research on ASL shows that this visual-gestural system exhibits formal structuring at the same two levels as spoken languages: a sublexical level of structure internal to the sign (the phonological level in spoken languages) and a level of structure that specifies the ways in which signs are bound together into sentences (the grammatical level). ASL does share principles of organization with spoken languages, but the realization of those principles occurs in formal devices arising from the different possibilities afforded by a language in three-dimensional space.

1.1.1   Sublexical Structure in the Hands

There is a sublexical structure to signs of ASL. Signs are composed of representatives of classes of sublexical components. The parameters within which sublexical contrasts in ASL signs occur are Hand Configuration, Place of Articulation, and Movement (Klima and Bellugi 1979; Stokoe, Casterline, and Croneberg 1965). These are roughly comparable to parameters of spoken language that provide for, for example, consonant/vowel distinction and, in languages such as Chinese, lexical tone. The number of configurations that the hand can physically assume, the number of possible places of articulation, and the number of possible different kinds of movements are large indeed. Yet ASL uses only a limited set of these sublexical components. Each parameter has a limited number of representatives, or values, which serve to differentiate lexical signs (figure 1.1). The sign forms that we gloss as CANDY, APPLE, and JEALOUS, for example, differ only in hand configuration (in the appendix we give the notation conventions used in this book); the signs SUMMER, UGLY, and DRY differ only in place of articulation (the forehead, nose, and chin, respectively); and the signs TAPE, CHAIR, and TRAIN differ only in movement. Like spoken languages, sign languages have a highly restricted inventory of elements and systematic restrictions on the ways in which sublexical components can combine. Although the values of the different parameters are arrayed concurrently with respect to one another in a layered fashion, there is sequentiality in the sublexical structure when more than one representative of a parame-

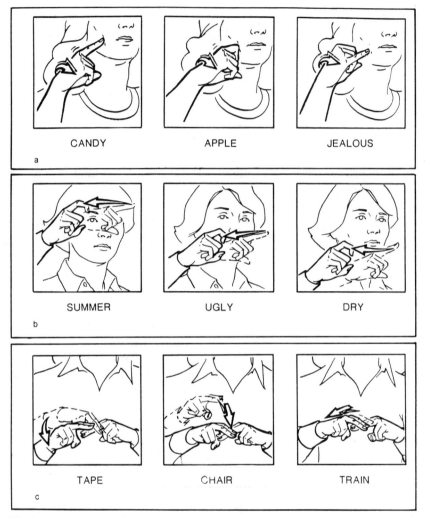

CANDY   APPLE   JEALOUS

a

SUMMER   UGLY   DRY

b

TAPE   CHAIR   TRAIN

Figure 1.1
Minimal contrasts illustrating major formal parameters of ASL sign: (a) Hand
Configuration, (b) Place of Articulation, (c) Movement.

ter occurs in a single sign: two Hand Configurations, for example, or two Movements (Liddell 1984; Liddell and Johnson 1985; Wilbur, Klima, and Bellugi 1983; Padden, in press; Supalla 1982, 1985).

Moreover, despite the vast differences in the transmission modalities of sign and speech, both language systems reflect the same underlying principles, principles that determine the internal organization of their basic lexical units. Clearly, these principles do not originate in the constraints of a particular transmission system. This sameness of principles suggests that the constraints determining linguistic structure arise at a more central level (Bellugi and Studdert-Kennedy 1980; Studdert-Kennedy and Lane 1980). In what follows we offer some evidence for the sublexical structure of sign and for the parallels between the structure of ASL and that of speech.

Studies of historical change in signs over the past century show that the direction of change in particular signs has uniformly been away from the more iconic and representational to the more arbitrary and constrained, hence toward conformity to a tighter linguistic system (Frishberg 1975). A classic example of this historical change is shown in the ASL sign HOME, originally a merged compound of the highly representative signs EAT and SLEEP (figure 1.2). In EAT an /0/ handshape moves as if bringing food to the mouth; SLEEP is an open palm laid on the cheek. Today, owing to processes of compounding and historical change, HOME is a unitary sign with a single handshape, touching two places on the cheek. The iconicity of the original two signs has been completely lost; HOME is one of the more abstract signs of ASL. Historical changes such as this one suggest that there are systematic pressures within ASL that constrain its lexical elements in regular, formationally based ways, resulting in more abstract, arbitrary forms.

Observational evidence for the sublexical structure of a sign language such as ASL comes from slips of the hands, which, like slips of the tongue (Fromkin 1973), yield valuable information about the organization of the language (Klima and Bellugi 1979, chapter 5; Newkirk et al. 1980). A subject intending to sign SICK, BORED (meaning 'I am sick and tired'), for instance, inadvertently switched the hand shapes of the two signs, keeping all other parameters the same (see figure 1.3a). This slip results in two possible but nonexistent sign forms. The figure also shows transpositions of Place of Articulation and of Movement parameters in slips of the hand from ASL signers. In such slips of the hand, the typical errors are not actual ASL signs but rather *possible* signs constructed from the restricted set of available Hand Configurations, Movements, and Places of Articulation making up the signs of ASL. They are never arbitrary errors, never movements or handshapes that do not occur in the language. The signer

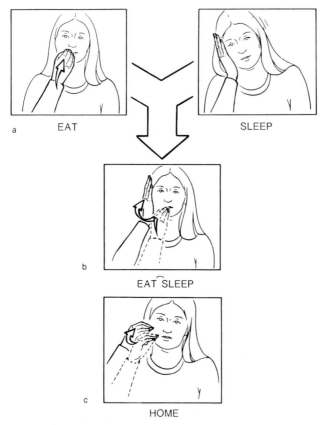

Figure 1.2
The suppression of iconicity through historical change in compounds. (a) Mimetic signs EAT and SLEEP. (b) The formal compound EAT and SLEEP meaning 'home.' (c) The modern opaque merged sign HOME.

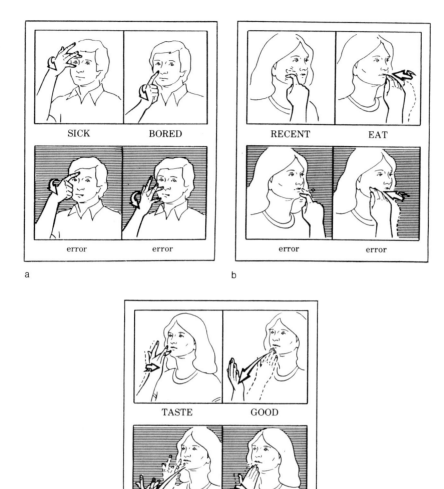

c

Figure 1.3
Transpositions of formal parameters in unintended slips of the hand, showing the independence of components in ASL signs: transpositions of (a) Hand Configuration, (b) Place of Articulation, and (c) Movement.

makes the erroneous form consistent with the systematically constrained combination of parameter values in ASL. Moreover, these are errors of combination rather than errors of selection; that is, they reflect a "reshuffling" of what was intended rather than an erroneous selection of a possible sign form. Slips of the hand thus provide impressive evidence that the sublexical components postulated have psychological reality as independent units at a level of programming prior to the actual articulation of a string.

A variety of experimental evidence also confirms the sublexical structure in sign. For example, deaf signers uniformly code ASL signs in short-term memory experiments on the basis of the component elements of signs. Intrusion errors in the immediate short-term recall of lists of signs share formational rather than semantic or iconic properties with the presented signs (Bellugi, Klima, and Siple 1975; Bellugi and Siple 1974). Commonly, the sign presented and the error differ by only one formational parameter. Moreover, just as phonological similarity among words causes interference in the short-term recall of lists of words, formational (but not semantic) similarity of signs interferes with the short-term recall of lists of ASL signs (Poizner, Bellugi, and Tweney 1981). These experimental studies indicate that the formational parameters of signs have significance in processing as well as structured significance linguistically.

Comparison of two different sign languages with independent histories, ASL and Chinese Sign Language (CSL), also shows parallelism with sublexical structure in spoken languages. Among spoken languages there are two kinds of systematic differences: differences in the elements that comprise morphemes and differences in the ways in which these elements can be combined. A sound or a sound combination that occurs in one language may be impossible in another. Figure 1.4a shows the different signs for FATHER and SUSPECT in ASL and CSL. Even the inventories of components (Hand Configurations, Places of Articulation, and Movements) differ in ASL and CSL, and, moreover, even when the two sign languages use the same elements, there are systematic differences in the ways in which the elements can combine. Figure 1.4b shows the same handshape and its differing uses in the two sign languages. In ASL the common contacting region for this handshape with another hand is with thumb and index finger, illustrated in the ASL signs COUNT, INTERPRET, VOTE, and JOIN. By contrast, in CSL the same handshape can make contact on or with the three extended fingers, as shown in figure 1.4b, in NAME, ENROLL, SUMMARY, and TOPIC. This contact region, perfectly acceptable and common in CSL, is not an allowed form in ASL. Thus we see that, even when the same component is used in the two

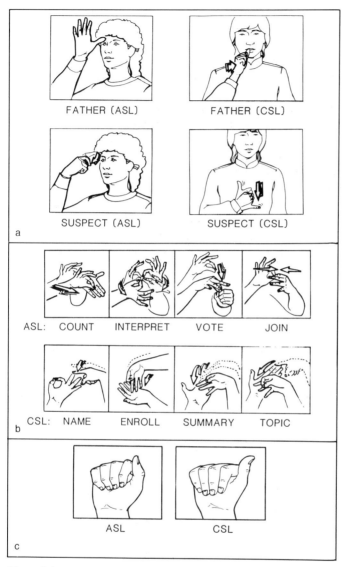

FATHER (ASL)   FATHER (CSL)

SUSPECT (ASL)   SUSPECT (CSL)

a

ASL: COUNT   INTERPRET   VOTE   JOIN

CSL: NAME   ENROLL   SUMMARY   TOPIC

b

ASL   CSL

c

Figure 1.4
Contrast between two different sign languages: Chinese and American Sign Languages. (a) Differing ASL and CSL signs. (b) Differing morpheme structure constraints in the use of the pinching handshape in ASL and CSL. (c) "Phonetic" differences between ASL and CSL Hand Configurations.

sign languages, there may be differing morpheme structure constraints. Furthermore, we have identified fine-level "phonetic" differences that occur systematically between the two sign languages, just as there are phonetic differences between spoken languages (as in the difference between American and French /n/ sounds). Even something as simple as hand closure differs systematically between CSL and ASL. Both signed languages use a closed fist handshape, which occurs in many signs, as shown in the Chinese sign for FATHER. However, there are characteristic differences in hand closure and thumb placement, as illustrated in figure 1.4c. The ASL handshape has a more relaxed closure with the thumb resting on the fist; the CSL handshape characteristically has a more tensed closure of the fingers into the palm, with the thumb stretched outward. These fine phonetic level differences lead to something like a foreign accent when native users of one sign language learn the other (Klima and Bellugi 1979; Fok, Bellugi, and Lillo-Martin 1986).

Finally, native signers reveal an awareness of the internal structure of signs in their creation of poetic sign forms and plays on signs (Klima and Bellugi 1978). The creative use of language regularly and deliberately manipulates sublexical sign components. In poetic sign, for example, one handshape may recur throughout a passage, forming a kind of alliteration or a play on signs. One value of a parameter may be deliberately substituted for another, producing wit. This deliberate manipulation of elements of a linguistic system clearly reflects signers' intuitive awareness of this aspect of linguistic form (Klima and Bellugi 1979).

There can be no doubt that both types of language system—sign and speech—reflect similar underlying principles. It is important to note, however, that signs and words do not have the same internal structure in all respects. Their sublexical units combine differently in the formation of morphemes. The elements that distinguish English words from one another appear in contrasting linear order; the elements that distinguish ASL signs are preferentially arrayed concurrently in a layered structure. The predominance of concurrent layering, however, is most evident in the morphological processes found in ASL.

1.1.2 Three-dimensional Morphology

It had long been thought that sign languages lacked grammar, but recent research has shown that ASL and other sign languages have highly articulated grammars that are as complex and expressive as those of spoken languages. It turns out, however, that the grammatical processes of ASL are conditioned in important ways by the modality. In particular, many grammatical mechanisms elaborately exploit the spatial medium and the possibilities of multilayered structure.

Like spoken languages, ASL has developed grammatical markers that serve as inflectional and derivational morphemes; there are regular changes in form associated with systematic changes in meaning across syntactic classes of lexical items. Some morphologically marked distinctions in ASL happen not to be marked by grammatical inflections in English—another indication of the autonomy of ASL—although they are so marked in other spoken languages. Morphological processes in ASL typically involve changes in features of movement of sign forms. Figure 1.5 shows a variety of these derivational processes; note that members of pairs or of triplets share the same root (Hand Configuration, Place of Articulation, Movement Shape) and yet differ from one another by features of movement, such as manner, speed, tension, and number and type of repetition. Figure 1.5 illustrates examples of some of the various derivational processes we have found in ASL, including the derivation of deverbal nouns from verbs (a form meaning 'comparison' related to a form meaning the sign COMPARE), nominalizations from verbs ('the activity of measuring' related to a form meaning MEASURE), derivation of predicates from nouns ('proper' related to a form meaning BUSINESS), sentence adverbials from signs ('unexpectedly' related to a form meaning WRONG), characteristic predicates from adjectival signs ('vain' related to a form meaning PRETTY), and derivations for extended or figurative meaning (a form meaning 'acquiesce' related to QUIET). Frequently, these devices result in whole families of signs that are related in form and meaning (Bellugi and Newkirk 1980). An example is shown in figure 1.5g: the sign CHURCH has a derivationally related predicate meaning 'pious' and a related idiomatic derivative meaning 'narrow-minded.'

We have described derivational processes in ASL that typically change grammatical category (for example, verb to noun). ASL verb and noun signs also undergo a wide variety of inflectional processes, again characteristically affecting patterns of movement and spatial contour co-occuring with root forms. As shown in figure 1.6, verb signs in ASL undergo inflections for specifying their arguments (subject and object), for reciprocity ('to each other,' for example), for distinction of grammatical number ('to both,' 'to many'), for distinction of distributional aspect ('to each,' 'to any,' 'to certain ones at different times'), for distinction of temporal aspect ('for a long time,' 'over and over again,' 'uninterruptedly,' 'regularly'), for distinction of

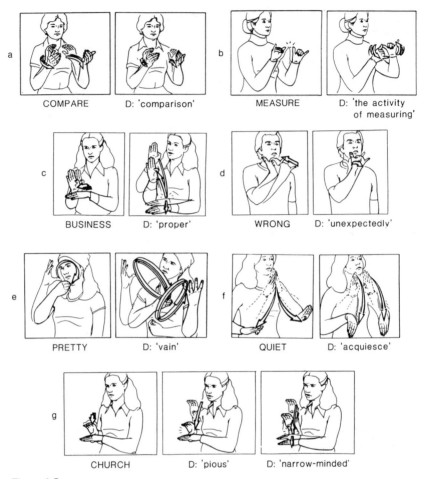

Figure 1.5
Derivationally related sets of forms in ASL. (a) The formation of deverbal nouns. (b) Nominalizations from verbs. (c) Derivation of predicates from nouns. (d) Sentence adverbials from basic signs. (e) Characteristic predicates from basic signs. (f) Derivations for extended or figurative meaning. (g) Predicate form of the sign CHURCH meaning 'pious' and a related idiomatic derivative meaning 'narrow-minded.'

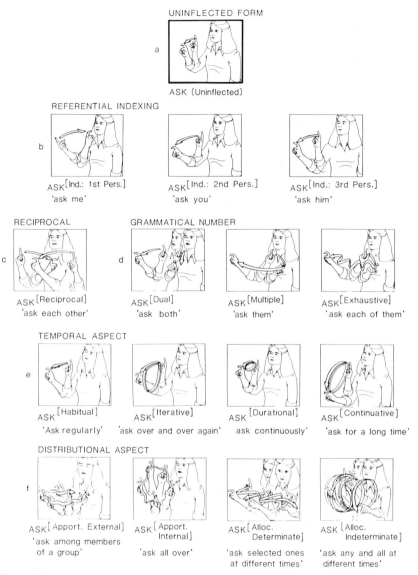

Figure 1.6
Layered inflectional processes in different grammatical categories stemming from a single root. (a) The uninflected sign ASK. (b) Distinctions of referential indexing. (c) A reciprocal form. (d) Marking for grammatical number. (e) Marking for temporal aspect. (f) Marking for distributional aspect.

temporal focus ('starting to,' 'increasingly,' 'resulting in'), and for distinction of manner ('with ease,' 'readily'), among others.

In ASL, which is rich in morphology, families of sign forms are related by an underlying root: The forms in figure 1.6 share a hand-shape /G/, a location (plane in front of body), and a local movement shape (closing of the index finger). Inflectional and derivational processes represent the interaction of the root with other features of movement in space (dynamics of movement, manner of movement, directions of movement); these, along with spatial array, doubling of the hands, and reduplication, are all layered, as it were, on the sign root. Thus a single root form—such as the one underlying ASK—has a wide variety of manifestations (see figure 1.6).

In the *kinds* of distinctions that are morphologically marked, ASL is similar to many spoken languages. In the *degree* to which morphological marking is a favored form of patterning in the language, ASL is again similar to some spoken languages. In the *form* by which lexical items are systematically modified, however, ASL may have aspects that are unique. What appears striking in ASL morphology is that the stem, derivational patterns, and inflectional patterns can co-occur as layered in the final surface form; these forms can be spatially (as well as temporally) nested within one another.

The numerous morphological processes in ASL are conveyed by combinations of a limited number of formal components; these components, which consist of the structured use of space and movement, are peculiar to the visual-gestural mode. Spatial components, such as geometric arrays (circles, lines, arcs), planar locus (vertical, horizontal), and direction of movement (upward, downward, sideways), primarily involve the manipulation of forms in space, and they figure significantly in the structure of inflections for indexing, reciprocity, grammatical number, and distributional aspect. Movement qualities, such as end manner (continuous versus hold), tension (tense versus lax), and rate (fast versus slow), figure significantly in the structure of inflections for temporal aspect, focus, manner, and degree. Two components—cyclicity (single cycle versus reduplicated) and hand use (one hand or two hands)—interact with other components to form inflections in several grammatical categories.

1.1.3   Recursive Rules: Nesting of Morphological Forms

In ASL inflectional processes can combine with root signs, creating different levels of form and meaning. In these combinations the output of one inflectional process can serve as the input for another (can be recursive), and there can also be alternative orderings, which produce different levels of semantic structure. Figure 1.7 shows the unin-

a   GIVE (uninflected)

b   GIVE [Durational]
     'give continuously'

c   GIVE [Exhaustive]
     'give to each'

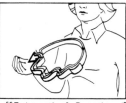

d   GIVE [[Exhaustive] Durational]
     'give to each, that action
     recurring over time'

e   GIVE [[Durational] Exhaustive]
     'give continuously to each in turn'

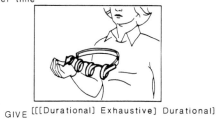

f   GIVE [[[Durational] Exhaustive] Durational]
     'give continuously to each in turn,
     that action recurring over time'

Figure 1.7
Recursive nesting of morphological processes in ASL. (a) The uninflected sign GIVE.
(b, c) GIVE under single inflections. (d) One combination of inflections (Exhaustive in
Durational). (e) Another combination of inflections (Durational in Exhaustive). (f) Recursive applications of rules (Durational in Exhaustive in Durational).

flected sign GIVE (figure 1.7a), the sign under the durational inflection meaning 'give continuously' (figure 1.7b), and, alternatively, the sign under the exhaustive inflection meaning 'give to each' (figure 1.7c). The exhaustive form of GIVE can itself undergo the durational inflection (figure 1.7d). The resulting form means 'to give to each that action recurring over time.' Conversely, the durational form of GIVE can also undergo the exhaustive inflection (figure 1.7e), the resulting form meaning 'to give continuously to each in turn.' And the output in figure 1.7e can once again undergo the durational inflection: The durational of the exhaustive of the durational of GIVE means something like 'to give continuously to each in turn that action recurring over time.' This creation of complex expressions through the recursive application of hierarchically organized rules is also characteristic of the structure of spoken languages. The form such complex expressions take in this visual-gestural language, however, is certainly unique: the sign stem embedded in the pattern created by a morphological process with that pattern itself nested spatially in a pattern created by the same or a different morphological process. The proliferation of co-occurring components throughout the language makes it obvious that ASL tends toward conflation, toward the systematic packaging of a great deal of information in co-occurring layers of structure.

1.2 *Spatially Organized Syntax and Discourse*

We now turn to a domain in which the nature of the apparatus used in ASL may have its most striking effect: the means by which relations among signs are stipulated in sentences and in discourse. The requirements of a spatially organized syntax may be especially revealing for the neurological substrate of language. The most distinctive use of space in ASL is in its role in syntax and discourse, especially in pronominal reference, verb agreement, anaphoric reference, and the referential spatial framework for discourse. Languages have different ways of marking grammatical relations among their lexical items. In English it is primarily order that marks the basic grammatical relations among verbs and their arguments; in other spoken languages it is the morphology of case marking or verb agreement that signals these relations. By contrast, ASL specifies relations among signs primarily through the manipulation of sign forms in space. A horizontal plane in front of the signer's torso plays an important role in the structure of the language and not just as an articulatory space accommodating hand and arm movements as the mouth accommodates the tongue. In this language space itself carries linguistic meaning.

Grammatical relations in ASL, such as subject and object of the verb, are specified in several distinct ways. One of these mechanisms involves the relative order of the signs in the clause. In clauses with transitive verbs in ASL, the subject noun phrase occurs directly before the verb. As a formal syntactic mechanism, this is equivalent to the determination of grammatical relations through word order. This is a mechanism also found in English. A second mechanism that identifies subject and object of the verb in ASL is essentially spatial in nature, and it is this device that we describe in more detail. The class of inflecting verbs in ASL is a large one; inflecting verbs are verbs whose paths are mutable with respect to points in signing space. In this way the subject and/or object of the verb is expressed. For many of these verbs, such as GIVE, the subject of the verb is defined by the initial point and the object is defined by the final point; however, there are ASL verbs for which the role relations with respect to the loci are reversed, as in WELCOME. Thus inflecting verb signs move between abstract loci in signing space to indicate the grammatical function (subject, object) of their arguments.

A nominal introduced into ASL discourse can be associated with an arbitrary locus in a horizontal plane of signing space, provided that another nominal in the discourse frame has not already been associated with that locus. Subsequent reference to that locus (by verb agreement or by pointing) is the equivalent of pronominal reference in ASL. In signed discourse pointing again to a specific assigned locus clearly "refers back" to a previously mentioned nominal, even with many other signs intervening. This spatial indexing allows explicit coreference and may even reduce ambiguity. In English the intended reference of lexical pronouns is often unclear. The sentence "He said he hit him and then he fell down" fails to specify which pronouns refer to the same noun, that is, which are coreferential. The spatial mechanisms used in ASL, by contrast, require that the identities of the referents be maintained across arbitrary points in space. In ASL the failure to maintain such identities results in strings that are ill-formed, rather than in strings that are simply unclear. Among the special facts about ASL pronouns to be borne in mind are (1) there is potentially an indefinite number of formal pronominal distinctions (because any arbitrary point in the appropriate plane of signing space can serve as a referential locus); (2) the referents are unambiguous, at least within the confines of a given discourse frame; and (3) linguistic reference, under a variety of circumstances, can shift (Lillo-Martin and Klima 1986).

We illustrate aspects of the use of spatial loci for referential index-ing, coreference, verb agreement, and the use of spaces embedded within spaces (figure 1.8). Figure 1.8a presents a sample sentence with an embedded clause, in which the subjects of the main clause and of the embedded clause differ. The same signs in the same order but with a change in the direction of the spatial endpoints of the verb would indicate a different grammatical relation. Figure 1.8b illustrates the spatial arrangement of the multiclausal sentence meaning John encouraged him to urge her to permit each of them to take up the class. Because verb agreement may be given spatially, sentences whose signs are made in different temporal orders can still convey the same meaning. Spatial indexing thus permits a certain freedom of word order (in simple sentences, at any rate) while providing clear specification of grammatical relations by spatial means. Different spaces may be used to contrast events, to indicate reference to time preceding the utterance, and to express hypotheticals and counterfac-tuals. It is also possible to embed one subspace within another sub-space, as in embedding a past-time context within conditional subspace, as illustrated in figure 1.8c.

Overall, then, the ASL system of spatialized syntax is similar in *function* to grammatical devices found in the spoken languages of the world (Bellugi and Klima 1982b). However, in its *form*—marking con-nections among spatial points—spatially organized syntax in ASL bears the clear imprint of the mode in which the language evolved (Padden 1983, in press; Lillo-Martin and Klima 1986; Lillo-Martin 1986).

This spatial referential framework for syntax and discourse is fur-ther complicated by interacting mechanisms. Although the referential system described is a *fixed* system in which nominals remain associ-ated with specific points in space until specifically "erased," the spa-tial referential framework sometimes *shifts*; for example, third-person referents may be assigned to the locus in front of the signer's torso, which otherwise denotes self-reference. When this shift occurs, the whole spatial plane rotates, and previously established nominals are now associated with new points, as illustrated in figure 1.9.

The different systems mentioned here (pronominal reference, verb agreement, coreferentiality, and spatial contexts) make complex and dynamic use of space. In each subsystem there is mediation between the visuospatial mode and the overlaid grammatical constraints in the language. Because the syntax of ASL relies so heavily on the manipu-lation of abstract points in space and on spatial representation, the processing of linguistic structures involves the processing of visuo-spatial relations. Obviously, no such processing is required in spoken

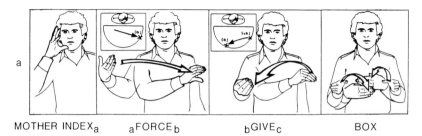

MOTHER INDEX$_a$ $_a$FORCE$_b$ $_b$GIVE$_c$ BOX

"Mother$_i$ forced him$_j$ to give him$_k$ the box."

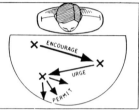

JOHN ENCOURAGE$_a$ $_a$URGE$_b$ $_b$PERMIT$_c$[Exhaustive] TAKE-UP CLASS

"John encouraged him$_i$ to urge her$_j$ to permit each of them$_k$ to take up the class."

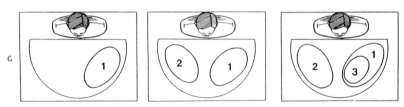

Figure 1.8
Syntactic spatial mechanisms in ASL. (a) A spatially organized sentence in ASL showing nominal establishment and verb agreement. (b) Spatial reference diagram for multiclausal sentence. (c) Embedded spatial references, one subspace within another.

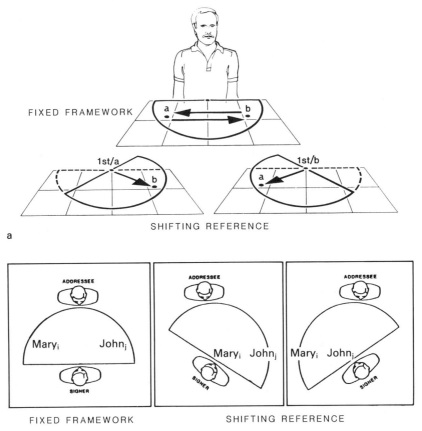

Figure 1.9
Fixed and shifting frames of reference in ASL syntax, as illustrated by (a) verb agreement, and (b) nominal establishment. The arrows in (a) represent different directions of
movement of the verbs, reflecting alternative ways of indicating 'a verbed b' and 'b
verbed a.' The diagrams in (b) illustrate the assignment of noun phrases to arbitrary loci
in signing space. In the fixed framework the third-person loci remain constant. In the
shifting framework the whole spatial plane rotates, and previously established nouns
are reassigned to new spatial loci.

languages. This difference between the surface form of syntactic mechanisms in spoken and signed languages may have important consequences for the way in which a visuospatial language is represented in the brain. We discuss some of these implications throughout the chapters that follow.

Despite the important differences in form, signed and spoken languages clearly share underlying structural principles. Like spoken language, sign language exhibits formal structuring at the lexical and grammatical levels, similar kind and degree of morphological patterning, and a complex, highly rule-governed grammatical and syntactic patterning. The implications of representation of a visuospatial language can be brought out by investigating the additional two perspectives that close this chapter: sign language acquisition and sign language perception and processing.

1.3   Acquiring a Visual-gestural Language

Studies of children's acquisition of spoken language have illuminated both the nature of linguistic systems and the child's natural propensity for linguistic analysis. Children who are learning a language analyze underlying grammatical rules, and their course of development can be revealing of the linguistic structure. Because visual-gestural language is unlike spoken language in the ways we have described, one might expect to find that sign language is acquired in radically different ways from spoken languages. In fact, the similarity in the acquisition of signed and spoken language is remarkable. The differences that do appear reflect the spatial nature of sign language organization. In what follows we discuss some developments in the acquisition of the spatial mechanisms of ASL by deaf children of deaf parents, including pronominal reference, the morphological inflections associated with verb agreement, and the syntactic system of referential spatial indexing (Bellugi and Klima 1982a, 1982b; Boyes-Braem 1981; Hoffmeister and Wilbur 1980; Lillo-Martin 1986; Loew 1982; Maxwell 1980; Newport and Meier, in press; Newport and Supalla 1980; Petitto 1983; Pettito and Bellugi, in press; Supalla 1982).

1.3.1   Pronominal Signs: The Transition from Gesture to Symbol

Deixis in spoken languages is considered a verbal surrogate for pointing; in ASL, however, it *is* pointing. The pronominal signs in ASL meaning 'I' and 'you' are, in fact, the same pointing gestures used by hearing people to give their words a nonverbal supplement. Thus we would expect the acquisition in ASL of pronominal reference to self and addressee to be easy, early, and error free, even though in the development of spoken languages pronoun reversal errors are found in young children. Instead, despite the identity of ASL pronouns with nonlinguistic gestures, the course of their acquisition is startlingly similar to that in spoken languages. Deaf infants between 9 and 11 months of age point freely for investigating and indicating and for drawing attention to themselves and others, as do hearing children. During the second year, however, something dramatic happens. The deaf children stop pointing to themselves or their addressee; in fact, they seem to avoid such pointing. During this period their language development evinces a steady growth in sign vocabulary, which they use stably in a variety of contexts and in multisign sentences. The next period sees the reemergence of pointing to self and addressee but now as part of a linguistic system. At this stage surprising errors of reversal appear in the children's pronominal signing; children sign (YOU) when intending self, patently ignoring the transparency of the pointing gesture. These pronoun reversals are also found in hearing children of the same age. By around the age of 2½ years, such reversal errors are completely resolved, just as they are in hearing children of the same age. Because the form of the pronominal sign is the same as the pointing gesture, these errors and their resolution provide evidence for a *discontinuity* in the transition from prelinguistic gesture to a formal linguistic system (Petitto 1983, in press).

1.3.2   Inflections: Verb Agreement

The ASL system of verb agreement functions is similar to that of spoken languages, but the form of verb agreement in ASL requires that the signer mark connections between spatial points. Around the age of 2 years, deaf children begin using uninflected signs, even in imitating their mothers' inflected signs and even in cases in which the adult grammar requires marking for person and number (Newport and Ashbrook 1977). So, even though the children are perceiving complexly inflected forms, they begin, like hearing children do, by selecting the uninflected stems. By the age of 3 years, deaf children have learned the basic aspects of verb morphology in ASL (inflections for person, temporal aspect, and number; see Meier 1981, 1982). At this age they make overgeneralizations to noninflecting verbs, analogous to overgeneralizations such as *eated* in the speech of hearing children. Such errors reveal the child's analysis of forms across the system (Bellugi and Klima 1982b; Meier 1981, 1982). So, despite the difference in the form of spatial marking, the development and the age of mastery of the spatial inflection for verb agreement is the same in ASL as for comparable processes in spoken languages.

1.3.3 Referential Indexing: Syntax and Discourse

The integration of the spatial verb agreement system in the sentences and discourse of ASL is highly complex. When deaf children first attempt to index verbs to arbitrary locus points in space, they index all verbs for all referents to a single locus. In telling the story of Rapunzel, for example, a child of 3½ years (evidently using her early hypothesis about syntactic rules) indexed three verbs in space—SEE, ASK, and PUSH (each of which has distinct referents)—but she indexed all three verbs at the same locus (figure 1.10a). In effect, she "stacked up" the three referents (father, witch, Rapunzel) at a single locus point (Loew 1982). In later developments the loci for distinct referents are differentiated, although occasional discourse problems still interfere with the establishment and maintenance of the one-to-one mapping between referent and locus (Loew 1983; Lillo-Martin 1986). Figure 1.10b gives a particularly complex example in which a deaf child is recounting an imaginary story in which she (Jane) has ten children, and another woman arrives to claim them as her own. Jane (in the role of the other woman) signed, "(I) WANT MY . . . YOUR . . . JANE'S CHILDREN." One can understand why in this situation she finally resorted to the use of her own name sign to clarify the reference! By the age of 5 years, however, children give the appropriate spatial index to nearly every nominal and pronoun that requires one, and almost all verbs show the appropriate agreement.

Deaf children, like their hearing counterparts, extract discrete components of the system presented to them. Furthermore, the evidence suggests that, even when the modality and the language offer possibilities that seem intuitively obvious or transparent (pointing for pronominal reference, for example), deaf children ignore this directness and analyze the language input as part of a formal linguistic system. Young deaf children are faced with the dual task in sign language of spatial perception, memory, and spatial transformations on the one hand and processing grammatical structure on the other, all in one and the same visual event (Stiles-Davis, Kritchevsky, and Bellugi, in press). Studies of the acquisition process have found that deaf and hearing children show a strikingly similar course of development if exposed to a natural language at the critical time. These data thus dramatically underscore the biological substrate of the human capacity for creating linguistic systems. These findings show powerfully how language, independent of its transmission mechanisms,

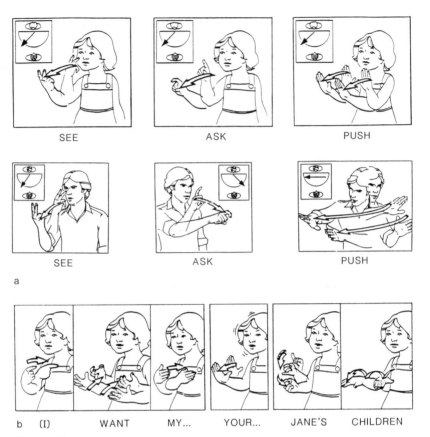

SEE   ASK   PUSH

SEE   ASK   PUSH

a

b   (I)   WANT   MY...   YOUR...   JANE'S   CHILDREN

Figure 1.10
The acquisition of spatialized syntax in deaf children. (a) Deaf child's incorrect "stack-ing" of referents (note that child has indexed verbs referring to three different referents at the same locus point) and adult's correct spatial reference for context. (b) Child's complex pronominal spatial reference meaning 'The old woman said to Jane, "I want my . . . your . . . Jane's children." '

emerges in children in a rapid, patterned, and, above all, linguistically driven manner.

1.4   Perception and Production of a Visual-gestural Language

1.4.1   Extracting Movement from Sign Form

The visual system is organized more for the analysis of changing events than for the analysis of static ones (Johansson 1973). As we have seen, in ASL superimposed patterns of movement and spatial contouring convey grammatical information. To study directly the complicated movement patterns within the linguistic system of ASL, we need to extract movement from sign forms. We adapted a technique introduced by Johansson (1973) for studying the perception of biological motion, by first placing nine small incandescent bulbs at the major joints of the arms and hands (shoulders, elbows, wrists, and index fingertips). We then recorded signing in a darkened room so that on the videotape only the pattern of moving points of light appeared against a black background. We found that, even with such greatly reduced information, deaf signers could quite accurately recognize and identify the inflections presented in these point-light displays, demonstrating that these grammatical patterns of movement form a distinct and isolable (but co-occurring) layer of structure in ASL. By removing various pairs of points, we found that movement of the fingertips, but not of any other pair of points, is necessary for sign identification. This study showed that the dynamic point-light displays accurately transmit linguistic information; they capture the subtleties of contrasts in movement that mark grammatical distinctions in the language and demonstrate the isolability of this co-occurring layer of grammatical structure in ASL (see Poizner, Bellugi, and Lutes-Driscoll 1981; Bellugi 1980).

1.4.2   The Interplay between Perceptual and Linguistic Processes

We have been using point-light displays to study the interplay between basic perceptual processes and higher-order linguistic ones. To pursue this, we have shown sign movements to both native deaf signers and hearing nonsigners in order to see what differences might exist in their perception of movement. Triads of basic and of inflected ASL signs were presented as point-light displays for judgments of movement similarity. Multidimensional scaling and hierarchical clustering of judgments for both deaf and hearing subjects revealed, first, that lexical and inflectional movements are perceived in terms of a limited number of underlying dimensions. Second, the perceived dimensions for the lexical level are generally different from those for the inflectional level. These results, with perceptual data, support our previous linguistic conclusion, namely, that the linguistic fabric of the two levels of structure in ASL is woven from different formational material. Furthermore, deaf and hearing subjects have different psychological representations of movement type within each level; the perception of movement form is tied to linguistically relevant dimensions for deaf but not for hearing subjects. Thus the data suggest that the acquisition of a visual-gestural language can modify the natural perceptual categories into which these movement forms fall (Poizner 1981, 1983, in press).

These experiments extend previous studies of the perception of other formational categories of ASL, that is, configuration of the hands (Lane, Boyes-Braem, and Bellugi 1976; Stungis 1981) and location of the hands (Poizner and Lane 1978). In these previous studies, however, the patterns of results for deaf signers and for hearing nonsigners were the same; no modification of perception resulting from linguistic experience was found for static sign attributes. The perception of ASL movement (and perhaps movement in general as a category) may be crucially different from the perception of static parameters, such as Handshape and Place of Articulation. It is important that the modification of perception of movement following sign language acquisition parallels processes found for spoken language. Experience with spoken language likewise can affect the perception of speech sounds. For example, the distinction between /r/ and /l/ serves to contrast words in English but not in Japanese, and, unlike infants and English-speaking adults, Japanese-speaking adults fail to discriminate these acoustic differences (Miyawaki et al. 1975). Thus modification of natural perceptual categories following language acquisition appears to be a general consequence of acquiring a formal linguistic system, be it spoken or signed.

1.4.3   Three-dimensional Computer Graphics and Linguistic Analysis

The modality of language interacts deeply with biological mechanisms for perceptual processing and movement control. In many ways the transmission system of sign language (visual-gestural) is radically different from that of speech and offers remarkably different possibilities and constraints. The study of sign language offers an opportunity for investigating language production because movements of the articulators are directly observable. By measuring sign language articulations, we can directly compare the physical structure of the signed and spoken signals. Nonetheless, it has been difficult to analyze and measure the subtle movements of the hands and arms in three dimensions. We have recently devised new techniques for such an analysis, and these techniques enable us to quantify the movement signal and thus help us to uncover the structure of movement organized into a linguistic system.

We currently analyze three-dimensional movement using a modified Op-Eye system (figure 1.11), a monitoring apparatus permitting rapid high-resolution digitization of hand and arm movement (Poizner, Wooten, and Salot 1986). Two optoelectronic cameras track the positions of light-emitting diodes (LEDs) attached to the hands and arms and provide a digital output directly to a computer, which calculates three-dimensional trajectories. From the position measurements the movements are reconstructed in three dimensions on an Evans and Sutherland Picture System. This system allows dynamic display and interactive control over the three-dimensional movement trajectories, so that various trajectory and dynamic characteristics can be calculated for any portion of the movement (Loomis et al. 1983; Jennings and Poizner 1986).

Figure 1.12 illustrates aspects of the measurement and analysis process, presenting the reconstructed movement of the hand and the associated velocity and acceleration profiles for two grammatically inflected signs, LOOK[Continuative] and LOOK[Durational]. Although ASL relies heavily on spatial contrasts, temporal contrasts are also used. The Continuative and Durational inflections, for example, are minimally contrasted by their temporal qualities and serve to elucidate a difference in timing between signed and spoken language. The Continuative inflection, meaning 'action for a long time,' is made with a tense, rapid outward movement with an elliptical slow return to the starting point. The Durational inflection, meaning 'continuous action,' is made with a smooth, circular, even movement that is repeated. The panels of figure 1.12b present for each inflection the reconstructed movement of the hand along with the associated velocity and acceleration profiles. The panels of figure 1.12c present characteristics of a single movement cycle. We find that the temporal contrasts underlying these inflections, as well as those for ASL in general, are typically stretched over much longer intervals than those found in speech. Sign language simply does not use the extremely rapid 40–50-msec temporal intervals found in spoken languages to contrast forms (Poizner 1985). Rather, temporal variation in sign language occurs over much longer intervals, and sign language heavily uses spatial contrasts.

Figure 1.11
Three-dimensional movement monitoring system showing the main hardware components and the position of infrared emitting diodes on a subject.

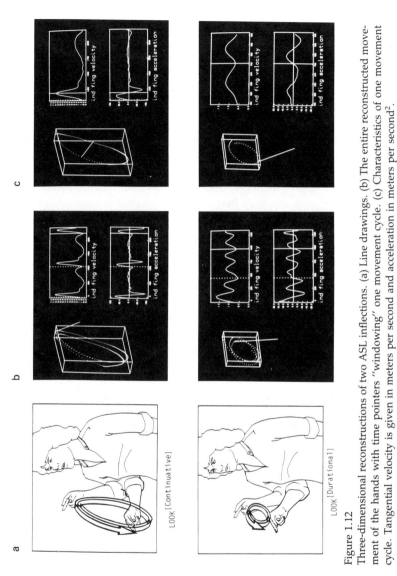

Figure 1.12
Three-dimensional reconstructions of two ASL inflections. (a) Line drawings. (b) The entire reconstructed movement of the hands with time pointers "windowing" one movement cycle. (c) Characteristics of one movement cycle. Tangential velocity is given in meters per second and acceleration in meters per second².

This difference in temporal structure between signed and spoken languages has important implications for our understanding of the basis of the specialization of the left hemisphere for language. The left hemisphere is specialized not only for language but also for the rapid temporal analysis that speech strongly requires. It has been proposed that the specialization of the left hemisphere for language is actually a secondary consequence of its more primary specialization for rapid temporal analysis. Theories basing the specialization of the left hemisphere for language on superior capacities for auditory processing and rapid temporal analysis would not predict left-hemisphere specialization for sign language. ASL pits linguistic function against stimulus form in a strong way because in large part it conveys grammatical relations through spatial relations. As we will show, ASL provides a special window into the nature of brain organization for language.

These studies lead to the following conclusions. ASL has developed as a fully autonomous language with a complex organization not derived from spoken languages, providing a new perspective on human language and the determinants of its organization. ASL exhibits formal structuring at the same two levels as spoken language (the internal structure of lexical units and the grammatical scaffolding underlying sentences) and similar kinds of organizational principles (constrained systems of features, rules based on underlying forms, recursive grammatical processes). The forms assumed by this manual language reflect its modality. The inflectional devices of ASL make structured use of space and movement, nesting the basic sign stem in spatial patterns and complex dynamic contours. In the basic lexical items, morphological processes, and sentences of ASL, the multilayering of linguistic elements is a pervasive structural principle. Spatial-locational contrasts and the manipulations of space have a crucial syntactic function in ASL. Rather than relying primarily on the order of items and fine temporal processing, sign language is organized in co-occurring layers and requires the processing of spatial relations. Sign language thus incorporates functions for which each of the cerebral hemispheres shows a different predominant specialization. How, then, is language organized in the brain when the language is inherently spatial? To answer this question, the following chapters report on our studies of six deaf signers with unilateral brain damage. We analyze the capacities of these patients to process nonlanguage visuospatial relations, to produce nonsign gestures, and to communicate in sign language. In the next chapter we turn to the issues involved, to previous studies performed, and to our methods of analysis.

Chapter 2
The Neural Substrate for Language

One of the most striking findings in the study of the relation between the structure of the human brain and behavioral functioning is cerebral dominance. Abundant evidence indicates that language processing is generally a left-hemisphere function, whereas the processing of visuospatial relations is generally a right-hemisphere function. Of course, this evidence was obtained with hearing subjects, whose language is a spoken one. In ASL, unlike spoken language, the signal is spatially organized. Let us recapitulate here briefly how in ASL spatial patterning figures in highly significant ways in the grammar of the language. The rich inflectional and derivational devices of ASL make structured use of space and movement, embedding signs in specific planes of space and spatial arrays. ASL conveys its syntax and discourse in large part by manipulation of space. Nominals introduced into the discourse may be associated with specific points in a plane of signing space; verb signs move between these points to specify subjects and objects of the verb. Pointing to a specific locus later in the discourse clearly "refers back" to a specific nominal, even after many intervening signs. Different subsystems of the language (pronominal reference, nominal establishment, verb agreement, and coreferentiality) thus rely on space and spatial representation (Klima and Bellugi 1979; Bellugi and Klima 1982b; Bellugi 1980).

Because ASL incorporates both complex language structure and complex spatial relations, it exhibits properties for which each of the hemispheres of hearing people shows specialization. Deaf people who have been deprived of auditory experience and who rely on a sign language for their principal mode of communication throughout their lives thus provide a privileged testing ground for investigating how the brain is organized for language, how that organization depends on language modality, and how modifiable that organization may be.

A great deal of evidence on brain organization for language has come from studies of speakers with brain lesions. We present here results of our studies of lifelong signers who have experienced brain damage. Because there is scarcely any previous research on sign language impairment in deaf signers, we have tested various hypotheses about the overall organization of the brain for sign. We wondered whether sign language is strictly unilaterally represented, as speech is, or bilaterally represented in congenitally deaf signers to a degree not characteristic of speech in hearing people. Alternatively, we wondered whether the left or the right hemisphere would be dominant for sign. Furthermore, when sign language breakdown occurs, would impairments be selective with respect to the structural components of the language? And, if we were to find left-hemisphere dominance for sign, would damage to the classical speech areas disrupt sign in the same manner as it affects speech? Because grammatical and spatial relations are so intimately interwoven in ASL, we consider it especially important to investigate not only how sign language breaks down but also how visuospatial functions break down; that is, we want to explore whether or not spatial functions are represented in the brain differently in deaf signers and to what degree spatial processing deficits affect sign performance.

Patterns of ASL impairments resulting from localized lesions in deaf signers can help illuminate the nature of neural organization for language. However, the brains of deaf people do not evolve independently of those of hearing people, and language mechanisms have certainly evolved in part to meet the needs of spoken communication. The neural organization for a visual-gestural language in deaf signers may therefore be determined in part by the evolutionary history of language development in the oral-auditory transmission modality. To the extent that specialized language structures developed for speech govern the representation and processing of ASL, neural mechanisms in deaf ASL signers will be similar to those found for hearing speakers. To the extent that the modality in which a language develops shapes the structure and processing of the language, modality-relevant neural structures may be implicated in its representation. The study of brain organization in deaf ASL signers allows us to address such fundamental questions regarding neural mechanisms for language.

2.1.1   Specialization for a Language in a Visual Modality

Besides its specialization for language, the left hemisphere seems better adapted than the right for processing sequential signals. As we pointed out in chapter 1, a major difference in form between ASL and most spoken languages is that ASL tends to transmit structural information in co-occurring layers rather than in sequence. The concurrent display of *linguistic* structure in ASL therefore allows study of the interplay of these (opposing) attributes: Will separate linguistic levels in ASL break down independently of one another, much as they do in spoken languages, despite the radical differences in the way in which the linguistic information is packaged in the signed signal? Will there be substitutions and transpositions involving sublexical components of signs? Will the syntax of ASL be disturbed independently of the lexicon?

Undoubtedly, the most distinguishing characteristic of ASL as a language is its reliance on spatial mechanisms to convey syntactic structure. Does right-hemisphere damage disrupt the processing of this linguistic signal? Are left-hemisphere mechanisms, some of which clearly involve sequential analysis, called into play for a language that preferentially packages its linguistic information in such a spatial, concurrent manner? Or is the underlying basis of left-hemisphere specialization for language tied to *function* rather than to *form*?

2.1.2   *Apraxia and Aphasia: Motor versus Linguistic Impairment*

The use of aphasias to reveal brain organization for sign language presents special problems. An important question involves the dissociability of sign aphasias from apraxias, neural disorders of movement not traceable to any motor weakness or lack of coordination. Because apraxias frequently co-occur with aphasias, some investigators have proposed that the two share a common underlying basis, namely, an underlying deficit in the control of movement or gesture. We use a number of tests, described in detail later in this chapter, to distinguish among impairments in linguistic, symbolic, and motor functions and to evaluate each separately. Results of these tests can illuminate the relation between aphasia and apraxia in both hearing and deaf individuals in a strong way by determining the dissociability of the breakdown of nonlinguistic gestural behavior and of gestural *language*.

2.1.3   *Specialization for Visuospatial Capacity*

The right hemisphere has long been considered a poor relation to the left; the left has been said to be dominant for language, skilled motor control (praxis), fine temporal processing, analytic analysis, and feature extraction, whereas the right has been considered to lack any significant specialization of its own. This view is still reflected occasionally. However, the work of Roger Sperry and his associates with split-brain patients and mounting case reports of patients with unilateral lesions to the right hemisphere converge to indicate that the right hemisphere has its own specialized abilities (Ratcliff and Newcombe 1973; Ratcliff 1982; Levy 1982). Rather than extracting features, the right hemisphere organizes parts into complex configurations, and rather than being dominant for speech, it is dominant for processing visuospatial relations. Its function with respect to processing spatial relations might be especially important in sign language, because many of the grammatical processes crucially involve spatial relations and the manipulation of space. What, then, are the consequences for brain organization when space functions linguistically?

To our knowledge, this is the first investigation of brain organization for nonlinguistic visuospatial processing in brain-damaged deaf signers. Our objective is to determine whether this organization is the same as or different from that in hearing-speaking individuals. We administered a battery of tests for nonlinguistic processing to deaf patients with brain lesions (and to matched deaf controls). The tests have proved in hearing patients to distinguish maximally the performance of those with lesions in the left hemisphere from those with lesions in the right. We investigate (1) whether lack of auditory experience and use of a spatial language affect the functional organization of the brain of deaf signers for nonlinguistic visuospatial processing, and (2) the degree to which impairments in nonlinguistic visuospatial processing affect sign performance.

Before describing the methods used in our investigations, we review previous studies of the effects of brain damage on deaf signers, including the limitations of these studies. At the end of the chapter we introduce the six patients with unilateral lesions (three with left-hemisphere lesions and three with right-hemisphere lesions), whose cases form the major focus of this book.

2.2   Background and Previous Studies

Until recently, little has been known about brain organization for sign language. Two lines of evidence have been used, one with normal deaf signers and the other with brain-damaged signers. Neither of these lines has proved definitive.

Experiments with non-brain-damaged deaf signers have generally employed tachistoscopic presentation of signs, following the paradigms developed for the differential presentation of visual material to the two cerebral hemispheres. In order to stimulate one hemisphere exclusively, in these paradigms it is necessary to present visual stimuli rapidly. But an important attribute of ASL lexicon and grammar is movement, and it is extremely difficult to capture movement in the brief exposure necessary to stimulate one hemisphere exclusively. This difficulty has meant that most investigators presented only static line drawings or photographs of signs tachistoscopically to the visual hemifields of signers (see Poizner and Battison (1980) for a review). These studies found more right- than left-hemisphere involvement. One study, however, presented signs in motion, as well as ones presented statically (Poizner, Battison, and Lane 1979), and found a shift from right-hemisphere dominance to a more balanced hemispheric involvement with the change from static to moving representations. A new experiment has, in fact, shown significant left-hemisphere dominance in normal deaf signers for the identification of computer-synthesized moving ASL signs (Poizner and Bellugi 1984). Nonetheless, it is impossible to capture much of the movement of sign language in the brief exposure durations available; only lexical signs have been presented, and no analysis of hemispheric specialization for grammatical processing or for language production has been possible. Furthermore, the weight of the evidence from the tachistoscopic studies shows greater right-hemisphere than left-hemisphere involvement, possibly because of greater right-hemisphere preprocessing of signs presented statically. In any case, these studies have not proved definitive.

The study of the breakdown of sign language following localized brain lesions in deaf signers can resolve these and many other issues. In the study of brain-damaged signers, there is no limitation on the presentation of movement; grammatical processing as well as lexical processing can be studied, language production as well as language comprehension can be studied, and analyses of brain function can be made not only in terms of left-hemisphere and right-hemisphere functioning but also in terms of the roles of specific anatomical structures within the hemispheres. Furthermore, the study of language breakdown under conditions of brain damage can reveal in a robust way the nature of brain organization for language. We first mention some historical aspects of the study of the breakdown of spoken language resulting from brain damage in hearing individuals and then review previous studies of brain-damaged signers.

As early as the time of Hippocrates in the fourth century B.C. in Greece, it was reported that injury to the brain could result in impairment of language capacities. In fact, even the ancient Egyptians knew that certain head injuries could result in loss of speech. Thus the recognition of the disturbance we now call aphasia has a long history.

Of more recent vintage are the aspects of aphasia most relevant to our concerns in this book: brain organization for language and its relation to modality.

It was in 1865 that Paul Broca, a French neurologist, made the seminal discovery that a lesion in a part of the *left* hemisphere resulted in sudden and long-lasting language disturbance in a previously normal individual and led to his statement that "we speak with the left hemisphere." Lesions to the corresponding regions of the *right* hemisphere were not accompanied by any observable language impairment.

A decade after Broca's work, the Viennese neurologist Carl Wernicke noted that lesions to different parts of the left hemisphere are accompanied by radically different patterns of language problems. Specifically, the lesion site that Broca had studied (the posterior regions of the frontal lobe) most noticeably involved language production: reduced output, slow and effortful articulation with articulatory errors, and omission of grammatical formatives. Comprehension did not appear to be affected. This constellation of symptoms came to be known as Broca's aphasia. By contrast, the lesion site that Wernicke had identified most noticeably involved problems in comprehension. Production showed fluent, rapid output and preserved syntactic markers, but the output was often irregular in the frequency of lexical and sublexical substitutions. In the most extreme cases, it constituted a sort of "word salad." This syndrome came to be known as Wernicke's aphasia.

One of the earliest researchers to address the issue of modality of language and brain organization was the British neurologist Hughlings Jackson. In an 1878 article Jackson predicted that, because of injury to some part of the brain, a deaf signer might lose his natural system of signs, that is, his sign language. This prediction remained purely speculative for a long time. The reason was that no relevant cases had been reported in the literature. Gradually, however, pertinent, if not decisive, cases did appear, and these few clinical reports of sign aphasia do show left-hemisphere involvement. Most of these reports, however, are not especially revealing because the linguistic impairments of these patients were usually extremely underreported and because testing procedures were insensitive to critical linguistic, psycholinguistic, and sociolinguistic issues of sign languages. Furthermore, most of these studies were carried out before the advent of computer-assisted tomography (CT scans), which has provided an extremely important means of localizing the site of brain damage. Without autopsy information, therefore, such studies had no way of specifying exactly where the brain damage occurred. As we turn to these earlier case studies, let us remind the reader that aphasia is to be understood as a language disorder that results from brain damage and cannot be accounted for by peripheral sensory or motor dysfunction or by general cognitive deterioration in attention or motivation. (More detailed reviews of the early case studies are in Poizner and Battison (1980) and Kimura (1981).)

Grasset (1896) provides the first report of a deaf man who experienced a left-hemisphere lesion. The patient was French. His right-handedness is implied but not specifically reported. Unfortunately, only his fingerspelling in French was evaluated, and not his use of French Sign Language. The patient had mild paralysis of the right arm and could not fingerspell with that hand; however, he showed no impairment in fingerspelling with his left hand and showed no comprehension loss. This patient's impaired right-handed fingerspelling apparently resulted from peripheral motor impairments of his right hand, rather than from a central language deficit. Thus Grasset's patient is not a case of aphasia. It is neither a true "fingerspelling" aphasia, in which case fingerspelling production in the nonparalyzed left hand would also have been impaired, nor presumably a case of sign aphasia. At any rate, no mention is made of the patient's use of sign language.

Burr (1905) likewise sheds little light on brain organization for sign language. The patient in this study became deaf early in childhood and learned to sign. She never learned to talk, but she did learn to read and write. She later suffered massive left-hemisphere damage that left her fairly unresponsive and with general intellectual deterioration that included loss of language. This case also does not demonstrate sign aphasia, for it lacks the appropriate selectivity of impairment.

Critchley (1938) provides a report of a right-handed deaf British man who experienced a left-hemisphere stroke. The patient could hear until the age of 7, at which time his hearing gradually diminished. By the age of 14 years, he was deaf. He communicated by means of sign language. Critchley reports that the patient's natural sign language was unaffected but no information on the testing of sign language is given. The patient's fingerspelling, however, was impaired. The patient was reported to have an initial paralysis of the right hand, which improved considerably with time. This case is difficult to interpret. Because the patient did not become completely deaf until the age of 14, hemispheric specialization might have been established on the basis of hearing and speech, before his learning of sign language. Furthermore, it is unclear how skilled the patient was in fingerspelling and in the sign language he used (presumably some form of British Sign Language) before his stroke, and no details are given of the testing of his reportedly unimpaired sign language.

Reider (1941) introduces a case of a hearing patient from the American Midwest who learned sign language from his deaf mother, possibly as a first language. Although few details of testing were presented, the patient reportedly was severely aphasic for speech but less impaired in sign, although he tended to perseverate in his signing. Autopsy revealed effects of diffuse encephalitis throughout the entire brain, without any focal lesions. This case also provides little resolution of the issues, because the patient did not have unilateral brain damage and because few test details are given.

Leischner (1943) presents an important and well-documented case of a congenitally deaf, apparently right-handed man from a deaf family who learned Czech Sign Language as a first language. Language testing was extensive. The patient was bilingual in written Czech and German but could speak neither well. The testing was carried out primarily in Czech Sign Language. The patient showed both difficulty in expressing himself in his sign language and loss of sign comprehension. He produced nonsense signs, perseverated in his signs, incorrectly named objects and pictures, and reportedly produced a superfluous number of signs, more than was necessary to communicate. He had difficulty signing automatic sequences; for example, when asked to sign the days of the week, he once signed SUNDAY, SATURDAY, FRIDAY, SEPTEMBER, APRIL. As mentioned, his comprehension of sign language was also impaired. In these respects his signing resembled the speech of a hearing Wernicke's aphasic. A strength in this study is that the brain was autopsied, so the precise areas of damage could be determined. There was damage to the left parietal lobe, including the supramarginal and angular gyri, and to portions of the temporal lobe. Unfortunately, there was also an older lesion to the basal ganglia of the right hemisphere, which prevents any conclusive interpretation of how sign language might be represented in the brain.

Tureen, Smolik, and Tritt (1951) present a case of a congenitally deaf right-handed man who lost his ability to fingerspell after sustaining an injury to the left hemisphere. A hemorrhaging tumor in the left frontal lobe was surgically removed. Posterior portions of the second and third frontal convolutions were excised. Tureen and his colleagues held common misconceptions of their time about sign languages, viewing them as a universal primitive system of gestures. They report that the patient lost and recovered his use of sign language, although no testing of sign language was performed because the interpreter knew only fingerspelling.

Douglass and Richardson (1959) present a case of 21-year-old congenitally deaf right-handed woman who learned sign language from her two older deaf siblings. She had attended an oral school for deaf children and later married a deaf man. It appears from reports of her clergyman, relatives, and friends that sign language was not her primary mode of communication; rather, fingerspelling seemed her superior skill. During an abortion, the patient experienced a stroke that caused extensive damage to her left hemisphere, with associated paralysis of the right arm. Clinical signs led the authors to infer that the greatest damage was to the posterior frontal region, with lesser damage to the parietal and temporal areas. Both the production and comprehension of signing and fingerspelling were impaired, but signing was the more affected. Reportedly, the patient could carry out nonlanguage movements with the left hand without difficulty. Although descriptions of fingerspelling errors were given, those for sign were not.

Sarno, Swisher, and Sarno (1969) present the case of a 69-year-old right-handed congenitally deaf man who apparently learned sign language and fingerspelling at the age of 7 at a school for deaf children. He had two sisters who were also deaf. Before his stroke he was reported to have intermixed speaking and mouthing with signing and fingerspelling. His stroke was to the left hemisphere, which left him with moderate paralysis of his right arm. After his stroke he was severely aphasic, with deficits in both production and comprehension. The patient's ability to express himself was apparently more impaired than was his comprehension. The authors report that his expressive impairment was worst in speaking, followed by fingerspelling and writing; he was least impaired in signing. Likewise, his comprehension of fingerspelling and lip movement was more impaired than his comprehension of print or signs. Although this case is fairly well documented, interpretations based on it are complicated by the mixed language system the patient apparently used before his stroke.

Meckler, Mack, and Bennett (1979) present the second case of a *hearing* signer who suffered brain damage. The patient was a 19-year-old man of deaf parents. He had learned sign language and speech concurrently. The patient was left-handed. An automobile accident left him with a dense paralysis of his right arm and a right-sided sensory deficit. He apparently had a generalized lesion to the left hemisphere. He was initially globally aphasic for both sign and speech; over time he showed improvement, but his comprehension in both modes improved considerably more than did his expressive capacities. Apparently, fingerspelling was more impaired than signing.

Battison and Padden (1974) and Battison (1979; discussed in Poizner and Battison (1980)) describe a 70-year-old right-handed man who became deaf at the age of 5. He learned sign language a few years later, after being enrolled in a school for deaf children in Canada. His brain damage was in the region of the left middle-cerebral artery. His signing, fingerspelling, and writing were all impaired. He showed hesitations, substitutions, formational errors, and perseverations in all three modes of expression.

Underwood and Paulson (1981) present the case of a left-handed signer, a 57-year-old congenitally deaf man. At the age of 7 he was enrolled in a school for deaf children, where he learned sign language. The patient reportedly was a skilled signer, although it is difficult to interpret Underwood and Paulson's statement that "in addition to American Sign Language, gestures were incorporated into his communication with deaf peers" (p. 286). The patient had a left-sided stroke with resulting right hemiplegia. No further information localizing the site of the brain lesion is given. The patient was severely aphasic for sign language, unable to express even his basic needs. His comprehension of sign was also impaired. Unfortunately, no description of his sign language errors is given, although errors in fingerspelling and writing are described.

Chiarello, Knight, and Mandel (1982) provide a well-documented case of a 65-year-old American woman who became deaf at 6 months of age after contracting scarlet fever. At the age of 5 years, she was enrolled in a residential school for deaf children, where she learned sign language. She had a stroke in the left hemisphere, with consequent paralysis of the right arm. A CT scan revealed a lesion to the left parietal region and some subcortical extension into the posterior portion of the middle frontal gyrus. Globally aphasic initially, her symptoms resolved somewhat to fluent signing with substitutions (paraphasias), difficulty in finding signs, and impaired sign comprehension and repetition.

There have been two reported cases of signers with damage to the right hemisphere. The first (Battison (1979); discussed in Poizner and Battison (1980)) involved a 68-year-old prelingually deaf man who was left-handed. He began signing in early childhood, either through contact with his older deaf sister or through his early entry into a school for deaf children. The patient experienced a right-hemisphere stroke with consequent paralysis of the left hand. He showed severe impairment in both production and comprehension of signs, fingerspelling, and writing.

Kimura, Davidson, and McCormick (1982) present the second case of a signer with right-hemisphere damage. This patient was a 52-year-old right-handed prelingually deaf woman from Canada. She learned to sign at age 7, when she entered a school for deaf children. She had mild neurological deficits, consisting of a slight weakness of the left arm and hand and a slight neglect of left hemispace. She apparently had no sign language deficits, as assessed primarily by family reports and conversations with a skilled sign language interpreter.

It is clear from this review of existing case reports that previous research has failed to assess the linguistic competence of signers with respect to such central aspects of language as syntax and morphology. Because it has only been in the last decade that the grammatical system of ASL has been elucidated, the shortcomings of these studies are to be expected. With sign language regarded as "primitive" or a "form of pantomime" instead of as a complex language system, many of these studies can supply little usable information about the nature of sign language breakdown following brain damage. It becomes difficult, after all, to assess a patient's skills in ASL when the interpreter for the testing knows only fingerspelled English. Most of the case reports, in fact, do not even provide a single description of any sign language error. Without any linguistic description of the signing behavior of these patients, it is impossible to reach any conclusions about the nature of aphasia for sign language. Furthermore, previous studies have not compared performance of left-lesioned patients and right-lesioned patients across a given array of tests. In this manner left- and right-lesioned patients can be directly compared. With our current understanding of the nature of ASL, we have been able to develop a battery of tests with which to analyze a signer's strengths and weaknesses. These tests are described in detail in the next section.

2.3   Methods

We have four basic groups of tests. (1) To begin to investigate sign aphasia, we adapted the Boston Diagnostic Aphasia Examination (BDAE; Goodglass and Kaplan 1972) to ASL in order to see whether the pattern of impairment following brain damage in deaf signers is at all comparable to that found in brain-damaged hearing individuals. (2) We also developed a series of tests directed toward production and comprehension of particular grammatical structures of ASL.

Specifically, we tested for the capacity to process sublexical structure, morphology, and spatialized syntax. (3) To determine the relationship between apraxia and aphasia in a user of a gestural language, we assessed the capacity for representational and nonrepresentational movements of the hands and arms. (4) Finally, we used an array of nonlanguage visuospatial tests that have been shown in hearing people to differentiate the effects of damage to the left as opposed to the right hemisphere.

The entire battery of tests was administered to six brain-damaged signers, who are our focus here, and to deaf controls matched in age, age of onset of deafness, and language background. A native ASL signer administered all tests (in order to make the subject feel at ease in using ASL), with responses videotaped for later analysis.

2.3.1   Evaluation of Sign Aphasia

We adapted a standardized assessment of language skills, the BDAE (Goodglass and Kaplan 1972), for use with deaf, signing patients. We first translated the BDAE into ASL, with necessary modifications. Edgar Zurif and Harold Goodglass, pioneering investigators of aphasia in hearing people, helped us adapt the test to a visual-gestural language. As an example of a modification, note first that the right-sided paralysis of many aphasics requires that they take the sign examination with their left hand only. We therefore built this constraint into our adaptation of the BDAE by using only one-handed signs. The fact that a deaf signing patient may have use of only one hand does not in itself produce a language impairment. In ASL there are no lexical contrasts based on the use of one versus two hands, and, indeed, left-handed signers have mirror image signing of those who are right-handed. Signers often have one or the other hand occupied and sign well nonetheless. We have, in fact, asked native signers to sign lists, stories, and passages with only the left or the right hand; not only have they found this to be an easy task, but other signers, when tested, can comprehend their signing without trouble. Linguistic ability and effective communication are not hampered by using only one hand instead of two (Vaid, Bellugi, and Poizner 1985).

Another change in adapting the BDAE was motivated because hearing patients had to make rapid repetitions of items ranging from easy (*mama*) to difficult (*huckleberry*). In our test the items were not direct translations into ASL but were chosen to range correspondingly from formationally simple (UNDERSTAND, MOTHER) to formationally complex (BEE, RESEMBLE, FOREVER). Certain linguistic facts obliged us to modify some test items, as is usual in translating a test from one language to another. In the responsive naming task, for example, the question, "What do you do with a razor?" calls for the answer, "Shave." The signs RAZOR and SHAVE, however, share the same root, so the question in ASL contains an obvious clue to the answer. We changed the item to WHAT DO YOU DO WITH A BOOK? because the answer, READ, is formationally unrelated to any sign in the question itself.

The BDAE yields more than an index of a patient's general communication or language capacity; it also provides a profile of language impairments. The first part of the BDAE consists of standardized tests assessing various aspects of language production and comprehension; the second part yields ratings of attributes of conversational and expository signing. We discuss results of the BDAE in chapters 3, 4, and 5.

Standardized Tests of the Boston Diagnostic Aphasia Examination
The BDAE, as adapted by us for deaf patients, consists of five tests having to do with sign language: sign fluency, sign comprehension, naming, repetition, and paraphasia. We describe each separately.

Sign fluency is based on three subtests: a rating of ease of sign articulation, a measure of the length of sign phrases in spontaneous signing, and a test of sign agility requiring rapid serial repetitions of single signs that vary in formational complexity.

Sign comprehension consists of four subtests. The first is sign discrimination, a multiple-choice test of sign recognition in which the examiner produces a single sign and the patient points to a picture of the sign's referent. In the second subtest, body part identification, the patient points to the appropriate body parts in response to their **?** names designated by the examiner. The third subtest requires the patient to carry out sign commands, varying from one to five significant informational units (such as "Put the pencil on the card, then put it back"). The final comprehension subtest, complex ideational material, requires yes/no answers to simple factual material and brief questions that explore the patient's comprehension of short, signed stories.

There are four naming subtests for evaluating word-finding ability. Responsive naming requires the patient to answer a signed question (such as "What color is grass?"). In visual confrontation naming the patient names pictures. In body part naming the examiner points to his or her own body parts, and the patient is asked to name the parts. **?** The animal naming subtest measures patients' facility in controlled association by having them produce as many names of animals as they can in 60 seconds.

In the repetition test the patient is asked to repeat single signs and to repeat sentences of either low or high probability, that is, referring to likely as opposed to unlikely situations.

Types of paraphasia (linguistic substitution) are tabulated in specific BDAE subtests. These substitutions include what is commonly referred to as "slips of the tongue" as well as substitutions of elements from outside the immediate string. These transpositions and substitutions can take several forms. In phonemic paraphasias there is transposition or introduction of extraneous phonemes in a spoken word. Phonemic paraphasias in sign arise from substitutions of one sublexical element for another (a change in Handshape, Location, or Movement). In speech, for example, the error might be the word "bindow" for "window." Verbal paraphasias involve the substitution of one sign for another, and neologistic distortions are substitutions or introductions of extraneous sublexical elements such that most of the intended word or sign is not recognizable as a unit.

Rating-scale Profiles of the Boston Diagnostic Aphasia Examination
The second part of the BDAE provides a rating scale for assessing certain aspects of spontaneous language production. To obtain a database for the rating-scale profiles, we transcribed and tabulated various characteristics from a 10-minute sample of each patient's conversation and expository signing. We measured the length of sign phrases, noted paraphasias, and classified and counted all grammatical and lexical morphemes.

We obtained ratings for six aspects of sign production: melodic line, phrase length, sign agility, grammatical form, paraphasia, and sign finding. In the BDAE for hearing individuals, what is termed the melodic line refers to the number of words within an intonational contour. Strictly, melodic line is not a property of signing or of gesturing. What is comparable, however, is the rhythmic flow of signing (as distinguished from simply unfaltering, fluent output). Rhythmicity is important as a measure because it provides evidence that a string of signs, whether fluently outputted or not, represents phrasal/sentential structure rather than merely a string of signs linked together associatively as opposed to syntactically. In the ASL adaptation the rating reflects the number of signs within a single rhythmic grouping. Phrase length is the maximum recurring number of signs in an uninterrupted run, bounded by pauses or sentence markers; the scale reflects the average of the longest number of runs of signs for every ten starts. Sign agility is the patient's ease of articulating signs and sign sequences. Grammatical form reflects the variety of grammatical constructions a patient uses. Paraphasias focus on substitutions or insertions of semantically inappropriate signs or neologisms. Sign finding reflects the informational content of the patient's signing with respect to the patient's level of motoric fluency; measurement is based on the proportion of substantives and specific action signs relative to the number of low-information signs (such as pronouns and other closed-class morphemes and indefinite signs, for example, THING). A seventh scale, sign comprehension, is based not on ratings but on test scores from the four BDAE comprehension subtests.

Five of the six rating scales are 7-point scales, in which 7 stands for normal and 1 for maximally abnormal language characteristics. For the sixth scale, sign-finding ability, both extremes reflect deviant language production, with normal performance in the middle. Our ratings closely follow the principles specified for hearing patients, outlined in Goodglass and Kaplan (1972), but adjusted for characteristics of ASL.

The Cookie Theft picture of the BDAE (figure 2.1) is typically used to elicit speech from aphasic patients; we used it to elicit signing. On the right-hand side the picture shows a woman standing beside an overflowing kitchen sink; the woman, drying a plate, appears oblivi-

Figure 2.1
The Cookie Theft elicitation card from the Boston Diagnostic Aphasia Examination. Copyright © 1972 by Lea and Febiger. Reprinted with permission.

ous. On the left-hand side of the picture a boy stands on a stool, attempting to reach a jar of cookies on a shelf above his head. The stool is tipping over and is about to fall. Also on the left-hand side is a girl reaching up to the boy, presumably for a cookie.

2.3.2   Tests for Processing the Structural Levels of American Sign Language

We designed the following battery of tests of language comprehension and processing for the levels of structure in ASL:

> 1. tests for processing ASL "phonology": the Rhyming Test and the Test for Decomposition of Signs;
> 2. tests for processing ASL morphology: the Comprehension and the Elicitation of Noun/Verb Distinction;
> 3. tests for processing spatial syntax in ASL: the Nominal Establishment Test, the Test of Verb Agreement with Fixed Framework, and the Test of Verb Agreement with Shifting Reference.

Our studies focus on morphological and syntactic processes because in these processes sign language makes the most widespread and distinctive use of the properties of the visuospatial modality. Some of these studies are outlined in what follows. (These processes and their measurement are also discussed in chapters 4, 5, and 6.) In the tests described in the following discussion we found that normal, deaf young adults and control subjects matched in age and background to the brain-damaged signers perform quite well. In addition, we gathered data on young deaf children and found that they have the requisite capacities early on.

Sublexical Tasks
The two tests for evaluating ASL "phonology" are Rhyming and Decomposition.

It has been argued that for hearing people phonological processing is one aspect of linguistic processing that is mediated primarily and preferentially by the left hemisphere. But is this left-hemisphere specialization based on the linear, temporal sequencing of phonemes in the words of spoken languages, or is it based on sublexical processing in general? Given the difference between the sublexical structure of English words and that of ASL signs (linear temporal contrasts versus co-occurring components in space), it becomes important to determine the nature of the errors that brain-damaged deaf patients make at this level and to assess their abilities to decompose signs into their component elements. In our test for impairment in phonological processing, the subject looks at three pictures of objects and identifies the two objects whose signs "rhyme" (that is, signs that differ in only one of the three major parameters of signing: Hand Configuration, Place of Articulation, and Movement).

In developing a test of the ability to decompose signs into their sublexical components, we used familiar signs that can be represented by pictorial objects. First, we assess the patient's ability to name the pictures. For each of the major formational parameters of ASL (Hand Configuration, Place of Articulation, Movement), there are five sets of items. The subject sees a sign and then a set of four pictures. He or she is asked to pick out the picture that represents a sign with the same Hand Configuration (or Place of Articulation or Movement; see figure 2.2). The arrays include a semantic distractor and a formational distractor (picture of an object representing a sign similar in another component to the target sign). The central question of interest is whether left-lesioned signers, but not right-lesioned signers, are impaired with respect to these phonological processing tasks.

Figure 2.2
Test for processing ASL "phonology": Decomposition of Signs. The subject is asked to select the picture whose sign has the same Hand Configuration as the target. The correct choice is (c), because the ASL sign TELEPHONE has the same Hand Configuration as COW.

Morphological Tasks

Two tests are used to evaluate the morphological processing of signs. The tests examine comprehension and elicitation of noun/verb distinction.

In ASL the formal distinction between the action-instrument noun-verb pairs, discussed in chapter 1, is marked by the patterns of movement. This derivational process relates semantically associated noun-verb pairs, such as SIT and CHAIR, FLY and AIRPLANE, and CUT and SCISSORS. In such pairs the members share the same Handshape, Place of Articulation, and Movement Shape (for example, back and forth, closing, and nodding) but are differentiated by movement features, such as frequency, end manner, and tension. Some verb signs have repeated movement, others single movement; but the related noun movement is always repeated, restrained, and small (Supalla and Newport 1978). Thus the morphological marker that distinguishes nouns from verbs involves manner, size, and repetition. The linguistic structure of these forms in the adult language has been well analyzed, as has its acquisition in deaf children (Lillo-Martin et al., "Acquisition," 1985; Launer 1982). We have developed tests to assess knowledge of this derivationally related distinction.

In the test for Comprehension of Noun/Verb Distinction, the examiner makes a single sign—a noun or a verb from a related pair—and the subject designates which one of four pictures illustrates the sign. The four pictures include the object referred to by the noun, the activity referred to by the verb, a sign distractor (something whose sign is similar to the target sign), and a semantic distractor (something similar to the thing referred to by the target sign). Figure 2.3 presents an example.

The second test, Elicitation of Noun/Verb Distinction, is designed to elicit the production of a noun/verb distinction. The subject sees a picture of an object or of an activity corresponding to the noun or verb, respectively, of a related pair. The examiner then prompts the production of the noun or verb, asking, "What is that?" or "What is she (or he) doing?"

Spatialized Syntax

Three tests examine the processing of spatialized syntax: the Nominal Establishment Test and two tests of Verb Agreement, one in a fixed framework and the other with a shifting reference.

The verb agreement tests we have developed provide a means for assessing selective impairment of the structural components of ASL. As described in chapter 1, for a large class of inflecting verbs in ASL, subject and object are signaled by reference to loci in the plane of

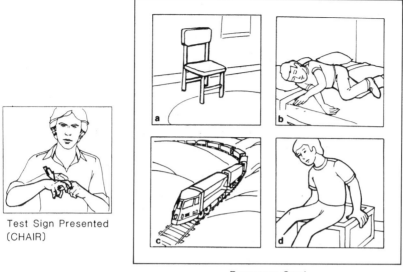

Test Sign Presented
(CHAIR)

Response Card

Figure 2.3
Test for processing ASL morphology: comprehension of the formal distinction between nouns and related verbs. The correct choice is (a). The sign for (d), SIT, is morphologically related to the sign CHAIR, differing only in features of movement (for example, repetition and restrained manner). The sign for (c), TRAIN, is a formationally related distractor.

signing space. Noun phrase referents are assigned arbitrary places in space (their spatial loci); verb signs, for which these nominals function as arguments, move between spatial endpoints that correspond to the loci. The movement of the verb proceeds either from the locus of the subject to the locus of the object (for example, GIVE) or in the opposite direction (for example, INVITE), depending on the verb class. In discourse referent identity is maintained through consistent indexing to established referential loci in space. Index maintenance and shifting is grammatically determined. Sentence structure in ASL can therefore be specified by the way in which verbs, nominals, and pronominal indexes are related to one another in space. Spatial contrasts play a central role in specifying grammatical relations in ASL. The tests we have developed for the processing of such spatial mechanisms have been given to normal deaf adults and to deaf children of deaf parents as additional normative data to that obtained from the elderly deaf control subjects (Bellugi, in press; Lillo-Martin et al., "Acquisition," 1985).

The test for Nominal Establishment probes perception and memory for spatial loci associated with specific nominals. The examiner signs a test item and asks two kinds of question (figure 2.4): (A) where a certain nominal has been established (to which the subject answers by pointing to a specific locus in signing space), and (B) what nominal has been established at a certain locus (which the subject answers by signing the nominal). Half of this test has two nominals on each list, and the other half has three. In associating loci with their nominal reference, this test assesses perception and memory for the assignment of loci to their nominal reference, a key aspect of coreference structure in ASL syntax and discourse. The graph in figure 2.4 presents results of testing young deaf children of deaf parents on the Nominal Establishment Test. As the figure shows, children of 2 years of age are unable to handle the test. When asked question A, for example, they look around the room for the real objects; they are unable to answer question B at all. By age 3, however, young deaf children can perform well the task of comprehending the association of nouns with arbitrary spatial loci.

There are two tests for verb agreement; they investigate the memory and processing of verb agreement markers in ASL. In the Verb Agreement with Fixed Framework test the experimenter signs a sentence describing an event with two participants, either of which semantically could be the subject or the object of the verb. Figure 2.5 shows two sample items selected from the test (presented at different times in the test administration), one of which shows a picture of a cat biting a dog and the other of a dog biting a cat. Sentence A, for example, is notated as DOG INDEX$_b$ CAT INDEX$_b$ $_a$BITE$_b$; for example, 'The dog bit the cat.' Note that the same signs presented in the same order but with different spatial endpoints of the verb (sentence B) means 'The cat bit the dog.' The spatial pronominal indexes and order of signs are maintained; thus the movement of the verb between spatial points is the only indicator of grammatical relations. The subject's task is to point to the picture described by the examiner's sentence.

A correct response involves processing and remembering the nominals and their associated spatial loci as well as the direction of movement of the verb between the spatial loci. Furthermore, so that subjects cannot use surface cues and therefore must grammatically decode the sentence, the spatial arrangement of items in the picture does not necessarily match the spatial arrangement set up in the experimenter's sentence.

The second test, Verb Agreement with Shifting Reference, again involves describing events with two participants, either of which semantically could be the subject or object of the verb, for example, the

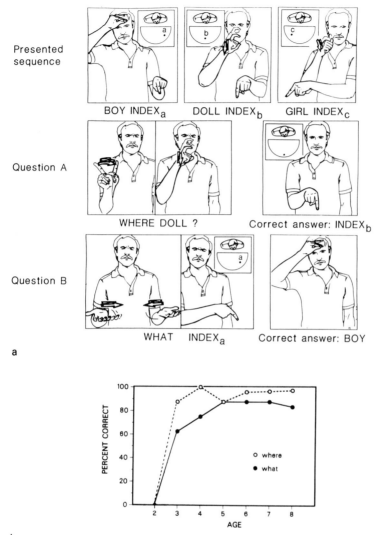

BOY INDEX$_a$ DOLL INDEX$_b$ GIRL INDEX$_c$

WHERE DOLL ?   Correct answer: INDEX$_b$

WHAT   INDEX$_a$ Correct answer: BOY

a

b

Figure 2.4

Association of nominals with spatial loci. (a) Two sample items from the Nominal Establishment Test in which three nouns, BOY, DOLL, and GIRL, are established at different points in signing space. In question A the experimenter asks for the locus of a specific noun sign. In question B the experimenter asks the subject to name the noun associated with a particular locus. (b) Results of the Nominal Establishment Test for sixty-eight young deaf children of deaf parents.

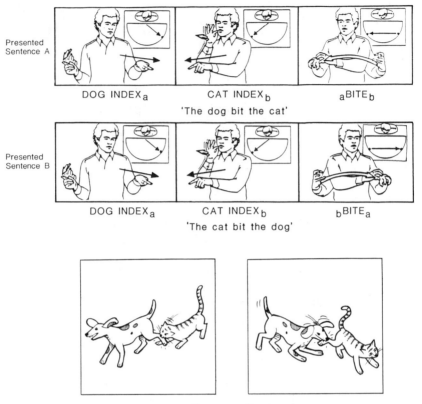

Response Card

Figure 2.5
Verb Agreement with Fixed Framework to test spatialized syntax. Grammatical relations are signaled by the spatial endpoints of the verb. We show here two sample items from the test and the corresponding response-choice card. The subject is asked to select the picture on the card that corresponds to the sentence signed. Note that the spatial arrangement of the nouns in the sentence need not match the spatial arrangement of the objects in the picture.

verb HIT and the two arguments BOY and GIRL. In this test the experimenter first signs a sentence involving nominals, each with an associated spatial pronominal index and an action verb whose spatial endpoints mark subject and object by means of the associated spatial loci, as in

(2.1)   GIRL INDEX$_a$, BOY INDEX$_b$, $_a$HIT$_b$.
        'The girl hit the boy.'

(2.2)   GIRL INDEX$_a$, BOY INDEX$_b$, $_b$HIT$_a$.
        'The boy hit the girl.'

The experimenter then asks the subject two questions in random order about the sentence (figure 2.6). These questions are equivalent to asking: (A) Who was the recipient of the action (that is, who got hit)? and (B) Who was the agent of the action (that is, who did the hitting)? Note that the only difference in form between sentence (2.1) and sentence (2.2), which differs from it in meaning, is in the movement of the verb between the spatial loci established for the nominals. In ASL answers to such questions involve the processing of nominals, the loci associated with them, and the direction of movement of the verb between spatial endpoints. In addition, the test question requires processing a shift of spatial reference, because there is no identity between the spatial loci of the presented sentence with those of the test question.

The tests for processing spatial syntax and coreference in ASL, the Verb Agreement Tests, thus require not only intact syntactic processing but also the intact spatial cognitive abilities that underlie these linguistic functions. Such spatial cognitive functions include perception and memory for spatial locations, for spatial relations, and for higher-order spatial transformations.

Linguistic Analysis
One of the main methods we used to analyze language capacity is the in-depth analysis of language samples of brain-damaged signers. Up to now, with almost no exceptions, previous studies of brain-damaged signers have not analyzed signing in terms of breakdown within the individual structural levels of the sign language.

We have used several sources of data for analyzing free conversation in brain-damaged signers: free interchange, eliciting commonly known stories or having patients retell stories from brief videotaped versions or from stories from books without words, having patients describe their apartments or rooms, and eliciting anaphoric reference in ASL. From this language material we have performed a detailed analysis of language capacity, language use, and language break-

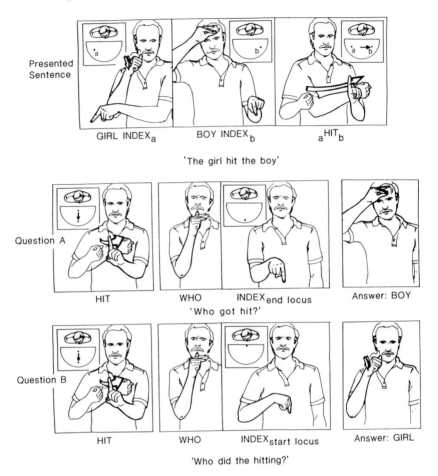

Figure 2.6
Verb Agreement with Shifting Reference to test spatialized syntax. We give a sample test sentence and two questions together with their appropriate responses. Note that the questions involve a shift in the spatial frame of reference relative to the test sentence.

down. We have used the array of techniques at our disposal to understand language structure, function, and breakdown.

2.3.3   Apraxia Tests

In order to investigate apraxias and their possible relation to sign aphasias we administered the following tests, which examine non-representational movements (the Kimura Movement Copying Test), representational movements (ideomotor apraxia tests of the BDAE), and pantomime recognition.

We administered a slightly abbreviated form of the Kimura and Archibald Movement Copying Test (Kimura 1982). In this test of nonrepresentational movement, the subject imitates unfamiliar, meaningless sequences of hand and arm movements.

For symbolic (that is, representational) movements we used the ideomotor apraxia tests of the BDAE, adapted for signers. As in the BDAE our adaptation divides tests of apraxia into three sections: buccofacial movements, intransitive limb movements (for example, "Wave goodbye"), and transitive limb movements (for example, "Throw a ball"). When subjects are unable to carry out a commanded movement ("Show me how you would . . ."), the examiner demonstrates the movement and asks the subject to copy it.

Varney and Benton's (1978) Pantomime Recognition Test was used to assess the ability of our patients to understand meaningful nonlinguistic gestural communication. The test consists of a series of videotapes of a person miming the use of common objects, such as a spoon, pen, or saw. The patient must point to a drawing depicting the object pantomimed from a test booklet containing four response choices per item.

These issues are developed further in chapter 6.

2.3.4   Nonlanguage Visual Processing Tests

We selected the following tests, which maximally distinguish the performance of right- from left-brain-damaged hearing individuals: visuoconstructive tests, visuoperceptual tasks, and visuospatial tasks. Again, our questions deal with the possible special interactions between the use of a visuospatial language and the processing of nonlanguage spatial relations.

Visuoconstructive Tests

In all four of the tests described in what follows (WAIS-R block design, drawing without a model, drawing to copy, and Rey-Osterreith complex figure), hearing patients with right-hemisphere damage are more severely impaired than patients with left-hemisphere damage and show different types of error.

The *block design* subtest of the Wechsler Adult Intelligence Scale (WAIS-R) has proved to be a sensitive means of distinguishing left- from right-brain damage in hearing patients. The subject assembles four or nine three-dimensional blocks with red, white, or half-red and half-white surfaces to match a two-dimensional model of the top surface. In the *drawing without a model* test, the patient draws from memory a clock with numbers and two hands, a daisy, an elephant, a box with three sides visible, and the front and sides of a house (Boston Diagnostic Aphasia Examination, Goodglass and Kaplan 1972). In the *drawing to copy* test the patient copies pictures of a daisy, an elephant, a cross, a box, and a house from models. And finally, in the *Rey-Osterreith complex figure* test the patient copies a drawing of the Rey-Osterreith complex figure (Osterreith 1944), a figure with much internal complexity.

Visuoperceptual Task: Benton Facial Recognition
In hearing people it is mainly the right hemisphere that mediates the discrimination of unfamiliar faces (Benton 1980; Rizzolati, Umilta, and Berlucchi 1971). There are several parts in the test of facial recognition (Benton et al. 1978). In one part the patient matches identical front-view photographs. The subject is shown one photograph of a face and an array of six different front-view photographs below it; the patient must pick the one of the six photographs that is the same as the sample. In the second part of the test the patient matches a front-view photograph with three-quarter-view photographs. He or she picks the three three-quarter-view faces that match from an array of six. In the third part the patient matches front-view photographs taken under different lighting conditions.

Visuospatial Tasks: Hemispatial Neglect and Line Orientation
Certain patients, primarily those with right-hemisphere lesions, have attentional deficits that result in their neglecting one half of the surrounding world, so-called hemispatial neglect. This neglect can extend to patients' ignoring one half of their own bodies. We use two tests of hemispatial neglect. In one test the patient marks the apparent midpoints of horizontal lines of different length. Patients with hemispatial neglect tend to put the mark off center, away from the neglected side, as if they were bisecting just the portion of the "unneglected" line (Benton 1979). In the second test, Albert's (1973) test of hemispatial neglect, the patient crosses out forty lines arranged pseudorandomly on a page. Patients with neglect tend to omit lines on the neglected side.

The perceptual capacity to judge the spatial orientation of lines is primarily mediated by the right hemisphere in hearing individuals. In the Benton Judgment of Line Orientation test, the patient matches the angular orientation of a pair of lines to a response-choice display of eleven lines. Five practice items consist of pairs of lines from the response-choice display that are shown in full length. The thirty test items consist of pairs of lines of partial length. Each partial line of the pair corresponds to the orientation of one of the lines appearing in the response-choice display below it. The partial lines represent either the upper, middle, or lower segments of the response-choice lines. The subject responds by pointing to or giving the numbers of the appropriate response-choice lines.

2.4   Summary Characteristics of Patients

The program of study just outlined is designed to investigate the effects of either left-hemisphere damage or right-hemisphere damage in deaf signers. All tests were administered entirely in ASL by deaf researchers from our laboratory. We videotaped all sessions for later analysis. We generally tested patients well after their cerebral injuries, so the deficits we encountered are likely to be stable ones. Testing requires several sessions, and with some patients we have been able to perform the entire battery more than once, although there are occasional gaps in our data. Because brain-damaged deaf signers are so rare, the patients we studied are scattered across the country. In selecting subjects, we studied only patients who were right-handed before their cerebral injury and who have unilateral damage. (Damage is assessed by CT scans whenever possible.) Subjects are preferentially prelingually deaf, have been signing throughout their lives, have deaf spouses, and are members of the deaf community.

In this book we report in depth on six deaf, brain-damaged signers, three with damage to the left cerebral hemisphere and three with damage to the right cerebral hemisphere. All were given the same range of tests, with occasional omissions. Furthermore, the entire battery was administered to matched deaf controls. (In chapter 8 we also provide results from some other cases of signers with right- or left-hemisphere damage to provide converging evidence for our first findings.)

Table 2.1 presents a summary of the characteristics of the six deaf signers who form the focus of this book. In order to protect the anonymity of the patients, we do not use their real names or initials,

Table 2.1
Summary characteristics of three left-lesioned and three right-lesioned deaf signers

Patient	Age at testing	Sex	Age at onset of deafness	Handed-ness	Language environment					Hemi-plegia	Lesion
					Parents and siblings	School	Spouse	Cultural group	Primary commu-nication		
Left-hemisphere-damaged signers											
Paul D.	81	M	5 yrs.	Right	Hearing	Residential deaf	Deaf	Deaf	Sign	—	Left subcortical; deep to Broca's area extending posteriorly beneath parietal lobe.
Karen L.	67	F	6 mos.	Right	Hearing	Residential deaf	Hard of hearing	Deaf	Sign	Right hemi-plegic	Left parietal; supramarginal and angular gyri; extending subcortically into middle frontal gyrus.
Gail D.	38	F	Birth	Right	Older deaf siblings	Residential deaf	Deaf	Deaf	Sign	Right hemi-plegic	Most of convexity of left frontal lobe; Broca's area damaged.
Right-hemisphere-damaged signers											
Brenda I.	75	F	Birth	Right	Hearing	Residential deaf	Deaf	Deaf	Sign	Left hemi-plegic	Right hemisphere
Sarah M.	71	F	Birth	Right	Hearing	Residential deaf	Deaf	Deaf	Sign	Left hemi-plegic	Right temporoparietal area; most of territory of right middle cerebral artery damaged
Gilbert G.	81	M	5 yrs.	Right	Hearing	Residential deaf	Deaf	Deaf	Sign	—	Right superior temporal and middle temporal gyri extending into the angular gyrus.

and we have changed identifying information, including appearance, in the illustrations. As table 2.1 shows, all the patients were right-handed before their brain damage; all received their entire education at residential schools for the deaf; all had deaf or hard-of-hearing spouses; all used sign language as a primary mode of communication with family and friends throughout all or most of their lives; and all were culturally members of deaf communities.

We first present individual case studies of the three left-lesioned signers, focusing on their language functioning in chapter 3. In chapter 4 we compare visuospatial language capacities across the three deaf signers and present results from the formal language testing. In chapter 5 we present case studies of the three right-hemisphere-damaged signers and contrast the effects of left- and right-hemisphere damage on sign language functioning. In chapter 6 we examine the relationship between apraxia and aphasia for sign language, and in chapter 7 we address the effects of left- and right-hemisphere damage on nonlanguage visuospatial capacities. Finally, in chapter 8 we provide results from a larger group of brain-damaged subjects and address broader questions about what the hands reveal about the brain.

Chapter 3

Signers with Strokes: Left-hemisphere Lesions

3.1 Gail D.: The Agrammatic Signer

When we first met Gail D., she was with her three deaf children, ages 9 to 14, all of them fluent in ASL, their "mother tongue." The children were holding a lively conversation in ASL, describing the events that led up to and followed their mother's left-hemisphere stroke some eight months before.

Our studies began with videotaping the children's signing, which we later submitted to linguistic analysis. We assumed that the family's signing would enable us to characterize Gail D.'s own prestroke signing and that the difference between her present signing and her children's would make clear the linguistic nature of her impairment. The children's ASL appeared to be rich and displayed all the appropriate inflectional and derivational morphology, including all the characteristic syntactic mechanisms of ASL, making full use of spatial contrasts to specify functions such as grammatical subject and object. In short, their colloquial ASL was perfectly full and correct. We felt assured that Gail D.'s prestroke language had been the same, a conclusion in which her brother, also a deaf signer, concurred.

At the time of the interview, Gail D., when compared to her children, presented us with a striking contrast. The difference between the mother and her children would have impressed even an uninformed outsider. The three bright-faced children were engaged in high-spirited, effortless interchange; their hands moved rapidly, smoothly, rhythmically. The commentary "changed hands" as each vied to take the conversational lead. Sitting between them, their mother looked from one to another as they took their turns. She, however, made almost no signs. She appeared to follow the conversation with eager attention, but even though she was its subject, she did not join in. An occasional nod, even an isolated sign came from her, but it was effortful, halting, and out of synchrony with the cadence of her children's free-flowing interchanges and completed after a false start or two. To us her signs seemed appropriate but limited, an indication that she was following the conversation—agreeing or disagreeing with what the children were telling us about her. Her frequent changes of facial expression registered her affective responses, but she seemed quite unable to initiate any communications about herself. We had the general impression that Gail D. was a vibrant, enthusiastic young woman, well tuned-in to the conversation, but her expression often turned into a grimace in the struggle to produce even an isolated sign—a pained reflection of her frustration.

Gail D. is a congenitally deaf woman, born of hearing parents. The etiology of her deafness, however, is hereditary; she has a deaf brother and a deaf sister. As a child she learned ASL from her deaf elder sister. She attended a school for deaf students and later worked as a postal employee and as a photograph retoucher. She was 38 at the time of testing, having experienced a left-hemisphere stroke some eight months before. Although initially her entire right side was affected, she had regained the use of her leg and face; her right arm, however, remained paralyzed. She had no apparent sensory deficit.

A CT scan performed eleven months after her stroke (figure 3.1) showed a left-hemisphere lesion:

CT Findings

There was a left-hemisphere lesion that involved most of the convexity of the frontal lobe, including Broca's area and the anterior portions of the superior and middle temporal gyri. The parietal lobe was spared, with the exception of the bottom of the postcentral gyrus and of small patchy lucencies in the white matter underlying the angular gyrus. The left internal capsule, putamen, and claustrum were also involved.

Gail D.'s children told us that her prestroke signing had been rich and effortless and much like their own but that after her stroke she suddenly became unable to communicate her thoughts through her language and certainly unable to formulate anything like a full statement. Even when she managed to bring forth a signed yes or no to signal agreement or disagreement, the ASL sign she produced occasionally seemed at variance with her intention, as when, in apparent agreement with someone else's claim about her, she nodded yes but signed no. Thus the lexical substitutions (so-called verbal paraphasias) that adversely affected her linguistic output did not always similarly affect her use of symbolic gestures in general.

By the time we began our testing, eight months after Gail D.'s stroke, the initial disabilities caused by the stroke had in many ways abated. Gail D. could now eat properly and could hold and manipulate objects, such as forks and pens, appropriately. She was also able to care for herself and for her family. Despite these recoveries in her

Gail D.

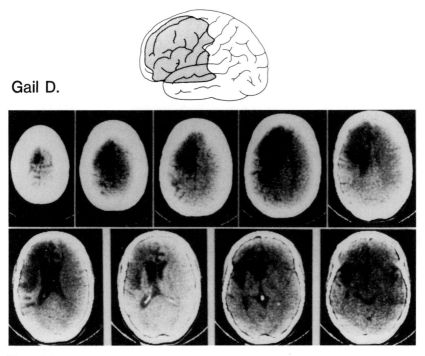

Figure 3.1
Lateral reconstruction of lesion and CT scan of left-lesioned patient Gail D.

physical condition, however, Gail D. was still virtually unable to express herself in sign (although her family reported that she understood them when they were signing).

We now present a translation from ASL of part of an interchange
between one of the examiners and two of Gail D.'s children:

EXAMINER: When did the stroke happen?
DAUGHTER: The first time it happened, I saw her. No, that time,
both of us happened to see her standing, and then fall. It was
hot, and it was in the summertime. She was standing in the
kitchen, and she staggered and fell by the corner of the door. She
lost her balance and fell on the floor. She was really dizzy. First I
told her to go to bed; and I pleaded with her, and told her that
she couldn't stand, and that I could cook for the family. "Go to
bed," I said to her, "I know how to cook." But she stood near the
corner, and then she just lost her balance and fell on the floor. I
ran and tried to catch her, but I failed. I was holding her, and she
was dizzy—it was terrible! We dragged her to the bed and tried

to pull her up on it. Her whole right side had become weak, and she had lost her ability to sign.

EXAMINER: What was her signing like after she returned from the hospital?

SON: It was hard to understand her language at first. I tried to catch what she meant. She seemed to know what she wanted to say, but it was hard for us to understand her. Sometimes her mind was confused at first. She could only answer yes or no, and even so we could not always be sure what she meant. She learned again, little by little, and now it is easier to make out what she is trying to sign. After her stroke, we had to take it step by step, and even to teach her the ABCs again.

Gail D. was 37 years old when she suffered this incapacitating stroke. From an interview with a close friend who was with the family throughout their problems, we learned more about the onset of the difficulties. Gail D. was in the hospital for three weeks after her stroke. At first, as the children indicated, she would not sign at all; communication for her was limited mostly to nodding her head to affirm or agree and to shaking her head to negate or disagree. Gail D. also had difficulty eating at first, not remembering how to hold a fork and trying to put the wrong end of it in her mouth. She would sometimes miss her mouth and try to direct her hand to her mouth. This lasted three to four weeks after the stroke. The children reported that the first sign Gail D. regained was CIGARETTE. Before the stroke she had been an inveterate smoker, which apparently provided enough motivation for this initial sign. Slowly she began to regain signs, one by one. Overall incapacitation and confusion such as this is not unusual during the initial recovery stage following a massive stroke.

Gail D. was born and raised in the West, the youngest in a family of five. Like her elder sister and brother, she has been deaf since birth. She went to the same residential school for deaf children as they did. Gail D.'s older siblings provided a sign language environment for her before she went to school. Her sign language environment was maintained during both elementary and high school, where the primary language used was ASL. She graduated from a residential high school with a vocational degree. During all those years her major form of communication was ASL—with classmates, dormitory counselors, friends, and other deaf adults. Gail D. married a deaf classmate and had three children, all of whom are deaf. These were the children we met during the first interview with Gail D. From childhood on, ASL has been Gail D.'s primary form of communication. Before her stroke Gail D. had been active in the local association for the deaf and had many deaf friends.

3.1.1   Agrammatic Language in Gail D.

As has been indicated, Gail D.'s spontaneous output was extremely sparse after her stroke. In order to elicit a richer sample that might reveal more clearly the nature of her language impairment, we asked Gail D. to describe the Cookie Theft picture. By allowing her to describe a picture, we provided her with a reference point from which she could formulate her description in sign as carefully and slowly as she desired. The examiner also presented her with prompts when necessary. The picture, taken from the BDAE, is reproduced in figure 2.1. The picture is a standard in studies of agrammatism across many different languages. In later chapters we examine all six patients' descriptions of the Cookie Theft picture.

Language Sample
The following is a sample of Gail D.'s interchanges with the examiner, all in ASL. The examiner's probes are given in English translation; Gail D.'s signing is in English gloss for signs. Figure 3.2 shows Gail D.'s awkward rendition and effortful articulation of the sign BROTHER, taken from her description of the picture.

> EXAMINER: What's that? [Pointing to the picture.]
> GAIL D.: THREE.
> EXAMINER: Who is that? [Pointing to the woman in the picture.]
> GAIL D.: MOTHER.
> EXAMINER: Who is that? [Pointing to the boy.]
> GAIL D.: BROTHER . . . BROTHER . . . .

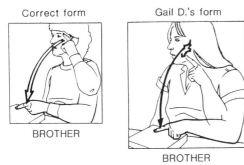

Figure 3.2
Effortful production typical of Gail D.'s signing.

EXAMINER: What's happening there? [Pointing to the water spilling on the floor.]
GAIL D.: WHAT? [Points, gestures, mouths "oh."]
EXAMINER: What is that? [Pointing to the water again.]
GAIL D.: F- . . . E- . . . F- . . . A- . . . L- . . . L. [Fingerspells "fall" laboriously.]
EXAMINER: What is the woman doing there?
GAIL D.: [Fumbles and gestures, then signs] PLATE T- . . . E- . . . O- . . . W- . . . L. [Attempts to fingerspell "towel."]
EXAMINER: What is the woman doing?
GAIL D.: TURN-OFF. TURN-OFF.
EXAMINER: What does the girl want?
GAIL D.: [Mouths "cookie" but puts finger to lips as does girl in picture.]
EXAMINER: What does the boy want?
GAIL D.: C- . . . A- . . . O- . . . O- . . . K- . . . E. [Attempts to fingerspell "cookie."]
EXAMINER: The boy wants what?
GAIL D.: [Points to boy, then to girl, then fingerspells] G- . . . A- . . . V- . . . E.
EXAMINER: The boy gave her a cookie?
GAIL D.: YES.
EXAMINER: What happened there? [Pointing to the stool about to fall.]
GAIL D.: [Mouths "off" and "fall" fumbles.]
EXAMINER: It is falling?
GAIL D.: YES.
EXAMINER: Okay. The boy is falling?
GAIL D.: YES.
EXAMINER: What about the girl?
GAIL D.: [Puts finger to lips.]
EXAMINER: She wants a cookie? [Prompting.]
GAIL D.: YES.
EXAMINER: What about the mother here?
GAIL D.: [Mouths "off" and pantomimes turning the faucet off, then attempts to fingerspell.] F- . . . D- . . . A- . . . S.
EXAMINER: [Guessing.] Dish?
GAIL D.: YES.
EXAMINER: Okay, fine. That's a funny picture. [Both smile.]

As the transcription shows, even with the picture before her and the prompting, Gail D.'s signing is exceedingly sparse. She tries to form ASL signs and to fingerspell English words, but even these simple words show transpositions and perseverations of the letters, for example, T-E-O-W-L for T-O-W-E-L. There are certain characteristics of Gail D.'s choice of means of communication that make her signing unusual, aside from the sparseness. First, there is an inordinate proportion of fingerspelled words. But more than that, for some of the items that she fingerspells, there are familiar and simple ASL signs that correspond to them. In such a passage the signs would be expected to occur rather than the fingerspelled words. These include the signs GIVE, COOKIE, and FALL, all of which Gail D. fingerspelled rather than signed. In other passages, though, Gail D. used these signs. In addition, she resorts to a variety of other methods of communication—the mouthing of English words, pantomime, and other nonsign gesturing. It is unusual that a combination of diverse communicative devices would occur in such an intermingled fashion within one description. Gail D. appears to be trying every device at her disposal to communicate, and after effortful attempts she appears blocked and continues to be so after switching from one mode of communication to another. This switching might well reflect a strategy that she adopted to bypass the blocking that rapidly develops within one mode of communication.

Gail D.'s signing consists largely of isolated open-class signs, without any of the grammatical apparatus of ASL. There are no grammatical inflections, no instances of derivational morphology, no compounding, no spatial indexing of nominals, and no verb agreement. Note, for example, that instead of signing the appropriate ASL verb GIVE, with its spatial inflections for verb agreement, Gail D. fingerspells instead. Her signed output is essentially a limited set of nouns and a few verbs, all in uninflected, simple citation form.

In fact, Gail D.'s signing of the Cookie Theft picture (figure 2.1) is similar to that of hearing patients who are classified as having Broca's aphasia. Goodglass and Kaplan (1972) present the following transcript for a case of an English-speaking Broca's aphasic describing the same picture.

EXAMINER: What happened?
PATIENT: Cookie jar . . . fall over . . . chair . . . . water . . . empty . . . . ov . . . ov . . . .
EXAMINER: Overflow?
PATIENT: Yeah.

The Contrast between Broca-like Signing and Autistic Signing
Deficits in language can take many forms. To sharpen our understanding of Gail D.'s language capacities, we found it instructive to compare her signing with the signing of another language-impaired

deaf woman whose signing bears some surface resemblance to that of
Gail D. This young woman, Judith M., is a deaf autistic signer, also
from a deaf family. She has deaf parents and two deaf elder brothers.
The family communicates in ASL only, and the young woman has
been surrounded all her life by ASL as a major form of communication. Her two elder brothers are native signers and college educated.

Judith M.'s first eleven months of life were, according to family
reports, normal, with no traumatic events. Then, at the age of 11
months, she began to exhibit autisticlike behavior; she no longer
made eye contact with the people around her. Instead of watching or
responding to facial expressions, she stared listlessly at inanimate
objects. She was diagnosed as autistic. Judith M. did not begin signing until the age of 5, when she produced the sign ICE-CREAM. We
interviewed her at home with her family when she was 21. Like Gail
D., Judith M. had a rich signing environment, in which her family
signed all the time.

In what follows we give a sample interchange between Judith M.
and her father (the father's ASL has been translated into English):

> FATHER: Do you want to see a train?
> JUDITH M.: SEE TRAIN. [An imitation of sign just produced by
> her father.]
> FATHER: First, we will . . . ?
> JUDITH M.: FIRST. [Imitation.]
> FATHER: Second, we will . . . ?
> JUDITH M.: SECOND . . . STORE.
> FATHER: Yes, we will go to the store. Third, we will . . . ?
> JUDITH M.: THIRD. [Imitation.]
> FATHER: Yes, we will be home soon.
> JUDITH M.: HOME, SOON. [Imitation.]
> FATHER: What will we do on Wednesday?
> JUDITH M.: STORE . . . TRAIN.
> FATHER: That again?
> JUDITH M.: AGAIN. [Imitation.]
> FATHER: Father and Judith M. will go to a store.
> JUDITH M.: STORE . . . FIRST . . . SECOND.
> FATHER: In the morning, we first go to the store.
> JUDITH M.: FIRST. [Imitation.]

Similarities in Signing of Gail D. and Judith M.
There are certain similarities in the surface output of the two young
deaf women communicating in ASL; the output of both is highly
restricted. The signed utterances of each consist of only one or two

signs, without syntactic relationships expressed. Both signers are from rich signing environments in which ASL is the primary form of communication among family and friends; yet in contrast to the grammatically rich and motorically facile signing evident around them in the home, the two of them exhibit marked signing deficits. Like Gail D., Judith M. shows not a shred of the complex grammar of ASL (no sentences, no inflections, no derivational processes, no compounding, no embeddings, and no spatial organization). The sign output of both is dysfluent, halting, effortful, and awkward, but in somewhat different fashions. Both emit signs somewhat effortfully, even stiffly. Both have highly restrictive vocabularies in their spontaneous signing, so their output is extremely sparse and limited. Despite these similarities, however, there are also differences between the two women that highlight the particular nature of Gail D.'s deficit in sign language.

Differences in Categorization

Some important differences between the language of the two young women were revealed by their responses to pictures. Almost all of Gail D.'s signed responses were the appropriate names for the objects in the pictures. In fact, in giving names for objects presented in pictures, Gail D. not only was accurate but even emitted responses relatively easily on many occasions. In contrast, Judith M.'s responses were often bizarre and limited to the same few signs given again and again as a response to a variety of different objects. For example, we showed her fifteen pictures of animals—dogs, cats, rats, snakes, monkeys, lobsters, insects, horses, and birds, and asked her to name each. To rat, monkey, insect, and bird, she responded BIRD; to all the others, she responded DOG. Her responses to pictures of people were even more bizarre. She misidentified all the pictures of people in her first response, focusing on some nonessential or irrelevant feature or activity: To a picture of a man running, for example, she responded HAIR. (It is revealing that Judith M. does not refer to any of her three brothers by name, but rather calls each of them BOY.) In contrast, her responses to inanimate objects were far more varied and often correct (she correctly named a helicopter, train, chair, book, church, airplane, spoon, store, iron, house, ring, hanger, and bicycle). Sometimes she responded with an item in a semantically related category (to a picture of a wreath, she responded TREE; to a picture of a car, she responded BICYCLE). These unusual naming responses reveal a curious distribution in Judith M.'s vocabulary, which appears to map to her interests. Autistic persons often show more involvement with things than with people. In contrast, virtually all of Gail D.'s responses, though short and discontinuous, were correct and appropriate, no matter what category of item she named (persons, places, things, colors, numbers, letters, activities, and so on).

Differences in Communicative Intent

When we consider Judith M.'s conversation, we note that much of her contribution is a kind of echolalia, imitating signs just made to her. In discourse with her family she rarely initiated topics of conversation. On the few occasions when she did initiate some conversational topic, a limited set of functions was involved; all the functions were situation bound and self-centered. Sometimes Judith M. initiated a topic to excuse herself from uncomfortable situations or to satisfy needs, such as eating, drinking, sleeping, and bathing. Furthermore, she interspersed all kinds of mannerism in her discourse. She rarely made eye contact and tended to avoid social interaction. The examiner had to make a gentle attempt to get her attention for each situation and each picture elicitation. As one family member wrote us, she "initiates communication only to serve basic wants and needs of her own." She shows no variation in facial expression or gesturing, nor does she attempt to mime or to communicate in other ways. The family member wrote us also that Judith M. "appears generally incapable of abstract thought, and shows no indication that she responds to the feelings of others, but only exhibits limited, largely echolalic signing." This echolalic signing is interspersed with meaningless repetitive movements that appear empty of communicative intent. Despite her rich signing environment, her own signing— and the cognitive capacities that underlie her language—is highly limited.

In summary, Judith M. is echolalic and avoids eye contact or any other contact with people. She rarely signs spontaneously except for the minimum necessary to satisfy basic needs; she appears to have little or no cognitive communicative intent. These are characteristics that Judith M. has displayed since infancy. She is "in a world of her own," as her parents put it. As is typical of autistic people, she is strikingly deficient in linguistic and cognitive functions. But unlike Gail D., she gives no indication that she is aware of her language shortcomings or of the feelings, intentions, or language of those around her.

3.1.2   A Broca-like Sign Profile

Although the surface form of Gail D.'s signing has some similarities to Judith M.'s, Gail D. tries every means at her disposal to communicate. She makes eye contact; she tries urgently to communicate, to indicate her ideas, and to engage in conversation with those around her. In her attempts to communicate, Gail D. not only struggles to express herself in signs but also attempts to mime, gesture, and even mouth or fingerspell English words. She is acutely aware of her difficulty in communicating and is constantly monitoring the responses of others, nodding vigorously when she is understood and indicating clearly when the addressee has misinterpreted her attempts to express herself. With a few signs and gestures Gail D. persists and often succeeds in communicating information about her past, family, childhood, and current experiences.

Gail D.'s signing output is limited to the expression of unadorned referential nouns and verbs, without any of the grammatical apparatus of ASL. It is clear that she has suffered a breakdown in specific aspects of linguistic functions that she once commanded. Despite her linguistic difficulties, she shows a zealous desire to communicate. Also, she shows the preservation of other cognitive functions, as the following results attest.

Lexical Retrieval
One important language function is the ability to access lexical items and associate them with their appropriate referents, that is, to bring up from memory the words that name specific things or actions or qualities. Gail D.'s spontaneous signing was extremely sparse, and what she did produce was almost exclusively uninflected nouns and verbs. In various tasks that we gave her, including some that required her to name pictures of objects, Gail D. showed that she could come up with the correct sign for the item presented. It is interesting that Gail D. often did not seem to have the same kind of effortful articulation on many of the naming tasks that she showed in spontaneous signing. She was rapid and, more important, accurate in naming objects. Figure 3.3 illustrates the kinds of effortful, awkward production Gail D. showed in her spontaneous signing of GIRL.

Because Gail D. was occasionally able to give a single sign response smoothly and rapidly, her deficit was clearly not a peripheral motor one but something more central. Furthermore, certain irregularities in Gail D.'s signing appear to depend on the linguistic function and structure of the unit she was attempting to produce, rather than on the form of the gesture itself. For example, a given gestural component, such as path movement directed toward her body, was preserved when that direction was a simple sublexical component of a sign, as when she signed ACCEPT. However, when that same path movement functioned as an inflectional morpheme (for example, indicating first person, as in BLAME-ME), she failed to produce it,

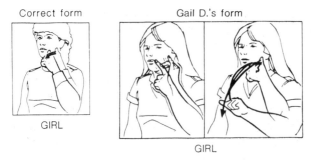

Figure 3.3
Articulatory difficulty characteristic of Gail D.'s signing. In the example Gail D. searches for the Hand Configuration and Movement of the sign, although on occasion she produces the sign smoothly.

signing instead the uninflected form. Thus her sign impairment cannot be simply a result of an inability to control and produce a given movement; it must be linguistically based.

As noted, Gail D. could produce many isolated signs if all that was required were morphologically simple, unmodulated open-class items. Her comprehension and memory for lexical items was good; she obtained a near-perfect score on a test of the comprehension of single signs. She was even readily able to give prompt and accurate answers to questions in ASL, such as "What do you do with a book?" and "What color is grass?" Likewise, on a test that requires comprehension and memory of two and three signs and their associated spatial loci, Gail D. performed similarly to controls. She was also able to follow many complex commands. In certain areas of ASL morphology, however, both her comprehension and her production were clearly deficient.

Morphology
Gail D.'s signing reflects none of the grammatical apparatus of ASL—none of the morphological inflections, for example, that are the markers for grammatical distinctions in the language. Recall that signs of ASL are related by a wide variety of inflectional and derivational processes. As discussed in chapter 1, a base lexical item often has a family of associated forms that are interrelated by formal patterning based on modifications of the movement of the signs in space. These different forms mark grammatical categories, such as person, number, reciprocity, temporal aspect, distributional aspect, and derivational processes. Gail D. not only consistently omitted these required inflectional morphemes in her spontaneous signing but also was unable to produce such morphologically complex forms in an elicitation

task. Her difficulty appears to come in assembling meaningful elements into a composite unit. Her primary problem is not in selecting the correct lexical morpheme but in combining the lexical morpheme with inflectional morphemes.

Gail D.'s morphological deficits extend beyond her inability to produce morphologically complex forms. One productive derivational process in ASL relates semantically associated noun-verb pairs, such as BROOM and SWEEP. On a comprehension test of the morphological distinction between these formally related nouns and verbs, Gail D. performed poorly compared to control subjects. She scored only 60 percent correct, below the range of scores of control subjects (the lowest score among sixteen young adult signers was 80 percent correct, and that among three elderly control subjects was 85 percent correct). Similarly, her performance was poor on a test of production of noun/verb distinction. In the testing we found that at times Gail D. made the appropriate formal distinction in specific individual noun-verb pairs (as in DOOR and OPEN-DOOR or BRACELET and PUT-ON-BRACELET); nevertheless, she did not appear to have control of this morphological distinction. The fact that her performance was poor in comprehension and production tasks makes it clear that her problems are at a morphological level, not at a motoric one.

Spatialized Syntax
As we have seen, Gail D. emitted only single signs without any of the inflectional apparatus of ASL or any of the other spatial-grammatical devices in the language, including those involving the manipulation of space. Even when we tried to elicit the production of relatively simple inflectional forms (such as that expressed by the change in direction of motion that signals a difference in subject-object relations), Gail D. was grossly impaired. The situation was different for comprehension of spatial syntax, however. Here, on many of our tests, she performed well. We note parenthetically that even her memory for nonlanguage spatial location was good. She was given two short-term memory tests; one required remembering the spatial locations of a series of randomly arranged blocks. In this test, the Corsi blocks test, there is an array of blocks before the patient. Patterns of an increasing number of blocks are formed by the examiner tapping out, on the blocks, the different spatial patterns. The patient taps out the same patterns until she reaches her spatial span. The second test, digit span, involves memory for sequences, not spatial memory. In this test the examiner signs series of numbers of increasing length, which the patient repeats until she reaches her digit span. Gail D. performed well on the Corsi blocks, with a spatial span of 5.

This score for spatial memory is well within the range of normal control signers. Her digit span, however, was 3, a sequence that is shorter than that of control subjects. Returning now to her language, we note that, although Gail D. could not produce a multisign utterance and although her signs were generally monomorphemic, she appeared to understand and grasp the gist of conversations, to understand instructions, to cope well with directives, and to correct the addressee's interpretations of her limited signs. Under these circumstances, however, one cannot be certain how much of Gail D.'s understanding is based on contextual cues, how much on the comprehension of selected words in the sentence, and how much on the comprehension of specific syntactic properties of a sentence.

To resolve this question, we administered a variety of comprehension tests. Among them were items from the standard BDAE, such as the ASL equivalent of "Put the watch next to the pencil and then turn the card over"—signed with an array of the objects in front of her. Gail D. performed all the tasks correctly. Thus we conclude that her comprehension is syntactically based.

To isolate aspects of her processing of ASL syntax, we used the two Verb Agreement Tests. These tests require the decoding of certain syntactic structures in ASL, namely, the spatial marking for verb agreement. In both tests we used reversible situations, such as a cat biting a dog and a dog biting a cat. Contrasts such as these are used to test for the processing of subject and object of active sentences in spoken English. In English it is the order of the items that signals subject-object relations. In ASL such grammatical relations may also be signaled by the manipulation of spatial relations, in which case the nominals are associated with specific points in the plane of signing space and the direction of the movement of the verb between spatial endpoints indicates subject-object relations. Gail D. had no difficulty comprehending these spatial relations in either test. When asked to point to the picture reflecting the relationship expressed in a signed sentence (Verb Agreement with Fixed Framework), she scored 80 percent correct. Furthermore, on the Verb Agreement Test with Shifting Reference, she had a flawless performance, comprehending all items correctly. These results stand in sharp contrast to her performance on the noun-verb comprehension test. Furthermore, the difference between the two performances is stable. A year and a half after our first testing of Gail D. (two years poststroke), we retested her on her comprehension of these two grammatical processes. At this later testing, the discrepancy was just as pronounced: superior performance (100 percent correct) on the verb agreement with fixed framework test but impaired performance (60 percent) on the comprehension of noun/verb distinction test. In the second testing, as in the first, Gail D. gave every indication that she could discriminate the characteristic movement of the verb from that of the related noun; her problem seemed to be one of associating each of the movement patterns with the appropriate grammatical category. Because there was no evidence at all of syntactic relations in her signing, this good comprehension of spatial verb agreement without reliance on contextual or semantic cues is striking.

3.1.3   Agrammatic English and Agrammatic ASL

Agrammatic English Writing

We have some samples of Gail D.'s prestroke written English, primarily from brief notes that she kept to indicate daily activities. As is common, deaf adults misspell many English words based on a lack of knowledge of their grapheme-phoneme correspondence. Spelling, of course, requires the ability to make productive use of English orthography. Hearing people tend to spell according to the pronunciation of words, as the frequency of phonetic misspellings testifies. Deaf people, of course, are less likely to rely on word pronunciation. Hoemann et al. (1976) tested deaf children in a recognition paradigm for the spelling of names for common objects. He found that only 19 percent of the errors for any age group were phonetically based, in contrast to up to 83 percent for hearing children on the same task. Hanson (1982) has studied the kinds of spelling error made by deaf adults and deaf children; she also found a predominance of errors that are not phonetically based. One type of error involved letter deletions in writing, as in "pinic" for *picnic*; "vehile" for *vehicle*. Another type of frequent and striking error was the transposition of letters within a word in ways that are not at all phonetically based. For example, "bapitze" for *baptize*, "hemipshere" for *hemisphere*, "surgrey" for *surgery*, "umberlla" for *umbrella*, and "agrue" for *argue*. Gail D.'s prestroke writing has misspellings of this kind; nevertheless the grammatical structure, even in these brief written reminders to herself, is intact. Here are some examples of her prestroke writing:

> I went to the hospital for blood trements.
> I went to the clinic for medince but it is all wrong.
> My husband buy medince for me. I don't have money.

The sentences have some complexity. There are pronouns, prepositions, some articles, and generally adequate grammatical structure, although the sentences are not without error, especially in the spelling; but the spelling errors, in general, cluster around the same few words (for example, "medince").

After her stroke Gail D. was able to write with her left hand, but her written English was radically different. Describing the Cookie Theft picture (figure 2.1) from the BDAE, Gail D. wrote the following:

Boy fell.
Girl want a cooker.
Mother turn off.

Her poststroke writing is extremely abbreviated, with little sentence structure. Her spelling deteriorated dramatically: She cannot spell her own name correctly or that of the city she lives in. The errors not only involve omissions or transpositions but also include radical and irrelevant intrusions ("Aution" for *Austin*, "Trex" for *Texas*, "firht" for *first*). The fact that Gail D.'s written English is impaired in a way similar to her signing points to a general loss of language capacities.

Agrammatic Signing
We present another sample of Gail D.'s poststroke signing:

GAIL D.: BROTHER . . . [Mouths "stove."] . . . C-O-A-T-T . . . [Mimes "flame burning."] . . . MANY C-A-A-T . . . FIRE . . . . [Face expresses surprise, gestures.]
[Examiner guesses that she means that her brother burned her on the stove.]
GAIL D.: YES.
EXAMINER: What did the brother burn?
GAIL D.: YES . . . C-O-A . . . .
EXAMINER: You mean the cat?
GAIL D.: YES. [Nods emphatically.]

This sample comes from our extended examination eight months after her stroke and typifies the extreme poverty of the output. Virtually all signs are either expletives (YES, NO) or open-class referential items, largely confined to nouns and to a limited number of them. The examiner guesses about the intent of the communication and in fact bears the brunt of the conversational interaction. Yet Gail D. clearly has a story about her childhood that she wants to convey and is able to indicate whether the examiner's guesses are correct or not. Although the communication is halting and effortful, with many interjections by the examiner, much information seems to have been exchanged.

3.1.4   Modality and Language

Indeed, Gail D.'s particular pattern of language impairment strongly resembles the pattern that is called Broca's aphasia in hearing patients. The characteristics of this syndrome include production that is awkward and dysfluent, lacks grammatical formatives, and is syntactically impoverished; comprehension, however, is relatively spared (see figure 3.4 for rating-scale profile). Although the modality is different, Gail D.'s signing fits the description of a Broca's aphasic remarkably well, and tests of her comprehension (the BDAE and her responses to the examiner in conversation) show that it is good; her scores on the BDAE comprehension test fall in the range typical of hearing Broca's aphasics. Closer examination with sensitive tests does reveal that Gail D. has some comprehension impairment for closed-class morphology. This is also consistent with the pattern of language deficits claimed for hearing Broca's aphasics (Zurif 1980).

There is one way in which Gail D.'s behavior appears to diverge from that of the conglomerate of impairments in language, including agrammatism, that has classically been referred to as Broca's aphasia. As indicated, Gail D.'s appreciation of one significant aspect of ASL syntax (conveyed through verb agreement) is not only good but in fact superior: her comprehension of syntactic relations conveyed spatially. For example, Gail D. obtained a perfect score on a test of verb agreement with shifting reference. This result differs from her performance on noun-verb and other morphology tests, in which she was impaired; verb agreement, however, is spatial. This difference may have to do with the site and extent of Gail D.'s left-hemisphere lesion. The CT scan shows that, although her lesion is massive, affecting the entire convexity of the left frontal lobe and parts of the anterior temporal lobe, the left parietal lobe is spared. Just this sort of lesion would cause typical Broca's aphasia in a hearing patient, with comprehension of closed-class morphology disrupted. This appears to be true across several different spoken languages (Kean 1985). It is important to note that Gail D. did not show intact comprehension of all grammatical processes. As described, she showed impaired comprehension on a morphological test of noun/verb distinction. Also, Gail D. showed severe impairment on a test to elicit production of morphological inflections. This pattern of impairment is similar to the kind of deficit seen across hearing agrammatic patients. Yet Gail D. has no trouble comprehending (although she could not produce) syntactic relations conveyed spatially. In fact, her performance on these tests was better than that of many non-brain-damaged young control subjects. This difference between Gail D.'s capacity to process morphology and syntax conveyed through spatial verb agreement in ASL, both of which are absent from her signing, may be a consequence of the modality through which these linguistic structures are conveyed.

Patient's Name___Gail D._____ Date of rating_____

                                                    Rated by_____

APHASIA SEVERITY RATING SCALE

0. No usable sign or sign comprehension.

1. All communication is through fragmentary expression; great need for inference,
    questioning and guessing by the listener. The range of information which can be
    exchanged is limited, and the listener carries the burden of communication.

2. Conversation about familiar subjects is possible with help from the listener. There are
    frequent failures to convey the idea, but patient shares the burden of communication
    with the examiner.

3. The patient can discuss almost all everyday problems with little or no assistance.
    However, reduction of sign and/or comprehension make conversation about certain
    material difficult or impossible.

4. Some obvious loss of fluency in sign or facility of comprehension, without significant
    limitation on ideas expressed or form of expression.

5. Minimal discernible sign handicaps; patient may have subjective difficulties which are
    not apparent to listener.

RATING SCALE PROFILE OF SIGN CHARACTERISTICS

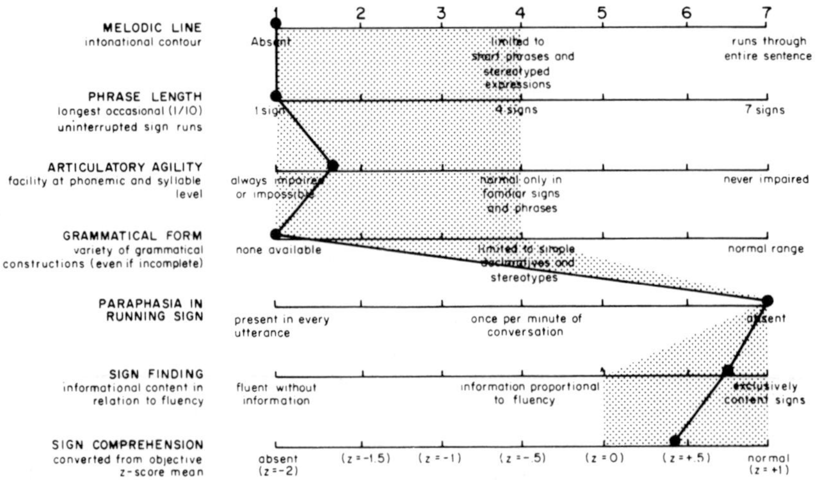

Figure 3.4
Standardized assessment of aphasia: rating-scale profile from Boston Diagnostic
Aphasia Examination for Gail D. The shaded region represents the range of profiles of
hearing subjects who are classified as having Broca's aphasia. Gail D.'s sign profile falls
well within this range.

Indeed, it is precisely in syntax that ASL makes the most dramatic use of space, and this is where Gail D.'s performance is unexpectedly good. Our interpretation is that syntactic function is nonetheless subserved by left-hemisphere structures. However, this case leads us to raise an interesting possibility: Will it turn out that the areas within the left hemisphere that are crucial for spatialized syntactic processing are more intimately connected to higher-order spatial processing in general? We examine this hypothesis in the light of the additional cases we present.

3.2   Karen L.: The Grammatical Signer

When we entered the room, Karen L. greeted us warmly and profusely, all smiles of recognition and pleasure. She began signing immediately, a tirade of talk, gossip, personal accounts of her experiences, complaints and praises about her surroundings. Her sign language flowed, hand moving freely and rapidly, in marked contrast to the halting, effortful, limited communication of Gail D. Karen L. told us stories about her background, her school days, and her personal history when we visited. Karen L. became deaf at the age of 6 months during an attack of scarlet fever. She attended a residential school for deaf children, and it was there that she learned ASL, which then served as her preferred way of communicating with others. ASL was her primary means of communication throughout her life with family and friends. She left high school at age 16, before graduating, and supported herself by working in manufacturing jobs. She worked throughout her adult life in relatively arduous surroundings. Karen L. married a man who, like herself, is deaf; thus in the family the communication was in ASL. Her close friends were deaf people, and sign language was their common mode of communication as well. In her most recent position Karen L. worked as a maid for a deaf couple, both of whom are professional educators; she had also been a baby-sitter and companion for deaf children. Karen L. regularly attended a church that had a deaf congregation and a signing minister. Her physician was one who knew deaf people and sign language. He conducted his examinations in sign language, and when he arranged to put Karen L. in a nursing home temporarily, he sought to find other deaf people for that home as well, so that she would have someone to communicate with.

During our test sessions Karen L. was happy to see the deaf examiners who visited with her, was eager to communicate with them in sign language, and was generally loquacious and gregarious. On five different occasions, we visited Karen L. and tested her; thus we had the opportunity to study the course of recovery of her abilities after her stroke. The results reported here are primarily from testing a year and eight months after her stroke, when Karen L. was 67 years old. Karen L.'s right side was paralyzed when we tested her; she had to walk with a cane or walker, and she had only limited use of her right arm. During testing and regularly after her stroke, Karen L. signed with her left hand, using the less functioning right hand as a base. Nonetheless, she had no problem producing signs.

Ten weeks after her stroke Karen L. had a CT scan (figure 3.5), which showed damage to the left hemisphere:

CT Findings
The scan showed primary impairment in the left parietal region. There was a left slit-like lucency in the region of the supramarginal and angular gyri that extended anteriorly and subcortically into the postcentral and precentral gyri, as well as into the posterior portion of the middle frontal gyrus.

Karen L. was described by deaf friends who knew her before her stroke as "warm, talkative [even garrulous in sign], and friendly." She exhibited the same characteristics after her stroke with the researchers who came to visit her at the hospital, the nursing home, and in the home of friends. She narrated events that occurred in the nursing home, in the hospital, and from her life before her stroke. She communicated well and freely, and for the most part, during our testing her memory seemed good; her signing was motorically fluent and in considerable part understandable (as we will explain).

We were able to interview a number of Karen L.'s deaf friends who had been in close communication with her both before and after her stroke, and thus we had a basis for evaluating her poststroke signing. A videotape filmed a few days after her stroke showed that Karen L. was nearly globally aphasic at first, using primarily gestures that were largely uninterpretable. There were hardly any recognizable signs at the time, only primarily vague gestures. To a series of questions she could indicate only that she did not know. We interviewed Karen L. six months after her stroke; she showed considerable improvement. By the time of our formal testing, Karen L.'s signing was once again effortless, grammatical, and interpretable; indeed, she was gregarious and even voluble. Her early symptomatology is reported in Chiarello, Knight, and Mandel (1982) and in Bellugi (1983). During our testing Karen L. appeared to be the least impaired of the three left-lesioned patients in her signing output; however, she often failed to understand instructions and showed some sign comprehension loss. Although she was ready and eager to communicate and al-

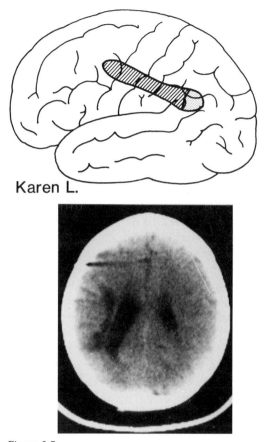

Karen L.

Figure 3.5
Lateral reconstruction of lesion and CT scan of left-lesioned patient Karen L.

though her signing was interpretable and for the most part under-standable, Karen L.'s signing contained numerous errors, which we analyze here. On testing she would often perseverate and sometimes fail to find the sign that she was searching for, but in contrast to her immediate poststroke signing, which was largely gestural, Karen L. was able to sign freely. Sampling from our numerous videotapes of Karen L.'s spontaneous signing, we examine her signing errors in two specific domains.

3.2.1 Sublexical Errors in Signing

Recall that Gail D. produced largely referential signs without any of the rich grammatical apparatus of ASL—the wide array of inflections that marks verbs and nouns for distinctions of person; the distinc-tions of number, temporal aspect, and distributional aspect; the rich assortment of derivational processes that elaborate the lexicon of ASL; or the spatially organized syntax that forms the framework for sentences and discourse in the language. On the other hand, Karen L.'s signing exhibited a range of grammatical markers, and she made use of the spatial organization provided by the language freely and correctly. We did, however, find an interesting array of errors that occurred in her signing, not at the grammatical level but primarily at the level of substitutions of sublexical parameters of signs—Handshapes, Movements, and Locations. Karen L. sometimes used an incorrect Handshape or an incorrect Movement for an intended sign; sometimes the Place of Articulation was incorrectly selected. Such sublexical errors are in some ways reminiscent of slips of the hand, which we have studied in the spontaneous signing of normal non-brain-damaged deaf people. Slips of the hand are analogous to slips of the tongue in spoken language (Newkirk et al. 1980). How-ever, these normal slips of the hand are inadvertent misorderings between intended signs within a given string, whereas Karen L.'s substitutions did not appear to have their source in other signs in the signing stream.

From analyzing videotapes of Karen L.'s free conversation, we found that virtually all her sublexical errors, which were numerous, produced well-formed nonsense signs in ASL, that is, sign forms that make use of the appropriate parameter values of ASL in allowable combinations but with the substitution of one parameter value for another. Table 3.1 presents examples of Karen L.'s sublexical sub-stitutions. These include selection errors within each of the major formational parameters of ASL: Hand Configuration, Movement, and Place of Articulation. Figure 3.6 illustrates three of these errors. As the figure shows, in signing CAREFUL, which has a /K/ Handshape,

Table 3.1
Sublexical substitutions of Karen L.

Sign	Parameter	Substitutions
CAREFUL	Hand Configuration	/W/ for /K/
FEEL	Hand Configuration	/B/ for /8/
BATHROOM	Hand Configuration	/A/ for /T/
ENJOY	Movement	/up-and-down/ for /circular/
GIRL	Movement	/contact/ for /downward brushing/
NAME	Movement	/back-and-forth/ for /downward/
SEE	Place of Articulation	/chin/ for /cheek/

Karen L. incorrectly used a /W/ Handshape. The resulting form is still recognizable from the context as the intended sign CAREFUL but is a nonexisting form in ASL, rather like saying *tareful* instead of *careful* in English. The ASL sign ENJOY has a flat /B/ Handshape and a circular Movement on the torso; Karen L. instead once produced it with correct Handshape and Place of Articulation but with an up-and-down Movement. The ASL sign FEEL has an open /8/ Handshape and a brushing Movement on the torso; Karen L. produced the sign with an incorrect Handshape, again producing a nonsense form in ASL (see figure 3.6). These were occasional errors, not consistent ways of forming a sign; at times Karen L. produced the same signs correctly, and at different times she made different sublexical substitutions.

One might well ask whether Karen L.'s sublexical errors might be attributable to motor difficulties. Like Gail D., she was right-handed before her stroke, and like Gail D., she relied on her nondominant hand for signing after her stroke. Because signing often involves the two hands as articulators in an intricately patterned fashion, this might raise some interesting questions. In ASL the two hands play important but differing roles; for most uninflected signs one hand is active or dominant. It has been noted that signers often use only one hand when the other hand is occupied with, for example, carrying packages. We investigated the capacity for signing under different experimental conditions in right- and left-handed deaf signers using only one hand in preparation for evaluating brain-damaged signers who may have paralysis of one arm. We found that deaf signers are perfectly able to convey linguistic information fully and without error using only one hand, even when that hand is their nondominant hand (Vaid, Bellugi, and Poizner 1985). We also tested control subjects matched with the left- and right-lesioned subjects in age and background, requiring them to use only one hand throughout our tests and conversational sessions, in order to evaluate linguistic per-

Correct form   Karen L.'s Sublexical errors

CAREFUL

Karen L.'s Handshape error
(/W/ for /K/)

ENJOY

Karen L.'s Movement error
(/ N/ for / ⊙ /)

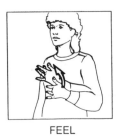

FEEL

Karen L.'s Handshape error
(/B/ for /8/)

Figure 3.6
Sublexical errors typical of Karen L.'s signing. Note selection errors within major formational parameters of ASL. These are the equivalent of phonemic paraphasias of
spoken language.

formance using the nondominant hand, and found no linguistic deficits. This gives us confidence that Karen L.'s linguistically motivated sublexical errors are not traceable to signing with her nondominant hand. Karen L.'s errors occurred within the context of unfaltering signing and involved substitutions of ASL formational parameters. The rule-governed nature of Karen L.'s errors and their occurrence in the context of fluent signing clearly confirm an aphasic disturbance.

3.2.2   Underspecified but Grammatical Signing

It is interesting that we found no instances of signing errors at other levels of Karen L.'s language: no substitutions of inflectional markers, no errors in grammatical construction, and no discernible errors in either sign order or verb markers, which serve as part of the spatial underpinnings of syntax in ASL. In great contrast to Gail D., Karen L. made full use of the grammatical properties of ASL and did so appropriately, without errors. Thus Karen L.'s signing is fully grammatical but shows primary impairment at the *sublexical* level of structure (the equivalent to phonemic errors in spoken language). Her grammar remains relatively well preserved.

Karen L. did, however, have two other sources of difficulty in signing and in conveying her intentions clearly. One source came from her occasional problems with accessing signs during our testing (for example, confrontation naming). When attempting to recall a sign, Karen L. would on occasion grope for the sign or use some circumlocution. Another source of difficulty in Karen L.'s signing gives rise to an impression of vagueness. In free conversation Karen L. uses all the spatial syntactic mechanisms (the means by which signs are related to one another in sentences, such as verb indexing, pronominal indexing, index shifting, and coreferentiality). She uses pronominal indexes freely and frequently. What she often *fails* to do is indicate the nominals associated with these indexes; that is, she fails to identify pronominal referents. Thus Karen L. would often have to be asked who or what was the topic of the syntactically correct description. The analogue in a spoken language such as English might be the use of pronouns when their antecedent is unclear or the overuse of indefinites (for example, "something" or "someone"). In ASL this is represented by frequent occurrence of spatial indexes—either on the verb or as spatially realized pronominals—without the prerequisite specification of prior referents. The passage that follows illustrates Karen L.'s failure to specify the nominals associated with her frequent indexes.

Karen L. is signing to the examiner about an event. Her signing is given in notation, followed by an English translation equivalent:

KAREN L.: LOOK-FOR FIND WITH ME, LIKE, ME. WITH ME DOG. ME MONEY, ALL-TOGETHER HOME. INDEX$_a$ WITH TWO-OF-US$_a$, EASY. $\overline{\text{WELL}}^{\text{neg}}$ INDEX$_{b-c['they']}$ LEAVE$_b$ LEAVE$_c$ LEAVE$^{[\text{Exhaustive}]}$. AND LOOK-FOR$^{[\text{Durational}]}$. INDEX$_b$ PUNISH INDEX$_b$. WELL, ME WRONG. LOOK-FOR$_b$$^{[\text{Durational}]}$ NOW LOOK-FOR$_b$$^{[\text{Durational}]}$ INDEX$_b$. ME OTHER GIRL HAVE-TO LOOK-FOR$_c$.

An English translation equivalent is:

KAREN L.: I'm looking, to find someone [unspecified] I like, with me and my dog. With my money, we could live all together at home. She [unspecified] could be with the two of us easily. They [unspecified, many] have moved out of this area from different places. And I'm still looking for someone. She/he [unspecified] was being punished. It was my fault. Now she/he [unspecified] is looking for him/her [unspecified]. I have to look for another girl myself.
EXAMINER: Who was looking? [that is, "Who are you talking about?"]
KAREN L.: LOOK$^{[\text{Durational}]}$ [meaning 'Someone [unspecified] was looking.']

Karen L.'s failure to specify the nouns associated with her many indexes gives rise to the impression of vagueness and lack of content in her signing. So far as we could ascertain, Karen L.'s frequently indexed verbs and use of pronominal indexes within the spatial reference framework of ASL show no errors of verb agreement. Her language pattern, then, shows preservation of the spatially encoded syntactic mechanisms of ASL but an overuse of pronominal indexes.

From our formal language testing we find that Karen L. suffers from impaired comprehension of ASL. Furthermore, she has marked difficulty in repeating signed sentences correctly. She was given signed sentences of increasing length and complexity and asked to repeat them exactly. She could handle the short sequences of three and four signs, but as the stimuli became longer and more complex, she would transpose signs and omit or add signs that had not been in the original stimulus. Her repetitions exhibited a variety of sublexical errors as well.

Gail D., the first person we described, is agrammatic; the few signs she produces are without any of the grammatical apparatus of ASL.

In contrast, Karen L.'s signing is morphologically rich and correct and shows a full range of correct grammatical constructions; however, she makes errors at the sublexical level. In addition, despite the grammatical richness, Karen L.'s signing is vague with respect to what and to whom she is referring. Her sign impairment differs not only from Gail D. but also from the next patient we present, Paul D., who has grammatical deficits of a different sort.

3.3.   Paul D.: A Paragrammatic Signer

The dignified old man at the entrance to our laboratory moved with no trace of the left-hemisphere stroke he had suffered ten years before. Paul D.'s spryness belied his 81 years, and his formal, good-humored, self-possessed manner reflected the self-assurance of a man who has gained a certain social prominence. He has edited and contributed to several literary publications. For many years he was a teacher of deaf children and an early champion of their educational rights, leading the fight against the purely oral method of education. As a fundraiser for deaf colleges and deaf causes, he was unsurpassed, traveling throughout the country to give signed lectures that were by all accounts elegant and spirited. This remarkable deaf man was a powerful communicator in ASL and had a great command of written English.

Paul D. was previously studied by Battison and Padden (1974), and Battison (1979, discussed in Poizner and Battison (1980)). We report here our own intensive investigation of his language capacities.

Severely impaired by the stroke to his left hemisphere, Paul D. had made a fiercely determined struggle to regain his use of language. He had in part succeeded, but his residual failures to communicate were puzzling and frustrating to him and his wife. Uncovering the precise nature of the deficit was an important and intriguing challenge for us.

Paul D. was born in Europe to a hearing family. When he was 5 years old, a high fever resulted in the loss of his hearing. The next year his family emigrated to North America, and he was enrolled in a residential school for deaf children, providing him with a community of signers. He began learning ASL and written English at the school. On leaving the school Paul D. entered a college for the deaf. After graduation he worked as a printer, editor, fundraiser, and teacher. He married a deaf woman, and the couple became influential members of the deaf community.

From conversations with Paul D.'s wife and daughter and from hospital records we have been able to piece together what his condition was like immediately before and after his stroke. The stroke produced dramatic changes. His wife reported that during his first week of hospitalization he was totally unable to communicate. Although after a few days he was able to get out of bed and walk, it was not until the second or third week that he could nod yes or no in response to his wife's questions.

The following is an English translation of his wife's signed description of the events immediately before and after the stroke:

> That day was supposed to be a holiday, but I decided to go to work anyway. My husband didn't have to work that day, and the two of us decided to meet for lunch. He would come to my office first, and then we would go downtown to have my passport picture taken. But about ten o'clock, he called me and said he couldn't come because he was too sick. Well, I said all right, and went on working until about two o'clock, when I just had a hunch that something was wrong. My daughter came and I told her that her father was really sick. She phoned a doctor for me, and made an appointment for five o'clock, after work. I drove home and found that he had messed up the whole apartment. He generally was a very neat and orderly man, but this time I found food messed up all over the kitchen. He was asleep on the bed, so I woke him up and asked what was wrong. He didn't say anything. I told him to get dressed, but he put his clothes on all wrong. I realized something was wrong with his mind, so I helped him dress. He kept falling down, and I tried to lift him up, all the while asking what was wrong. He didn't communicate at all. He couldn't walk, so I helped him get to the living room, but then I realized I couldn't get him down three flights of stairs. I was frightened and had to run for help, to ask a friend to phone the doctor. The doctor ordered an ambulance to bring my husband to the hospital. There they found he had had a stroke.
>
> After two days in the hospital, they got him up out of bed to walk. He could walk all right, but he was weak. But in all this time, there was no communication, absolutely *none*. I would tell him a story, and there was just no response from him at all, for one whole week. I would come every morning, noon, evening, because I wanted to feed him. The first time that he attempted to communicate in any way was when I came in and he pointed to his sleeve several times, to show me that it was all wet. I found that he didn't even know that he had no strength in his arm. He had picked up a cup of hot coffee and it spilled over his shoulder and burned him. He was trying to tell me about it. But even after

that, there was still no communication from him. The second week, he tried to fingerspell my name for the first time. That was great, because then I knew he knew my name.

I tried to communicate with him a lot, telling him things. He seemed to understand me, but he himself didn't communicate, except for nodding his head for yes and no. That was all. Once I arrived and saw a box of candy by his bedside. I asked him, "Who brought the candy, your girlfriend?" He laughed, so I knew he understood, but he couldn't tell me. So I said, "Was it a woman?" He nodded yes. "With her husband?" He nodded no. "Alone?" Yes. "Well, who was it?" He seemed to know but couldn't tell me. Finally I gave him a list of names, and some clues, like "Does she have children?" That way, I was able to figure out who brought the candy.

He stayed in the hospital two weeks, and then one day he sort of moved his hand downward trying to get something across to me, and I finally guessed what he wanted by asking different things. I asked "Do you want to go home?" and he nodded yes and gestured again, moving his hand downward. On the last day before he was to go home, a speech therapist came to work with him. She showed him cards with different objects on them, like a pencil, pen, clips, and asked him to identify them. He couldn't. I showed him the signs, and he even pointed incorrectly to the cards. He didn't know. He also couldn't give the names for the objects. I just cried.

Anyway, we brought the cards home, and my friend and I worked with him. We drew pictures and words on flash cards, but nothing happened at first. He kept looking around and seemed happy, but I didn't even know if he understood that he was in his own home.

I started to teach him, one sign at a time. I would point to a table and sign TABLE, point to a chair and sign CHAIR, and identify all the things around him. But he didn't know any of the signs. I showed him things, signs, and words all the time. I had a deaf woman stay with him for a month and told her to communicate with him all the time, to teach him signing, talking, anything. Just to keep his mind alert.

About three weeks later, he decided to go for a walk, and he found his way back home. I came home from work and asked what happened—I noticed that his hair was cut. I know he must have gone to his barber himself, and that meant he really must be improving. I asked, "What did you do?" He gestured to me, and then he turned his pants pocket inside out, to show me that it was empty. He was trying to tell me that he didn't have any money to pay the barber. I understood, and we drove back together to pay. I thought it was a really good indication that he was improving, but still it required a long time for him to relearn sign.

During that time, he couldn't write words at all. I had a hearing woman come to help him with different things for about six weeks, and then he had a chance to pick up some words again; she wrote notes to him. We had to teach him for a long time until he started to write English words again. He didn't use the TTY [teletypewriter for the deaf] for about two years. I think he was afraid to, but step by step we taught him. I would ask him, "Please call me. I want you to phone me so I know you are all right at home," because he was staying alone at the time while I was working. He knew how to dial the phone, so finally one day he called me. I typed "How do you feel?" He typed back something all garbled, because he couldn't yet write clearly, but that way I at least knew that he was there and able to phone.

3.3.1 Neurological Information

At the time of testing we asked a neurologist to examine Paul D., who had made an excellent recovery. The neurologist reported that he was alert, attentive, and cooperative, with normal good spirits. Strength, sensation, and coordination were normal. Paul D. had no loss of vision or loss of eye movement control. There remained slightly higher reflexes of his right extremities, but there was little evidence of the former paralysis of his right side. He had good use of both hands. We obtained a CT scan ten years poststroke (figure 3.7):

> CT Findings
> Paul D. has a subcortical lesion in his left hemisphere. There is an anterior focus deep to Broca's area, and included is the head of the caudate nucleus, putamen, globus pallidus, part of the thalamus, anterior limb of the internal capsula, and corona radiata. The lesion extends posteriorly into the white matter underlying the supramarginal and, to a lesser extent, angular gyri. The superior extension of the lesion involves the white matter deep to the motor strip and primary sensory areas representing the face. Finally, there is an enlarged left Sylvian fissure.

We examined Paul D. over a period of two years on many different occasions. Paul D. showed that, although his signing and written English had improved greatly over the ten years since his stroke,

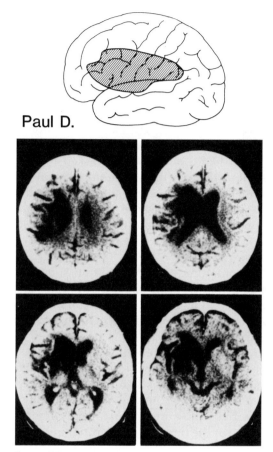

Paul D.

Figure 3.7
Lateral reconstruction of lesion and CT scan of left-lesioned patient Paul D.

linguistic deficits in both remained quite evident. When we tested him, Paul D. was signing long sentences, telling narratives, telling us about his recent travels, and performing well on some of our language tests. He signed smoothly with both hands, although there were still times when he searched for the correct sign.

We have an anecdotal account of his ability to hide his deficits. One of our research assistants, a young deaf woman, had gone to visit Paul D. at her college. Because he is an elder of the deaf community, she was seeking his advice about her study program. The assistant did not know that Paul D. had had a stroke. When asked for her impressions of him and his linguistic capacities, she remarked on his spry, dignified, courtly manner, not mentioning anything unusual about his signing. On further questioning, however, it transpired that the assistant had done all the signing and Paul D.'s role had been limited to signing YES, FINE at appropriate intervals—an effective strategy for hiding language impairment!

As soon as Paul D. tried to communicate beyond simple routines, his impairment was strikingly evident—facile signing but full of linguistic substitutions (paraphasias). In fact, even his wife continued to have difficulties understanding what he was saying. On the day of their first visit to the laboratory, his wife told us that he had tried to talk to her about an experience they had shared on their trip abroad. "He remembered something," she signed, "that I did not remember myself and wanted to tell me about it. But his signing was all mixed up, and I couldn't understand him. Now he generally signs quite well, and he understands me, but I can't always understand him."

Uncovering the precise nature of the deficit was an intriguing challenge for us. Our analysis of Paul D.'s conversation, narratives, stories, and interviews revealed impairment at all levels but, most important, at the *grammatical* level. We compared his written English and his ASL signing to determine what effects his brain damage had on the two different languages.

3.3.2   Wernicke-like Writing in a Deaf Signer

Impeccable Prestroke Writing
Befitting his occupation as an editor and journalist, Paul D.'s prestroke command of written English was excellent. Recall that he had learned English only *after* he became deaf and after the family emigrated to America. We give two examples from handwritten letters penned before his stroke (figure 3.8).

> This is a fraternal organization of, by and for the deaf, offering life insurance and disability benefits to deaf policyholders. Its

a. Prestroke writing

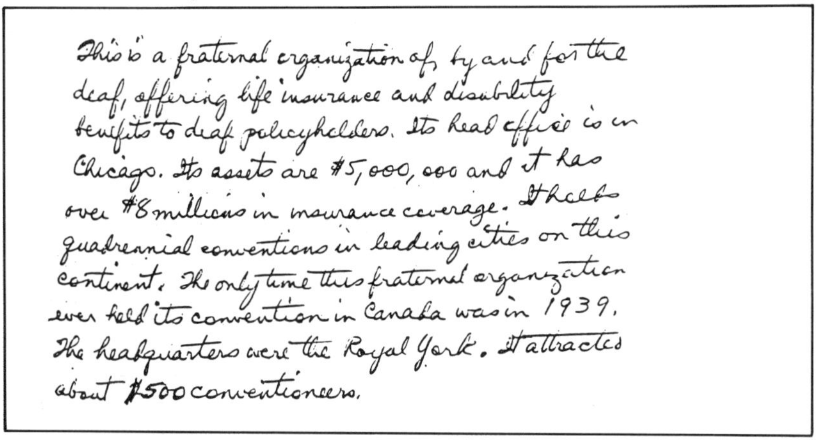

> This is a fraternal organization of, by and for the deaf, offering life insurance and disability benefits to deaf policyholders. Its head office is in Chicago. Its assets are $5,000,000 and it has over $8 millions in insurance coverage. It held quadrennial conventions in leading cities on this continent. The only time this fraternal organization ever held its convention in Canada was in 1939. The headquarters were the Royal York. It attracted about $500 conventioneers.

b. Poststroke writing

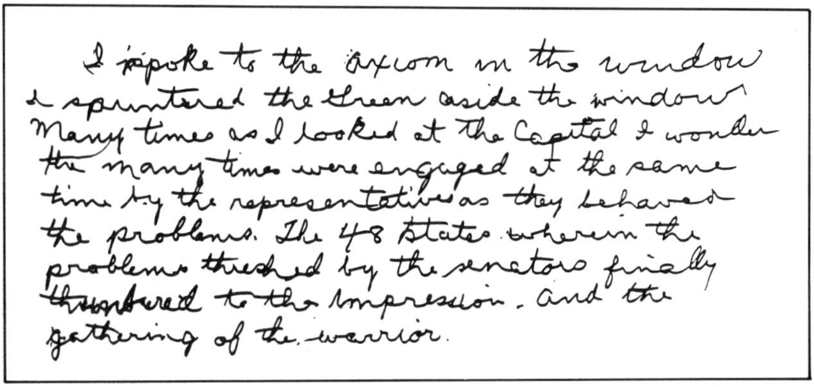

> I spoke to the axiom in the window I sprintered the three aside the window. Many times as I looked at the Capital I wonder the many times were engaged at the same time by the representative as they behaved the problems. The 48 States wherein the problems threshed by the senators finally thumbered to the impression. And the gathering of the warrior.

Figure 3.8
(a) Paul D.'s prestroke writing is in impeccable English. His poststroke writing (b) approaches jargon.

head office is in Chicago. Its assets are $5,000,000 and it has over $8 million in insurance coverage. It holds quadrennial conventions in leading cities on this continent. The only time this fraternal organization ever held its convention in Canada was in 1939. The headquarters were the Royal York. It attracted about 2,500 conventioneers.

The Society was organized in 1901 because of widespread discrimination against deaf applicants for life insurance coverage.

The second prestroke letter is:

I have never liked splinter groups. They weaken rather than strengthen an important cause, especially when the good of ALL people is concerned. You hit the nail on the head when you stated with truth that Judaism is synonymous with humanitarianism. Humanitarianism can best be served when everyone is pulling together to enhance the cause rather than to maintain "a house divided against itself." This is especially applicable to our deaf world where the need is acute for the people of all faiths and ideals to work hand in hand to better their welfare.

As these selections show, Paul D.'s writing is forceful, clear, and incisive, and in impeccable English.

Wernicke-like Poststroke Writing
The samples of Paul D.'s prestroke writing contrast sharply with his poststroke writing, although both include full grammatical sentences and express—or attempt to express—complex ideas. The following are a few selections written three years poststroke.

In the first selection Paul D. is describing the Capitol:

I walked toward the Capitol and entered the way up the stairs. I noticed the rooms were for the wayfarers and entered the deliberation room. The senators were in a huddle of a question.

I spoke to the axiom in the window. I sprintered the Green aside the window. Many times as I looked at the Capitol I wonder the many times were engaged at the same time by the representatives as they behaved the problems. The 48 states wherein the problems threshed by the senators finally thunbured [or thundured, not clear] to the impression. And the gathering of the warrior.

A second selection is from a letter to a friend.

> I have five days ahead of putting ideas together and I believe you have an altogether idea of putting to dress it. Here I am to greet you back at home. You are fit to become a partner in the game of gameship. Here you have had a fine game at home. One week you held a week in one whole part. You have molded your brother and sister and trusted in their lucky way. How is your mother and father? Have you steered their way to welcome home and hail their stay? Have they questioned their way into their broadened life?
>   . . . Finally you come right out to face the life as it is. Are you serenely the inspiring way you are set to it? Why are you not so annoying to have such an pest here to you?

Paul D. also wrote in a letter:

> I suppose I was driven on a sheet from which to gather a handful of facts. The sheet is way back at home—the first time I brought back. I prevented it here as I just am to pick up. This is my memory time to bring the back of the sheet. What a humming weather it was to take me to sum it up. It was a humid sum. Now the weather takes me to seal it off.

These poststroke samples show that Paul D.'s writing has become highly convoluted but is nevertheless couched in elaborate (unimpoverished) grammatical structure. The complexity of structure within the sentences and the variety of structure is essentially the same as in the prestroke writing. There are, of course, many incorrect word selections and many semantic misusages. The preservation of grammatical structure shows that there is no general impoverishment of syntax, nor avoidance or underemployment of any particular grammatical construction.

Within the generally well-preserved grammatical structure, however, there are substitutions of words and formatives (paraphasias). These substitutions are, for the most part, errors of selection rather than errors of combination; thus his errors in written English are unlike "slips of the tongue" carried over into writing. Another characteristic error in Paul D.'s written English is the inappropriate repetition of a given lexical item (perseveration). Some of Paul D.'s selection errors are illustrated in table 3.2.

Paul D.'s written English exhibits characteristics common to those made, in both speech and writing, by hearing Wernicke's aphasic patients. Although not exactly gibberish, Paul D.'s written language contains many incorrect word selections in a stream of generally well-

Table 3.2
Writing errors

Error	Examples
Lexical substitutions	Rooms for the *wayfarers*
	entered the *deliberation* room
	in a *huddle* of a question
	spoke to the *axiom*
	as they *behaved* the problems
	you have *molded* your brother
	an *altogether* idea
Morphological irregularities	sprintered
	gameship
Grammatical irregularities	such *an* pest
	of *putting to* dress it
	a *girl* washes *his* dishes
	the gathering of the *warrior*
Perseverations	many *times* as I looked at the Capitol I wonder the many *times* were engaged at the same *time*
	A partner in the *game* of *gameship*. Here you have a fine *game* at home.

preserved grammatical sentences. In some cases the incorrect selections are semantically related to what Paul D. probably intended to write: "huddle" for something like "conference" or "committee"; "of the question" for "about" or "on the question"; "rooms for the wayfarers" instead of, perhaps, "rooms for the visitors"; "behaved the problems" for "acted on. . . ." Other selections seem harder to interpret: "I spoke to the axiom" and "and the gathering of the warrior." As we have seen, there are also perseverations: "Many times as I looked at the Capitol I wonder the many times were engaged at the same time. . . ."

We were eager to see whether Paul D.'s signing showed similar kinds of semantic error and whether ASL's syntactic structure would be similarly preserved in his signing.

3.3.3   *Paragrammatic Signing*

The first thing we noticed about Paul D.'s poststroke signing was that he communicated generally well, using long complex sentences. He told stories about the past and conversed freely (although with occasional searching for signs). We sometimes had trouble understanding the details of his conversation. There were many strange, inappropriate, and even occasionally jargonlike signs. At first we were struck by the similarity of his signing to his written English. Some of his errors were unlike any we had seen before (and we have examined errors in signing from a great variety of sources and under many circumstances—in short-term memory, in children learning sign language, in slips of the hand, in the perception of signs under noise, in shadowing, and so on; indeed, deaf people have complained that we are interested *only* in their errors).

Two selections from his signing follow. The examiner's signs are translated into English. The patient's signs are presented in glosses using special notation and then translated into equivalent English. In the first selection, the examiner is asking questions for conversation and asks about Paul D.'s plans for the future (for example, what trips he and his wife are planning to take). Instead, Paul D. responds with something quite irrelevant and opaque:

> EXAMINER: What are your plans for the next few months?
> PAUL D.: I *PLAN[Habitual] T-O SEARCH [Durational] FIND MISTAKE. PLAN *H-A-Y H-A-V-E TO TELL-YOU EVERYTHING. ALL-WORKED-OUT. PAPER . . . *NOT. WELL . . . .
> ['I (have been planning) to always search to find mistakes. Planning, (hay) have to tell you everything. Make it all work out. The paper . . . (it isn't).   So . . . .']

The examiner is clearly puzzled and attempts to find out what Paul D. is talking about.

> EXAMINER: What paper are you referring to?
> PAUL D.: TALK BACK-FORTH *MY *W-A-Y LIST[Seriated External] PAPER, JOT-DOWN. BEFORE IN THERE_a CALIFORNIA. *SIT-DOWN_b IN *THERE_b. . . .
> ['We were talking back and forth (in my way). Lots of lists and papers and writing down. Back in California, I sat down.']

The conversation took place in Paul D.'s home in another state, but he appears to refer back to the time, some months earlier, when he visited in California. There are errors in his signing, including errors of spatial agreement, as when he set up a locus for California at point a, but apparently referred to that locus two signs later at point b.

The examiner again tries to clarify what Paul D. is referring to.

> EXAMINER: Oh, you're talking about our sessions in California. Have you been working on your signing?
> PAUL D.: PRACTICE. *SEE_a SIGN[Emphatic] *SEE_a.
> ['Yes, practicing. (I see it.) I work hard on my signing. (I see it.)]

In the second selection Paul D. is describing the layout of his apartment, in particular, a glass-enclosed patio adjoining his living room.

> PAUL D.: AND HAVE ONE *WAY-DOWN-THERE [unintelligible]. MAN WALK, MAN SEE THAT *DISCONNECT E-X-T-E-N-S-I-O-N O-F *EARTH ROOM. HAVE FOR MAN CAN *LIVE ROOF, LIGHT, SHADE[Seriated Plural] *PULL-DOWN[[+ Dual] + Habitual] AND HAVE GLASS WALL. . . . FOUR DIFFERENT. . . . TO-HAMMER[Habitual] MAN MAKE *HAND *MAKE M-O-B-I-L-E-S. ROUND-OBJECT-WALL[Allocative]. WONDERFUL *BRILLIANT[Predispositional] MAN. ['And there's one (way down at the end) [unintelligible]. The man walked over to see the (disconnected), an extension of the (earth) room. It's there for the man (can live) a roof and light with shades to (keep pulling down). And there's a glass wall with four different. . . . He hammered. The man (makes hands), makes mobiles, many on the wall. A wonderful (always brillianting) man.']

The errors that first impressed us involved Paul D.'s surprising tendency to use morphologically complex forms where simpler ones would have been appropriate. Figure 3.9 illustrates one such error: a morphologically illegal combination, *BRILLIANT[predispositional], meaning something akin to 'always brillianting.' The inflection for the predispositional aspect applies to signs referring to transitory qualities

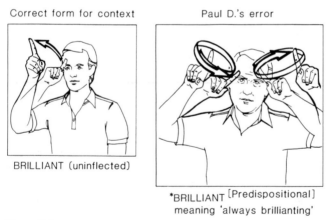

Correct form for context   Paul D.'s error

BRILLIANT (uninflected)

*BRILLIANT [Predispositional]
meaning 'always brillianting'

Figure 3.9
Example of Paul D.'s morphological errors. In the context the uninflected sign BRILLIANT is appropriate. Paul D. produced instead a morphologically complex form *BRILLIANT[Predispositional]. This is an illegal combination of sign and inflection based on a violation of a semantic restriction.

changing their meaning to permanent or inherent qualities; for example, the sign QUIET modulated for the predispositional aspect means 'quiet by nature' or 'taciturn.' However, because the sign form glossed as BRILLIANT already denotes an inherent quality, it is blocked from undergoing the inflection for the predispositional aspect in ASL. Thus Paul D. has produced an illegal combination of sign and inflectional form based on a violation of a semantic restriction. One might well expect simplifications (the substitution of a simpler form or the reduction of a morphologically complex form to a simpler one), but what we found instead was morphological overelaboration, along with various other kinds of error. We found Paul D.'s morphological errors most interesting. Before turning to these, we first consider some of the lexical substitutions that he made.

Lexical Substitutions
The lexical substitutions in Paul D.'s signing are similar to those in his writing. He produces signs that are semantically bizarre in the context, such as EARTH where the appropriate sign would have been ROOM, BED where the context called for CHAIR, DISCONNECTED where the context suggested EXTENSION, QUIT where an appropriate sign would be DEPART. Some examples are:

EARTH for ROOM
BED for CHAIR
DAUGHTER for SON
DISCONNECT for EXTENSION
QUIT for DEPART
HANDS for MOBILE
FINALLY for LAST
WIFE for HUSBAND
YEAR for HOUR
MISPLACE for LOSE-GAME
FINISH for LAST

It is clear that an overall characteristic of Paul D.'s lexical substitutions is that the errors are within the same lexical category as the form appropriate for the context. Nouns are substituted for nouns; verbs for verbs, and so forth. The within-category nature of these substitutions extends even further to semantically related items within the same lexical category (BED for CHAIR, YEAR for HOUR, and even EARTH for ROOM). This sort of thing is what makes his signing seem coherent but yet either not appropriate for the context or nonsense; that is, as opposed to Gail D., Paul D.'s impairment primarily involves selection at the lexical and the morphological levels.

Classifier Substitutions

Another clear example in which the basis for the substitution seems to respect divisions dictated by grammatical class are substitutions within the classifiers of ASL. In ASL signs a limited number of differentiated handshapes mark the semantic category or the size and shapes of nominals associated with them in sentences. These handshapes function similarly to morphemes known in spoken languages as *classifiers*, as has been argued by Newport and Supalla (1980) and by Supalla (1982). ASL classifiers, for example, those shown in figure 3.10a, mark semantic categories, such as human, animate nonhuman, vehicle, and upright object. These classifiers function as verbs of motion and location in sentences of ASL, specifying path and direction of movement of their noun referent.

Paul D., but not the other left-hemisphere-lesioned patients we studied, made grammatical errors in classifier forms. In signing the ASL equivalent of 'I saw the car pass by,' Paul D. signed CAR

a

UPRIGHT-OBJECT-   VEHICLE-Classifier   PERSON-Classifier
Classifier

b

CAR   *PERSON-Classifier-GO-BY

Figure 3.10
A classifier error of Paul D. (a) Three correct ASL classifiers. (b) Paul D.'s incorrect selection of PERSON-classifier for VEHICLE-classifier. The correct form, VEHICLE-classifier-GO-BY is shown in the inset.

*PERSON-classifier-GO-BY (figure 3.10b), using PERSON-classifier, which is incorrect for that context, instead of the correct vehicle classifier, shown in the inset. The choice of classifier is determined by the particular noun sign that occurs in the utterance. The noun sign CAR selects the vehicle classifier. Even if a person had been in the car, this nonetheless would not have sanctioned the use of the person classifier in this context. What governs the use of classifiers are grammatical rules determined by lexical classes, not the pragmatics of the situation. Paul D. makes relatively frequent substitutions of classifier morphemes in his signing. These selection errors within this domain are a prelude to his more striking errors of substitution and, in fact, augmentation within the morphology of ASL inflectional and derivational processes. The following is a list of some of Paul D.'s substitutions in this category.

> WOMAN LOCATED-AT-X-CL:/G/ *WALK CL:/B/
> [flat object classifier instead of person classifier]
> MOTORCYCLE *DRIVE-UP-CL:/B/
> [upright object classifier instead of person classifier]
> CAR *PASS-BY-CL:/G/
> [person classifier instead of vehicle classifier]
> B-U-S DRIVE *FLY-OFF-CL:/Y/
> [airplane classifier instead of vehicle classifier]
> ANIMATE-LAY-FLAT *PRANCING-CL:/V/
> [animate nonhuman classifier instead of person classifier]

Morphological Substitutions
Besides the classifier errors, we found that Paul D. also made a number of errors in which he substituted one morphological form for another. The nature of these morphological errors brought up interesting questions about the differences between sign and speech. In ASL, unlike English and many other spoken languages, morphological and lexical information are conveyed concurrently. ASL has, for example, an inflectional form that changes a class of predicate signs referring to temporary states so that they refer to inherent characteristics; we call this form the inflection for the Predispositional Aspect. When the sign QUIET is used with this inflection, its meaning changes to 'characteristically quiet' or 'taciturn'; the sign WRONG[Predispositional] means 'error prone,' and the sign SICK[Predispositional] means 'characteristically sick' or 'sickly.' The uninflected sign SICK is made with soft repeated contact with the forehead. In the inflected form SICK[Predispositional], the hand moves in a repeated, smooth, circular motion near the forehead. The inflectional form is conveyed by the pattern of movement—smooth, circular, and

repeated—which co-occurs with the lexical stem (handshape, target locus, and movement stem). As is typical for ASL morphology, the forms of inflection for specifying grammatical relations are intimately tied to the visual modality: The form involves contours and dynamic attributes of *movement* co-occurring with sign stems. This kind of organization—layered as opposed to linear—is characteristic of lexical stems and of derivational as well as inflectional forms. For example, the uninflected sign UNDER and a derived form meaning 'subordinate' share Handshape, Place of Articulation, and basic Movement shape, but they differ from one another only in features of movement (onset and offset, tension, and quality); otherwise, the two forms are identical.

Paul D.'s poststroke morphological substitutions often involved an appropriate root form with an inappropriate inflection or derivation. He also, on occasion, substituted one inflectional form for another and even produced nonsense inflections. Figure 3.11 and table 3.3 show some examples of morphological augmentation. In a sentence whose context called for the simple meaning 'under,' Paul D. signed UNDER[Idiomatic Derivative], a form meaning 'subordinate,' instead of the appropriate uninflected sign UNDER; he signed HARM[Idiomatic Derivative], meaning 'hazing,' instead of the appropriate uninflected sign HARM; he signed WALK[Durational], meaning 'walk continuously,' instead of the appropriate uninflected sign WALK. An example of inflectional substitution occurred when he signed LOOK[Habitual], meaning 'look regularly,' in a context that required instead LOOK[Multiple], meaning 'look at them.'

Neologisms in Morphology
It has been suggested that a breakdown in sign language should not result in neologisms, because in spoken language neologisms are based on reorderings of linear segments of words. But even with the concurrent packaging of structural information in ASL, we did find a number of neologisms based on substitutions within one or another of the major parameters of ASL; we even found impossible morphological forms (for example, a legal sign that has undergone an inflectional movement not permitted with that form).

In the examples in the preceding section the particular combinations of inflections or derivations with root forms were morphologically legal ones, although inappropriate for the sign context. It is interesting, however, that Paul D. also created morphologically illegal combinations, for example, 'characteristically brillianting,' as discussed earlier. Both the sign BRILLIANT and the inflection for Predispositional Aspect (which changes reference from transitory states to

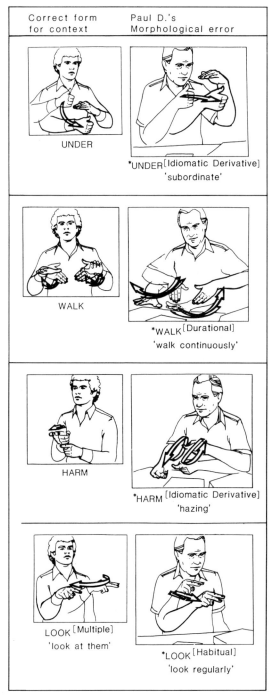

Figure 3.11
Morphological augmentations typical of Paul D.'s signing.

Table 3.3
Morphological elaborations

Sign form appropriate for context	Morphological augmentations and substitutions	Form of morphological modulation co-occurring with basic sign
UNDER (uninflected)	*UNDER[Idiomatic Derivative] ('subordinate')	Tense sharp movement
HARM (uninflected)	*HARM[Idiomatic Derivative] ('hazing')	Alternative brushing movement
WALK (uninflected)	*WALK[Durational] ('continuously')	Englarged movement
CARELESS (uninflected)	*CARELESS[Predispositional] ('characteristically careless')	Smooth circular movement
WRONG (uninflected)	*WRONG[Idiomatic Derivative] ('unexpectedly')	Soft wrist twist
DEBATE (uninflected)	*DEBATE[Multiple] ('debate all of them')	Addition of arc sweep
LOOK[Multiple] ('look at them')	*LOOK[Habitual] ('look regularly')	Substitution of soft repeated movement for arc sweep

that of inherent properties) occur separately in ASL and are well formed in Paul D.'s signing, but the combination of the sign and the inflection (shown in figure 3.9) is illegal in ASL on the basis of a semantic restriction: The sign BRILLIANT does not refer to a transitory state but to an inherent quality and thus cannot undergo the inflection. We know that Paul D. has semantic problems because he produces so many semantic substitutions; we suggest that a dampening of semantic values may also be the basis for his productions of illegal combinations of root signs and inflections. Paul D. selected an uninflected sign and an inflection that together form an illegal combination based on a semantic restriction; this incorrect selection may be due to Paul D.'s inability to differentiate clearly semantic values of morphemes, a kind of semantic dampening.

Figure 3.12 and table 3.4 show examples of neologisms in morphology in which Paul D. selected an appropriate root but combined it with a nonsense inflectional form. The figure shows an existing morphologically complex form, MONTH[Seriated Plural], meaning 'month after month,' and Paul D.'s nonsense form, a kind of morphological neologism.

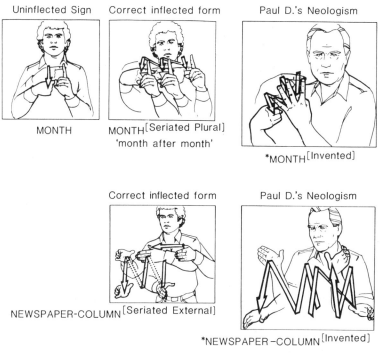

Figure 3.12
Neologisms in morphology from Paul D.'s signing.

Many of Paul D.'s errors in signing, then, are morphological elaborations—morphologically complex forms appearing where simple ones would have been appropriate for the context. In this regard the errors in his signing are equivalent to those that impressed us in his written English. Because these linguistic errors appeared in both language modalities, we conclude that the errors do not result from features peculiar to sign or speech but from a more central linguistic deficit.

3.3.4   Similar Breakdown in ASL and English: Lexicon and Morphology

Paul D.'s ASL signing and written English exhibit similar lexical and morphological errors. In both ASL signing and English writing there is a preponderance of semantic (as opposed to sublexical) paraphasias and, more important, morphological augmentations. Indeed, there is no impoverishment; among the substitutions in both sign and speech, one finds a strong tendency toward overelaboration in the choice of items substituted. In Paul D.'s signing the semantic and morphological substitutions occur as if whole families of related

Table 3.4
Morphological neologisms

Sign form appropriate for context	Sign form produced by Paul D.	Formal property
BRILLIANT (uninflected)	*BRILLIANT[Predispositional] ('characteristically brillianting')	Smooth circular movement
MONTH[Seriated Plural] ('months passing')	*MONTH[Invented Form] ('months passing')	Repeated movement on each finger substituted for repeated movement at different loci
NEWSPAPER-COLUMN[Seriated External]	*NEWSPAPER-COLUMN[Invented]	Inappropriate spatial alternation between the two hands

forms are simultaneously activated (see McClelland et al. 1986). A similar process is evident in his writing. The different types of families include semantically related lexical items, inflectional formatives, and derivational formatives (for example, "huddle" might be simultaneously activated with the semantically related word "conference") and similarly with perseveration; a previously activated item might retain a high level of activation and hence might be incorrectly selected subsequently.

Semantic errors that occurred in Paul D.'s signing and writing include the following.

English: *Huddle* might be simultaneously activated with the semantically related word *conference*.

ASL: The ASL sign QUIT might be simultaneously activated with the semantically related (but formally unrelated) sign DEPART.

Morphological errors that occurred in Paul D.'s signing and writing include the following.

English: In describing the Cookie Theft picture, Paul D. wrote, "I see a girl outstretching her arms." The two words *stretching* and *out* might be simultaneously activated.

ASL: UNDER[Derivational], meaning 'subordinate,' might be simultaneously activated with the semantically and formally related basic sign UNDER.

3.3.5 Modality and Language

A major difference in form between ASL and English is that ASL tends to transmit structural information in a simultaneously layered fashion rather than in a temporally sequential fashion. Because the left hemisphere seems better adapted than the right for processing sequential rather than simultaneous signals (Bradshaw and Nettleton 1981; Levy 1982), the simultaneous display of linguistic structure in ASL allows the study of the interplay of these opposing attributes. This major difference in form between ASL and English, namely, a primarily multilayered concurrent organization rather than a sequential, linear one, presents a challenge and an opportunity for insight into the fundamental basis of left-hemisphere specialization for language. It has been claimed by some that in humans the left hemisphere is fundamentally specialized for temporally sequential analysis and that it is this capacity that underlies left-hemisphere specialization for language. Our analysis of Paul D.'s poststroke signing suggests that these claims are questionable. Our initial questions included the following: Do separate linguistic levels in the signed signal break down independently of one another, as they do in spoken languages, despite the radically different way linguistic information is packaged in the signed signal? The special layered organization of sign language at the lexical and morphological levels might in fact preclude left-hemisphere specialization with respect to this special aspect of the grammar. Accordingly, one might expect markedly different patterns of language impairment. Paul D.'s breakdown within ASL morphology thus indicates that the temporal sequential organization of the spoken languages considered and the rapid temporal processing that such an organization requires cannot be the basis for left-hemisphere specialization for language.

Let us summarize what has been discussed. There is a parallel breakdown at the morphological level in Paul D.'s signing and writing, as we have shown. This demonstrates that morphological breakdown in aphasia can be independent of language modality. Sign language, however, in a striking way shows its roots in the visual modality through the special spatialized organization underlying its syntax. We show in chapter 4, when we compare sign aphasia deficits across the three left-hemisphere-damaged signers, that Paul D. has problems with the spatialized syntax of ASL that differ from his impairment in English syntax. We propose that this sign-specific syntactic breakdown may be intimately related to requirements of a syntax that is specifically spatially organized.

Initially, we were interested to see what, if any, the effects of left-hemisphere lesions for deaf signers might be, because the implications of this question have significance for a fuller understanding of brain organization for language in general. What is the effect of a radical change in the modality for brain organization for language? Sign language is, after all, so different from spoken language; not only do root and grammatical markers co-occur in time, but also spatial contrasts play a crucial role at all levels. Is there, for example, evidence of anything similar to aphasia for sign language?

In the first three patients examined here we found marked breakdown of their sign language resulting from left-hemisphere lesions. Furthermore, their sign language is not impaired across the board, but each of the signers shows evidence of *differential* impairment. One patient (Karen L.) shows errors primarily of the equivalent of phonology in her signing but maintained most of the grammar of the language. Even more interesting is that we find two different kinds of grammatical impairment for this sign language: one resulting in agrammatism with omissions of virtually all grammatical markings (Gail D.) and another resulting in paragrammatic signing with abundant but incorrect substitutions of grammatical markers (Paul D.). Components of this sign language thus appear to be differentially affected by different left-hemisphere lesions, despite whatever surface differences may obtain between sign and speech. Our first case studies indeed suggest clear aphasias for sign language.

The data that we have presented so far have come from our first examination of the spontaneous signing of three deaf patients. In the next chapter we present aspects of our formal language testing and standardized aphasia examination of these patients in order to come to a clearer understanding of the basis of their language impairments.

Chapter 4

Language across Left-lesioned Signers

The left cerebral hemisphere is closely connected with speech. In patients with split brains (that is, persons whose corpus callosum has been severed, with consequent elimination of neural transmission between the two hemispheres), the left hemisphere has total control over speech production and phonological processing (Sperry 1974; Zaidel 1977). The planum temporale, a portion of the auditory association cortex known to mediate language, is larger in the left hemisphere than in the right, even at birth (Geschwind and Levitsky 1968). Prelingual infants show left-hemisphere specialization for speech sounds (Entus 1977; Molfese, Freeman, and Palermo 1975). Thus the question arises of whether the specialization for language of the left hemisphere is unique for speech and sound: What is the effect of brain damage to the left hemisphere in persons whose primary language is in a different modality, a language not of the vocal tract and ears but of the hands and eyes?

To address this question, we first compare the language behavior of the three signers with left-hemisphere lesions in order to bring out the nature of the differences in their language impairments. We administered a wide array of tests (described in chapter 2), some of which were adapted from standard tests used with hearing brain-damaged patients and some that were specifically developed for use with deaf signing patients. The entire battery was administered to all six brain-damaged signers and to matched deaf controls. A native ASL signer administered all tests, with responses videotaped for later analysis. In addition to storytelling, picture description, and analysis of free conversation, the tests involved the following four areas:

1. The BDAE (Goodglass and Kaplan 1972). The BDAE provides a careful assessment of aphasia. The ASL version of the BDAE is not a direct translation but an adaptation we made for use with deaf signing patients.
2. Structural levels of ASL. We have developed a series of tests that assess the capacity to produce and comprehend indi-

vidual structural components of ASL. Specifically, we test for the capacity to process sublexical structure, grammatical morphology, and spatial syntactic structure.

3. Apraxia. We assessed capacities for both representational and nonrepresentational arm and hand movements in order to investigate the relationship between apraxia and aphasia for a gestural language. This will be further elaborated in chapter 6.

4. Nonlinguistic visuospatial processing. We selected an array of standard tests that assess capacity for visuospatial analysis. Hearing patients with right-hemisphere damage tend to be impaired on these tasks. This will be further elaborated in chapter 7.

4.1 Standardized Assessment of Aphasia: The Boston Diagnostic Aphasia Examination

4.1.1 Fluency, Comprehension, and Paraphasia

The BDAE provides a z-score profile for a variety of language subtests, standardized for a large group of hearing aphasics. Figure 4.1 presents profiles for our three deaf patients and three matched deaf control signers on three key BDAE subtests: fluency, comprehension, and paraphasia. This figure presents a general picture of the aspects of the patients' language behavior. The dashed line at $z = 0$ in the figure represents the mean score of hearing aphasics on each task (Goodglass and Kaplan 1972). Positive z-scores reflect performance that is a given number of standard deviations above the mean; negative scores indicate performance below the mean. Thus, except for paraphasias, the farther the score is to the left-hand side of the profile, the more impaired the performance. The opposite is true for paraphasias, because positive z-scores reflect an increased number of paraphasias and hence impaired performance.

As figure 4.1 indicates, the performance of elderly control signers is generally accurate. The three left-lesioned patients, however, show impaired sign performance. All three patients were tested well after their strokes, so the deficits we see are stable. The severity of the communicative impairment ranges from moderate to severe. Gail D. is the most severely impaired. Her fragmentary expression requires extensive inference, questioning, and guessing by the examiner (severity rating of less than 1). For Gail D. the range of information exchanged is severely limited and the listener carries the burden of communication. Paul D. received a severity rating of 3, indicating that he is able to discuss most everyday problems with little assistance. Even so, his impairment in production makes conversation difficult at

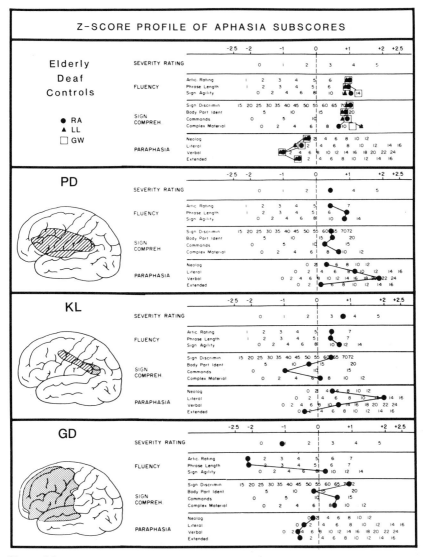

Figure 4.1
Standardized assessment of aphasia. z-score profiles of subscores from the BDAE for three deaf, left-lesioned signers and three deaf controls. PD stands for Paul D.; KL, Karen L.; and GD, Gail D.

times. Karen L. is slightly less impaired than Paul D., receiving a severity rating of 3.5, which indicates obvious losses in signing ability and, in particular, in sign comprehension.

The three brain-damaged signers have extremely different patterns of language breakdown. Paul D. and Karen L. have fluent sign output, whereas Gail D. is dysfluent. In contrast to her severe dysfluency in spontaneous signing, Gail D. showed only moderate impairment on a test of sign agility, which requires rapid serial repetitions of single signs varying in formational complexity. Gail D.'s relatively preserved ability to repeat signs rapidly and continuously indicates that her sign dysfluency cannot be accounted for by a peripheral motor dysarthria.

Tests of sign comprehension revealed a different pattern of breakdown. These subtests consist of a multiple-choice sign recognition test (sign discrimination), identification of body part names, the capacity to carry out sign commands varying from one to five significant informational units, and tests of complex ideational material, which require yes/no answers to simple factual material (such as "Will a cork sink in water?") and to brief questions testing comprehension of short signed stories. Paul D. and Gail D. showed only mild impairment in sign comprehension; Karen L.'s impairment was more marked, with a notable lack of comprehension of sign commands.

The patients' comprehension of printed English closely paralleled their comprehension of ASL. Paul D.'s mean z-scores for sign comprehension and reading comprehension were $+0.54$ and $+0.50$, respectively; Karen L.'s were -0.18 and -0.06, respectively; and those of Gail D. were $+0.47$ and $+0.38$, respectively.

The paraphasia scores show that Paul D. has a preponderance of semantic paraphasias, although he also produces some sublexical paraphasias (figure 4.1); Karen L., in contrast, produces almost exclusively sublexical paraphasias. Gail D. has few paraphasias of any kind.

In summary, Paul D. has fluent sign output with fairly well-preserved comprehension but with many semantic paraphasias. Karen L. also has fluent sign output, but her comprehension is impaired and she produces many sublexical paraphasias. Finally, Gail D.'s sign production is extremely dysfluent, with relatively well-preserved comprehension and few paraphasias. We argue that the language deficits of the three aphasic signers are, in general, related to impairment of specific linguistic components of ASL, rather than to an underlying motor disorder or to an underlying disorder in the capacity to express and comprehend symbols of any kind (this will be discussed further in chapter 6).

4.1.2   Rating-scale Profiles

The BDAE also provides rating scales for assessing a patient's spontaneous, natural signing in six aspects of sign production (melodic line, phrase length, articulatory agility, grammatical form, paraphasias in running sign, and sign finding) and in sign comprehension. Five of the six rating scales provide a 7-point scale in which 7 stands for normal and 1 for maximally abnormal language characteristics. Both extremes of the scale for sign-finding ability reflect deviant language production. Our ratings closely follow the principles specified for hearing patients, outlined in Goodglass and Kaplan (1972), but adjusted for characteristics of ASL. To obtain the ratings, we transcribed and tabulated characteristics of signing in 10-minute samples of each patient's conversation and expository signing. We measured phrase length, noted paraphasias, and classified and counted all grammatical and lexical morphemes. Figure 4.2 presents these rating-scale profiles for the brain-damaged signers and for the controls.

The profiles clearly show that the three left-lesioned patients have impaired sign language. (The elderly control subjects show normal sign characteristics, indicating that the impairment in the left-lesioned patients is not due to age.) The patterns of impairment of the three left-hemisphere-damaged patients are different. Karen L.'s phrasal grouping of signs (melodic line) is normal, Paul D.'s is near normal, but Gail D.'s is absent. This contrast between normal or near normal levels for Paul D. and Karen L. and extreme impairment for Gail D. is also characteristic of phrase length (six and seven occasional uninterrupted sign runs for Paul D. and Karen L., respectively, but utterances of only one sign for Gail D.). In articulatory agility Paul D. and Karen L. have fluent signing, whereas Gail D.'s signing is effortful and awkward. In a variety of grammatical forms Paul D. and Karen L. show a wide range of grammatical inflections and syntactic constructions (although not without error). Gail D., however, is decidedly agrammatic, producing only single sign utterances.

Both Paul D. and Karen L. have many paraphasia-type substitutions in running conversation. Gail D. was assigned a rating of 7 (no paraphasias), because she has no runs of fluent signing. Figure 4.2 shows that all three patients differ from one another in sign finding, the informational content of signs in relation to fluency. Paul D. has a rank of 4.5, reflecting his relatively high proportion of substantives to grammatical forms. Karen L., however, has a rank of 2.0, reflecting the absence of content signs in her otherwise grammatical signing; these missing signs make for vague communication. In contrast, Gail

RATING SCALE PROFILE OF SIGN CHARACTERISTICS

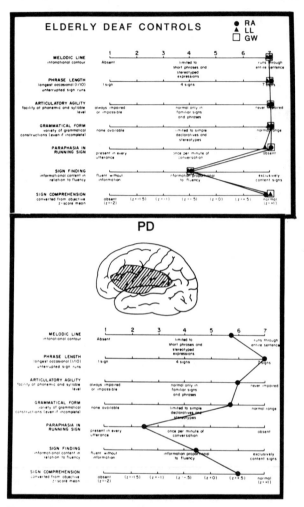

Figure 4.2
Rating-scale profiles of sign characteristics from Boston Diagnostic Aphasia Examination. Three deaf left-lesioned signers show marked sign impairment in comparison to deaf controls. PD stands for Paul D.; KL, Karen L.; and GD, Gail D.

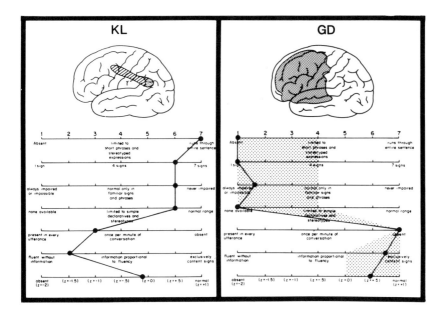

D.'s rank of 6.5 reflects her almost exclusive use of substantives and action signs. Finally, the sign comprehension ranking is the mean z-score of the four comprehension subtests of the BDAE. Here, Gail D. is no longer differentiated from the other two patients. Her comprehension is quite good. Both Gail D. and Paul D. have sign comprehension scores that fall just below those of the control subjects. Karen L., in contrast, has a more marked sign comprehension loss, with a mean z-score of -0.18.

Clearly, all three left-lesioned patients have impaired signing relative to the elderly deaf control subjects, but what is significant for our studies is that their signing did not break down in a uniform manner. The shaded area shown on Gail D.'s profile in figure 4.2 reflects the range of profile ratings characteristic of hearing Broca's aphasics (Goodglass and Kaplan 1972). Gail D.'s pattern of sign impairments—severely dysfluent, agrammatic sign production with relatively preserved sign comprehension—makes her profile of sign impairment classically similar to those of hearing Broca's aphasics. Paul D. and Karen L. show patterns of sign impairment markedly different from that of Gail D. and also different from each other in specific areas. Both are motorically fluent with fairly good phrase length, melodic line, and variety of grammatical forms, but Karen L.'s sign comprehension is considerably worse than Paul D.'s; in fact, her mean z-score across the comprehension tests fell more than two-thirds of a standard deviation below Paul D.'s. He makes a substantial number of semantic paraphasias, whereas Karen L. does not. Finally, Karen L. has less informational content relative to fluency than Paul D. These differences between the rating-scale profiles may not appear dramatic, but our linguistic analysis of these patients' signing, reported in what follows, reveals important differences in the layers of structure affected.

4.2   Tests of American Sign Language Structure

We tested patients across the range of structural levels of ASL. In general, consistent with their impaired performance on the BDAE, the patients with left-hemisphere damage showed breakdown on our tests assessing specific structural levels of ASL, with some individual sparing of capacities that we report here. We turn first to tests at the sublexical level, including a test in sign language that is analogous to rhyming in spoken language; next we look at tests of morphological distinction in ASL; and finally, we turn to tests of processing aspects of the spatial syntax.

4.2.1   Sublexical Tests

Two tests were designed to probe the subjects' abilities to decompose signs into parts: a Decomposition test and a test that taps the functional equivalent in ASL of rhyming. In the Decomposition test subjects are presented with a sign made by the experimenter and with four pictures of items. In the test for Decomposition of Handshape, for example, the subject is asked to choose the picture that represents a sign made with the same handshape as the presented sign. In the Rhyming test the subject is presented with four pictured items and is asked to select the two pictures representing signs that are similar in all but one parameter (Hand Configuration, Place of Articulation, or Movement). On the Decomposition test Gail D. scored 70.6 percent and Karen L., 57.1 percent; Paul D. did not take the test. On the Rhyming test Gail D. scored 47.8 percent; Karen L. did not take the test, and Paul D. obtained a very low score of 31.6 percent. In these sublexical tasks all three left-lesioned patients were impaired on one or the other test compared to normal signers and our control subjects.

4.2.2   Morphological Distinction

There is a productive morphological process in ASL by which noun-verb pairs are derivationally related; in these pairs (for example,

CHAIR and SIT, COMPARE and COMPARISON), the signs share the same handshape, place of articulation, and movement root; they differ from one another only in features of movement. In a test of elicitation of the formal distinction between nouns and verbs, the three left-hemisphere-lesioned patients performed quite poorly: Paul D. scored 61.1 percent; Karen L. scored 72.2 percent; and Gail D. had the low score of 40 percent. Two of the left-lesioned patients took the test of comprehension of the formal noun/verb distinction: Karen L. scored 70 percent and Gail D., 60 percent. Control subjects on both these tests performed well, none lower than 85 percent. Thus left-hemisphere damage appears to impair the capacity to comprehend and to produce this nonspatial derivational distinction.

4.2.3   Processing Spatialized Syntax

Sentence structure in ASL is specified in part by the way in which verbs, nominals, and pronominal indexes are related to one another in space; spatial contrasts play a central role in specifying grammatical relations. To evaluate comprehension of spatial syntax, we administered three tests: one test for Nominal Establishment and two tests for Verb Agreement.

The Nominal Establishment test evaluates perception and memory for the spatial loci associated with specific nominals in a horizontal plane of signing space, a part of the spatial referential framework of ASL. In this test the examiner establishes nouns at distinct spatial loci in signing space. The subject is then asked two kinds of question: (1) where a certain nominal has been established (which the subject answers by pointing to a specific locus), and (2) what nominal has been established at a certain locus (which the subject answers by signing the nominal). Paul D.'s performance on this test was extremely poor; he scored 40.9 percent correct overall. This level of performance is less than half that of the lowest scoring elderly deaf control signers who also took the test. Karen L. and Gail D. performed well (overall average of 84.1 percent and 81.1 percent correct, respectively). Thus Karen L. and Gail D. do not seem impaired in the primary ability to perceive and remember spatial loci and their referents. Paul D., however, is quite impaired, having poor immediate memory for locations and their associated nominals.

For the two tests of processing verb agreement, correct performance requires perception of spatial location, memory for spatial locations and for direction of movement of the verb between spatial endpoints, and appreciation of grammatical relations, such as subject and object of the verb signaled by spatial relations. In one test, Verb

Agreement with Fixed Framework, the experimenter signs a sentence describing an event with two participants, establishing locations for the two noun arguments and indicating grammatical relations through the direction of movement of the verb between the spatial endpoints. The subject's task is to answer by pointing to the picture described by the examiner's spatially organized sentence. The spatial arrangement of the items in the pictures need not match the spatial arrangement set up in the sentence. Similar items have been used in tests of the grammatical knowledge of hearing children to investigate the appreciation of grammatical relations signaled by word order (Brown, Fraser, and Bellugi 1962). The same pictures can serve to investigate preservation of grammatical relations signaled by spatial relations in ASL. On the test of Verb Agreement with Fixed Framework, two of the left-lesioned patients scored poorly and one scored well. Paul D. scored only 57.1 percent correct, and Karen L. scored only 55.3 percent; however, Gail D.'s score is surprisingly high—80 percent correct.

The second test, Verb Agreement with Shifting Reference, requires the additional ability to shift spatial framework in order to process correctly grammatical relations. In this test the experimenter signs a sentence involving nominals and their associated spatial loci and an action verb, whose spatial endpoints mark subject and object with respect to the spatial loci. The spatial relations indicated in the question involve a shift in spatial reference. On this test two left-lesioned patients were greatly impaired: Paul D.'s score was only 43.3 percent, and Karen L.'s was 42.8 percent. Gail D. performed extremely well on the test, obtaining a perfect score.

The results of these two tests are interesting in view of these patients' performances in other situations. Paul D. appears to have memory problems in general; thus it is not surprising that he performed so poorly on the Nominal Establishment Task. Paul D.'s low performance on the Verb Agreement tests converges with our linguistic analysis of his use of verb agreement in signing, discussed in the following section. As noted earlier, Karen L. has an ASL comprehension deficit. Her low scores on the Verb Agreement tests are consistent with her profile on the BDAE but show that at least part of that deficit lies in her comprehension of particular spatially realized grammatical relations in ASL. Karen L. makes spontaneous and widespread use of space for grammatical purposes, proliferating pronouns and indexed verbs. Her general visuospatial abilities are relatively intact (see chapter 7). In addition, she showed good performance on the Nominal Establishment Test, which taps the processing of spatial locations that can later be used linguistically. Thus her problem with the Verb Agreement tests may well lie in extracting the syntactic relations. Gail D., in contrast, shows surprisingly intact comprehension on these tests in the face of flawed, agrammatic, and sparse production.

Thus, on the tests that we developed to isolate processing of specific structural layers of ASL, equivalent to phonology, morphology, and syntax in spoken language, signers with lesions to the left hemisphere generally perform poorly (with the exception of Gail D. on the verb agreement tests). The implications of these patterns for hemispheric specialization become much clearer after linguistic analysis of the subjects' spontaneous language.

4.3   Linguistic Analysis of Aphasic Signing

The formal language testing just reported yields standardized measures of language capacities, with profiles of language impairments. The results indicate frank sign language aphasia in each of the three left-lesioned signers. In the nature of their language impairments, they differ greatly. In order to contrast the grammatical deficits of the three patients with left-hemisphere damage, we turn to a linguistic analysis of their signing.

4.3.1   Gail D.: Agrammatic Signing

Gail D.'s description of the Cookie Theft picture (figure 2.1) is characteristic of her signing output and stands in marked contrast to the responses of the other two patients: Gail D.'s responses were starkly abbreviated, and continuous prompting by the examiner was required to obtain some small output. Her sparse description is not due to any reluctance to communicate on her part but to the extreme effort her signing seems to require; she is clearly frustrated in her attempts to communicate. She tries to produce not just signs but also gestures, mime, fingerspelling, and the mouthing of English words; however, she is no better at producing these other means of communication than she is at signing. Gail D. can at times make single signs fluently and with little hesitation, for example, as single sign responses to comprehension tests. In expository conversation, however, she experiences great difficulty in expression; her narratives are severely limited, effortfully produced, and without any of the grammatical apparatus of ASL.

The following is a sample of Gail D.'s attempt to convey an incident from her childhood:

EXAMINER: What else happened?
GAIL D.: CAR . . . DRIVE . . . BROTHER . . . DRIVE . . . I . . .
S-T-A-D. [Attempts to gesture "stand up."]
EXAMINER: You stood up?
GAIL D.: YES . . . I . . . DRIVE . . . . [Attempts to gesture "wave
goodbye."]
EXAMINER: Wave goodbye?
GAIL D.: YES . . . BROTHER . . . DRIVE . . . DUNNO . . . .
[Attempts to gesture "wave goodbye."]
EXAMINER: Your brother was driving?
GAIL D.: YES . . . BACK . . . DRIVE . . . BROTHER . . . MAN . . .
MAMA . . . STAY . . . BROTHER . . . DRIVE.
EXAMINER: Were you in the car?
GAIL D.: YES.
EXAMINER: Or outside?
GAIL D.: NO.
EXAMINER: In the car.
GAIL D.: YES.
EXAMINER: You were standing up with your mother?
GAIL D.: NO . . . BROTHER . . . DRIVE . . . . [Points in back.] . . .
DEAF BROTHER . . . I . . . .
EXAMINER: Your brother didn't know you were in the car?
GAIL D.: YES.
EXAMINER: Your brother was driving and saw you in the back
seat?
GAIL D.: YES, YES. [Laughs.]
EXAMINER: Oh, I see.

It is clear that communication with Gail D. proceeds largely by guess-
work on the part of the addressee. Gail D. does not, however, have
difficulty indicating whether the examiner's interpretations are correct or not.

The most salient characteristic of Gail D.'s signing is that it is
agrammatic and effortful; it is composed of short utterances, largely
single, open-class items. She omits all grammatical formatives, including most pronouns (with the exception of I), all inflectional and
derivational processes, and all aspects of spatially organized syntax.

Toward a Model of Gail D.'s Sign Aphasia
In the spontaneous signing that we recorded of Gail D., most of the
utterances consisted of only a single lexical item and there were no
utterances with more than three lexical items. Many of the lexical
items that occurred were fingerspelled English words. These
fingerspelled items are particularly interesting because of the rela-

tively long, rich gestural sequences that they represent, for each fingerspelled letter is, in form, a separate signlike gesture. Thus the fingerspelled item G-A-V-E, which Gail D. used in describing the Cookie Theft picture, consists of a sequence of four separate hand-shapes; her somewhat scrambled T-E-O-W-L, meaning 'towel,' consists of a sequence of five handshapes. We must conclude, then, that an incapacity for linearly sequencing separate gestures is not at the heart of Gail D.'s language difficulty. This being the case, it is all the more striking that her multisign utterances give no indication of having an internal sentencelike structure; rather, they appear to be a simple concatenation of signs.

There are two explanations suggested by these observations. One is in terms of formal structure. The utterances that show any complexity in terms of the number of concatenated units are largely limited to those with the simplest type of internal structure: mere concatenation. What is largely absent is hierarchical structure. This is true of both fingerspelled words and utterances consisting of a sequence of lexical signs. There is little evidence of the sort of hierarchical structure characteristic of sentences.

The other explanation is semantic in nature (and may in fact be simply the semantic counterpart of the formal structural explanation). The individual gestures of the multigesture fingerspelled words are the mere concatenation of meaningless items. Within a given fingerspelled word, there is no combination of meanings into a meaning of the whole; the meaning of the fingerspelled word is not compositionally derived from any meaningful subparts. Similarly, few of Gail D.'s multisign utterances give any indication of having a sentence structure, whereby the meaning of the sentence as a whole is derived in a principled way from the meanings of the parts and their syntactic function in the sentence, for example, as subject, predicate, and direct object.

Either explanation provides a possible key to another irregular aspect of Gail D.'s sign production: the nearly complete absence of any of the inflectional morphology of the language, even though such inflectional morphology is not conveyed "horizontally" through a linear sequence of units but rather "vertically" through the layering of form components. Thus a unified account of major aspects of Gail D.'s impairment begins to emerge. Central to that account is her difficulty in combining separate meaningful components hierarchically. The basis for combination, whether it is linear, as in many spoken languages, or layered, as in ASL, does not seem to be a crucial factor.

4.3.2   Karen L.: Grammatical Signing with Sublexical Impairment

Karen L.'s signing output has always been rich and fluent, even after her stroke. She communicates well and freely, carrying on a conversation (indeed, a monologue) with normal rate, flow, and range of grammatical structure. Karen L. signs freely without prompting. What follows is a sample of her signing that relates some incident in her past.

> KAREN L.: *THERE$_a$ NOT-YET SEE. *THEY$_{b-c}$ SAY PRETTY *THERE$_a$. THIS$^{[+ to\ front]}$ BETTER THAN *THAT$_d$. TROUBLE *THERE$_d$ THAN HERE. QUIET HERE, *THERE$_e$ TROUBLE. RIOTS$^{[Allocative]}$ DRINK$^{[Habitual]}$.

An English translation equivalent is:

> KAREN L.: I have not yet seen what's over there. They [unspecified] say it is pretty there [unspecified]. This is better than that [unspecified]. There was more trouble over there [unspecified] than here. It's quiet here. Over there [unspecified] was trouble—riots in different places and regular boozing.
> EXAMINER: Where was the trouble? [Examiner is lost in terms of the referents of the conversation.]

On viewing the videotapes of this exchange, the examiner, and other researchers as well, indicated that it was often impossible to tell what Karen L. was talking about because she used pronominal indexes so freely without specifying in any way their antecedents. Of the three left-lesioned patients, Karen L.'s signing appears to be the least impaired. Her signing is grammatical with appropriate morphological inflections, including those for indexing. We noted that she frequently uses pronouns and verb indexing. Yet her signing shows two specific deficits: paraphasias in ongoing signing involving substitutions within the parameters of signs and failure to specify the nominals associated with her indexes.

4.3.3   Paul D.: Paragrammatic Signing

We asked Paul D. to describe the Cookie Theft picture in ASL and in written English. His written description is:

> I see a kitchen where a girl washes *his dishes and a big cookie jar *jarring a boy in the kitchen and a young girl *outstretching her arms *at the cookie and *jar the cover and I notice the *award of the water washing toward the floor.

Paul D. was asked to describe the scene in ASL, and part of his response is:

> PAUL D.: GIRL SPILL (THERE) [points to woman in picture]. WATER OVERFLOW, WATER. (SHE) [points to woman] *CARELESS[Predispositional]. (HE) [points to boy] *FALL-LONG-DISTANCE-DOWN. (SHE) [points to woman] *GIGGLING. (SHE) [points to woman] WORK, THERE. (SHE) [points to woman] *SPILL-ALL-OVER-SELF.

Paragrammatisms in each passage are starred (*) and include a number of forms that are inappropriate or ungrammatical for the context. An English translation of Paul D.'s signing is:

> The girl spilled there [pointing to the woman]. The water overflowed, the water. She is always careless by nature. He [referring to the boy] fell in a double somersault to the ground. She [referring to the woman] is giggling. She [referring to the woman] is working; she spilled water all over her dress.

Before his stroke Paul D. was articulate, even eloquent. After his stroke his output was still fluent but filled with inappropriate signs. Both his writing and his signing display errors of selection at the lexical and morphological levels. His written description contained inappropriate selections, such as "jar *jarring," "girl *outstretching her arms," "and *jar the cover," and "the *award of the water." Similarly, instead of a sign meaning 'starting to fall,' he used a form that means 'fall a long distance'; instead of a sign form meaning 'spill on the floor,' he signed a form that means 'spilled all over herself,' and so forth. Figure 4.3 shows Paul D.'s written version of the story and an error from his signed version. He used the morphologically complex form meaning 'characteristically careless,' when the sign form that would have been appropriate for the context is CARELESS (the uninflected form).

Paul D.'s aphasia is shown primarily in an abundance of lexical and morphological paraphasias. He often uses an appropriate root form but an inappropriate inflection or derivation. On occasion he substitutes one inflectional form for another and even produces nonsense inflections.

4.4 Spatial Syntactic Breakdown in Signing

In this section we focus specifically on the left-lesioned patients' capacities for spatialized syntax because it is in this domain that the three patients differ most dramatically.

*I see a kitchen where a girl washes his dishes
And a big cookie jar faning a boy in the kitchen
and a young girl outstretching her arms at the ___
cookie and for the stove and I notice the award
of the water working toward the floor.*

a

Correct form for context   Paul D.'s Morphological Augmentation

*CARELESS (Uninflected)

*CARELESS [Predispositional]

b

Figure 4.3
(a) Paul D.'s written version of the Cookie Theft picture and (b) an error from his signed version. Note the morphological errors in both.

1. Gail D.'s signing is the most impaired, and indeed she is completely agrammatic. There are no spatially indexed pronouns in her signing, and the few verbs she produces never have any spatial marking; the verbs that occur are either fingerspelled or in uninflected form only. Given this extreme paucity of signing, there is no possibility of any form of verb agreement or any other aspect of spatially organized syntax.

2. Karen L. is at the other extreme from Gail D. She is garrulous and loquacious, converses freely, and uses the spatial organization underlying signing profusely and, so far as we can ascertain, correctly in terms of verb agreement markings.

3. Paul D.'s deficits are particularly telling in this domain. We therefore discuss his use of all aspects of syntax in ASL in some detail here, in order to bring into focus the nature of his deficits.

One way to characterize the differences among the patterns of impairment of language in the three left-hemisphere-damaged patients comes from their patterns of communication. The same deaf researcher performed all three examinations. After we analyzed the videotapes, we found that the examiner played a different role in communicating with each of the three patients. With the agrammatic patient, Gail D., the interviewer had to guess, prod, probe, and finally supply much of the information at each point to understand what Gail D. wanted to impart. In contrast, with Karen L. and Paul D. the interviewer was able to maintain a flowing conversation, although she could not always follow the gist of their signing because of their linguistic impairments. With Karen L., whose signing is grammatical, the interviewer frequently asked, "Who are you talking about?" or "What is at that point?" because Karen L. often failed to specify the subjects of her many established pronouns. With Paul D., on the other hand, the interviewer sometimes had to ask, "How does this connect with what you said before?" This puzzlement on the examiner's part reflects the lack of explicit connections in Paul D.'s discourse, which we now discuss.

In order to understand the nature of Paul D.'s deficits in connected discourse, we first examine a domain in which he is not impaired, namely, the use of sign order to convey syntax. ASL allows a powerful test of brain mechanisms for syntax that may in part be modality bound. Within ASL syntactic relations can be conveyed in two different ways: by spatial organization, as we have discussed, and by the use of temporal sequence, or sign order. Thus, within one and the same language, we can contrast sentential relations conveyed by spatial relations (in which sign order is relatively free) with those conveyed by order of signs within the clause.

We looked at Paul D.'s syntax to uncover his use of sign order. Although it was sometimes difficult to follow the thread of his conversation because of his frequent paragrammatisms and lack of connections between topics, we found no instances of sentences that were ungrammatical because of an incorrect *sequence* of signs. His use of sign order to convey syntactic relations is well preserved. Where noun phrase arguments are specified, they are never in inappropriate order in his signing. Thus there is a similarity in his signing and his English writing in the preservation of syntax conveyed by order. We previously noted an equivalency between the kinds of paraphasia in his signing and in his English writing at the level of lexicon and morphology. Clearly, then, these language capacities and impairments are independent of particular transmission modalities.

Paul D.'s correct use of order to convey syntactic relations stands in marked contrast to his use of spatial relations to convey syntax and discourse functions. One important use of space is the placement of a nominal in a given locus in the signing plane, with subsequent references to that noun by referring back to that locus with, for instance, a pronoun sign. Paul D. showed an unusual pattern of use of nouns and pronouns. For example, in one passage of signing Paul D. used 105 nouns and only 8 pronouns. He uses the same nouns repeatedly when use of a pronoun is called for. This high ratio of nouns to pronouns is characteristic of his conversational and narrative signing. The paucity of the pronouns in his signing led us to investigate his use of verb agreement, the verb movement between spatial loci that is integral to the spatialized grammatical relations in ASL. In several passages of signing, all verbs that could be indexed spatially were examined. In one passage Paul D. used seventy-four verbs that could be indexed, thirty-five of which were made in citation form. Of those thirty-five, thirteen should have been indexed; these were failures of omission, using a citation form where an indexed form was appropriate and required. Paul D. did index thirty-nine verbs, but ten of those were *incorrectly* indexed! Thus there were failures not only of omission but also of commission in Paul D.'s use of verb agreement for spatialized syntax.

Some examples of his failure to maintain spatial agreement are given in table 4.1 and in figure 4.4. In signing the ASL equivalent of "We arrived [in Jerusalem] and stayed there," he produced the signs ARRIVE, STAY, and THERE, indexed to three different spatial loci, when, of course, all three signs should have had the same locus. Figure 4.4 shows Paul D.'s signing of this sentence and the correct way of signing it.

4.4.1 *Different Breakdown in Sign and English Syntax: Order versus Space*

The fact that Paul D. suffered a breakdown in spatialized syntax but retained intact his use of sign order to convey syntactic relations implies that his syntactic difficulties in signing are not general but are intimately connected with the requirements of that aspect of syntax in ASL that is specifically spatialized. Paul D.'s preservation of sign order to convey grammar is in agreement with our findings about his written English. Although he makes many incorrect selections of lex-

Table 4.1
Paul D.'s Agreement Errors

Error	Correct form
*ARRIVE$_a$ STAY$_b$ (THERE)$_c$	ARRIVE$_a$ STAY$_a$ (THERE)$_a$
*$_a$PARK-OVER-THERE$_b$, WALK, $_c$GO-THERE$_b$	$_a$PARK-OVER-THERE$_b$, WALK, $_b$GO-ELSEWHERE$_c$
*GET-OUT-OF$_a$, $_b$PEOPLE-FILE-OVER-TO$_c$	GET-OUT-OF$_a$, $_a$PEOPLE-FILE-OVER-TO$_b$
*$_a$GO-HOME$_b$, $_c$DRIVE-AWAY$_d$	$_a$GO-HOME$_b$ $_b$DRIVE-AWAY$_c$
*RUN$_a$ $_b$THROW BASKETBALL	RUN$_a$ $_a$THROW BASKETBALL

Correct form

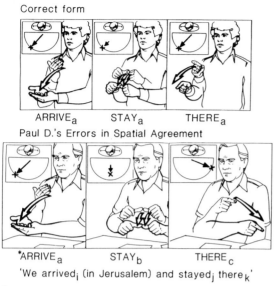

ARRIVE_a   STAY_a   THERE_a

Paul D.'s Errors in Spatial Agreement

*ARRIVE_a   STAY_b   THERE_c

'We arrived_i (in Jerusalem) and stayed_j there_k'

Figure 4.4
Paul D.'s failure to maintain spatial indexes in ASL.

ical items, the syntactic structures of English are generally well preserved in his writing and in his fingerspelling. In his written English,
verbs are appropriately inflected for tense and number, and Paul D.
makes few noticeable omissions.

The preservation of word order and of sign order in Paul D.'s
spontaneous production shows that he is able to assign to a given
nominal a position in the order of sentence constituents that is appropriate to its grammatical function as subject or object of the verb; that
is, his stroke did not impair his conceptual system or framework at
the level of abstraction of grammatical relations (grammatical subject
and object). Also intact is that part of his *realization* system that involves among other things the relative order of constituents to express these grammatical relations. There is obviously a marked
difference in Paul D.'s impairments across the differing possibilities
offered by the language modalities: Where order information is required for syntactic purposes, whether in English or in ASL, his language is unimpaired; where spatial manipulation is the basis for
syntactic organization (as in ASL, in certain contexts), Paul D. shows
a marked deficit.

To understand Paul D.'s deficit, it is instructive to note that in
conversation he rarely asks questions and does not seem to be ex-
changing information or really communicating with the addressee.

His conversation wanders, leaving gaps in information, even within sentences. It is as if he expresses one proposition at a time, with the next proposition somewhat related but not connected across a stretch of discourse. There is a clear parallel between this characteristic and his verb agreement errors: Even when he does establish the nominals associated with indexes, he is inconsistent in maintaining them. It is as if he cannot maintain referents during a discourse. As suggested in what follows, such problems may well be related to the organizational requirements of spatial planning and spatial memory involved in planning discourse.

In ASL the formal means for indicating pronominal reference is negotiated on-line and is spatialized. One aspect of this processing is that the signer has to negotiate the placement of points as he or she goes along, because there are no predefined points to choose from in sign. (In English and in most spoken languages there is a closed set of pronouns.) The abstract pronominal indexes in and of themselves are semantically empty; that is, they have no semantic content or value outside of the particular linguistic context. Thus for spatial indexes in ASL there is no related family of items in the internal lexicon that can be activated.

A second aspect of this processing requires that the signer plan ahead to establish abstract loci so that they are suitably placed for subsequent reference. And, of course, a signer must remember where each locus exists in the signing plane. Sign language interpreters (people performing on-line simultaneous translation from spoken language to signed language) often report that they have certain special problems in translating into ASL. A sign interpreter made the following comment to us:

> Very often when interpreting into ASL for deaf people, we don't know what the speaker has in mind or how he is going to present the information. So we sometimes find ourselves setting up a situation where the people or things involved are set up in the wrong locations, or we find that they introduce new information that should change the relationships among points in space. Then we need to reorganize, and must change the spatial locations. This mostly comes into play when we are using directional verbs, and we need to get from one locus to the other, and we would have done it differently if we had known how it was planned.

In recasting a system of fixed pronouns into a system of loci negotiated on-line, interpreters have difficulties because they do not know in advance how many distinct contrasting loci will be required and what the relationships among them will be. Thus they frequently find themselves with inappropriate spatial reference; they find themselves locked in, lacking enough hands, signing in crowded spaces, and the like. In ASL each individual point is referentially distinct, so that there is no ambiguity of pronominal reference.

As we have seen, Paul D. has difficulty with the entire system of spatial indexes in ASL. He underuses the spatial indexes for purposes of pronominal reference and verb agreement, and he incorrectly indexes verbs. He also performed poorly on a test of the comprehension of nominals and their associated spatial loci and on a test of spatially organized syntax. Paul D.'s difficulties here may be due in part to the special requirements of spatially organized syntax in sign—spatial memory, spatial planning, and syntactic and discourse structure.

4.5   Brain Mechanisms and Language Modality

In summary, the three left-hemisphere-damaged patients are clearly aphasic for sign language. This is demonstrated by converging evidence from multiple sources: a standardized aphasia examination adapted for sign language, formal language testing of different structural layers of ASL, and linguistic analysis of subjects' spontaneous signing.

The impairments of these signers are not uniform. They show remarkably different patterns involving impairment at different structural layers of the language. One left-hemisphere-lesioned patient (Gail D.) is grossly impaired. She is the only signer whose output is nonfluent, in sharp contrast to her prestroke signing. Her signing is limited to single signs in an utterance. Her output is effortful, and she often gropes for the sign. Her difficulties are clearly not due to peripheral motor problems, because she produces the same signs normally in some contexts. There is not a trace of the grammatical apparatus of ASL in her signing; signs are made singly and in uninflected form, with selection almost exclusively from referential open-class signs. She produces primarily nouns and some verbs but with no grammatical inflection, no grammatical use of space, hardly any closed-class items, and none of the spatial apparatus that links signs in sentences. This language profile is identical with that of hearing Broca's aphasics.

The second left-hemisphere-lesioned patient (Karen L.) has fluent signing and communicates well and freely. She can carry on a conversation (indeed, a monologue) with normal rate and flow and can exhibit a full range of grammatical structures. Her deficits in expression are confined primarily to impairment in the *sublexical* level (the equivalent of phonemic errors in spoken language). She shows no tendency to make semantic or grammatical errors in her ongoing conversation; indeed, she has relatively preserved grammar (but impaired comprehension). In many ways her signing appears to be the least impaired of the left-hemisphere-lesioned patients; however, she frequently fails to specify who or what is the subject of her freely and correctly used indexical pronouns and indexed verbs.

The third left-hemisphere-lesioned patient (Paul D.) also shows fluent, effortless signing after his stroke. He carries on conversations smoothly and with nearly normal rate and flow and does not appear frustrated, although he has occasional sign-finding difficulties. The content of the conversation, however, is revealing. His expressive language deficit is shown primarily in an abundance of paragrammaticisms, including semantically bizarre constructions and neologisms. Furthermore, he has a tendency to use morphologically complex forms where simple ones would be appropriate, for example, adding an inflection for the temporal aspect or using a derivationally complex form. And yet, at the same time, he fails to use the spatialized syntax of ASL (pronominal indexes and verb agreement markers). His signing is marked by an overabundance of nominals, a lack of pronominal indexes, and the failure to mark verb agreement correctly or at all. This appears to be an impairment of spatially organized syntax and discourse. Thus two left-hemisphere-lesioned patients have primary impairment at the *grammatical* level, the one agrammatic (Gail D.) and the other *paragrammatic* (Paul D.).

How are lesions of these signers related to their differing language breakdowns? Recall that Paul D. has a large subcortical lesion with a primary focus in the frontal lobe and extending to under the anterior portion of the parietal lobe. This lesion is not a commonly occurring one (or at least not a commonly reported one); it is entirely subcortical, and, in addition, no clearcut syndrome is classically associated with it. There is little basis for predicting the effects of such a lesion in a hearing person. We do note, however, that subcortical lesions can cause language impairment in hearing individuals (Damasio 1983b). Furthermore, the lesion involves portions of the left frontal lobe, an area that has been considered important for planning of activities (Damasio 1983a). This might be related to Paul D.'s difficulties in negotiating and planning discourse in signing, given the particular problems that ASL presents in negotiating the spatial underpinnings of syntax and discourse. In addition to Paul D.'s lesion, there is cortical atrophy, compatible with his age, which cannot be excluded as a contributing factor to the total picture. The severity of Paul D.'s language impairment, however, is unlikely to be attributable to such age-related factors alone. His case is an important one, not so much because it illuminates particular brain-behavior relations with respect to sign language but because of the intriguing modality-specific grammatical deficits that he exhibits.

Gail D., however, has a massive lesion that in hearing persons is typically associated with a lasting agrammatic aphasia. Her lesion involves not only the traditional Broca's area but also much of the surrounding cortex of the frontal lobe. Gail D. has a severe agrammatic aphasia for sign language. Her case points to the fact that there is an anterior region of the left hemisphere that is important for sign language. Whether or not this will turn out to be the same as the anterior region for speech is not clear, because her lesion is so large that it includes not only Broca's area but also much of the surrounding cortex. Broca's area is adjacent to that part of the motor strip that controls movement of the vocal tract. An analogous area that controls movement of the hands is located just superior to Broca's area, and Gail D.'s broad lesion includes both of these areas. Whether or not the same sign symptomatology would appear if one or the other were spared cannot be answered from this case. Gail D.'s case is an important one, however, because a comparable lesion in hearing people is typically associated with agrammatic aphasia. Indeed, she has a clear-cut aphasia for sign language that is remarkably similar to that of hearing agrammatics. Furthermore, she was young at the time of testing (38 years), and thus her symptoms are not complicated by the possible effects of advancing age. In these respects Gail D.'s case is different from Paul D.'s.

The case of Karen L. points to a possible difference between those neural structures that may underlie spoken language and those for signed language. Her lesion is in the left parietal lobe (supramarginal and angular gyri) with a subcortical extension into the frontal lobe. Her lesion is well circumscribed and spares the traditional Broca's and Wernicke's areas. Although a hearing patient with this lesion might have some initial speech comprehension difficulties and might suffer from word-finding difficulties, we would not expect a lasting speech comprehension deficit. Karen L., however, has such pronounced and lasting deficit in the comprehension of sign language. It may well be that anatomical structures of the inferior parietal lobule of the left hemisphere play a greater role for sign language than for spoken language. These structures are intimately involved with higher-order spatial analysis as well as with gestural control and may have been recruited in the service of sign language, because in sign language grammatical relations and spatial relations are so intertwined. Both Leischner (1943) and Chiarello, Knight, and Mandell (1982) have speculated on the special importance of anatomical structures in the left parietal lobe for sign language. If anatomical structures underlying languages in the two modalities do in fact differ, then it will be clear not only that structures within the left hemisphere are crucial for language in its various guises but also that the modality in which a language occurs may influence how the left hemisphere is organized for processing language.

Having examined these three left-hemisphere-damaged patients, we are warranted in coming to the following conclusion: Certain areas of the left hemisphere are crucial to language function in deaf signers whose primary language is a sign language. Without examining the effects of right-hemisphere damage, however, we cannot conclude that the left hemisphere is dominant for sign language, and we certainly cannot conclude that the left hemisphere is specialized specifically for sign language functioning. In fact, the brains of deaf signers might be bilaterally organized with lesions to the right hemisphere producing similar aphasias, or other aphasias, but aphasias nonetheless. We explore in the next chapter the different results produced by damage to the right hemisphere in deaf signers.

Chapter 5
Signers with Strokes: Right-hemisphere Lesions

As we have seen, the three signers with left-hemisphere lesions show marked sign language impairment, reflecting the essential role that the left cerebral hemisphere plays for sign language. What, however, is the consequence of right-hemisphere damage on language in the visual mode? Right-hemisphere lesions often produce pronounced visuospatial deficits. Do they also produce linguistic deficits for a language that makes such intricate use of spatial relations? Do clusters of language deficits appear, or does sign language break down by linguistic components in right-lesioned signers? Is sign language in fact bilaterally represented in the brains of deaf signers? Our studies of three signers with right-hemisphere lesions provide insights into these issues and are crucially important in helping us to understand the nature of language representation in the brain.

As with the left-lesioned signers, the three right-lesioned signers were right-handed before their strokes; they grew up signing, were intimately involved with the deaf community, and married deaf spouses. All use sign language as their primary mode of communication. They differ in occupational background. One was an artist before her stroke, another a key punch operator, and the third an airline mechanic.

5.1 Sarah M.: The Artist

Sarah M. is a delicate, gentle-looking woman, 71 years old at the time we saw her. Before her stroke she worked in ceramics and turned out skillful, spirited paintings. She also especially enjoyed the ancient art of egg decorating and produced over two hundred distinct and intricate designs; some samples appear in figure 5.1. Because her right-hemisphere damage produced a profound effect on her visuospatial capacities (to be discussed in chapter 7), she was not able to continue her artistic work after her stroke. Her drawings were simplified, reduced to a few unorganized lines, and she gave up her painting

Figure 5.1
Sarah M.'s prestroke artwork. Decoration of eggs (Fabergé) showing excellent visuo-spatial capacities.

altogether. She did attempt ceramics, but soon gave up there as well; the relatively simple designs on the few items she started were distorted, with colors and patterns omitted, particularly on the left-hand side.

The stroke occurred a year before we saw her. Deaf from birth, Sarah M. entered a residential school for deaf children at age 11 and was graduated from high school with honors at age 21. Her husband is also deaf, and the two are members of the deaf community in a large city. They have two children, a son and daughter. The daughter works as an interpreter and counselor for deaf people and has been an interpreter for her parents since she was young.

At our first meeting Sarah M. was with her husband and daughter. The daughter was sitting on Sarah M.'s right, engaged in a signed conversation with her mother. But Sarah M. was not looking at her daughter, as the normal pattern of eye contact in signed conversation would dictate. Instead, her gaze drifted sideways and down to the floor.

In ASL conversation the person being addressed is expected to keep eye contact with the signer and to screen out visual distractions from outside the conversation. If the addressee is approached by someone announcing a phone call, for example, the addressee holds up his hand to prevent the interruption, never taking his eyes from the signer. In our own laboratory there are constant visual "noises" and distractions, people walking about, holding conversations, and the like. No matter, it is considered rude of an addressee to lose visual contact with the signer. For hearing people, looking in another direction while someone is talking is not a breach of etiquette, because receiving the linguistic information does not require that one look at the person speaking. In fact, prolonged and unrelieved eye contact between speaker and listener is unusual—reserved probably for special relations, such as two people in love—and is inappropriate for casual conversation. A short span of eye gaze is fine, but constant eye contact may make a hearing person uneasy. For deaf people direct immediate eye contact is the rule, and any violation may be interpreted as an insult.

Sarah M. is a gentle, sensitive woman. She has always had a close relationship with her daughter and would certainly not want to offend her. Although, according to the daughter, Sarah M.'s signing is quite unchanged by her stroke, one aspect of communicating with Sarah M. is disturbing, namely, Sarah M. no longer looks at the signer while she is being signed to. Figure 5.2 illustrates some aspects

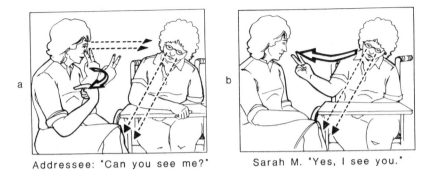

Addressee: "Can you see me?"   Sarah M. "Yes, I see you."

Sarah M. "I feel like I have three eyes."

Figure 5.2
Special issues relevant to testing deaf signers with right-hemisphere lesions. (a) Note unusual downward deflection of eye gaze of Sarah M. as she reads addressee's signs. (b) The contrast between sign direction (appropriate) and eye gaze direction (inappropriate) in Sarah M.'s response. (c) Sarah M.'s own description of her unusual eye gaze patterns.

of an interchange that took place during one of our sessions after Sarah M.'s stroke. The daughter was signing to her mother, but during this time the mother kept her gaze fixed toward the floor, rather than looking at her daughter's signing. The daughter stopped, appeared upset, and asked her mother (in ASL), "Can you see me?" (figure 5.2a). Sarah M. sighed, and signed, "Yes, I see you," but she continued looking downward at the floor and not at her daughter. Figure 5.2b illustrates the unusual behavior: Sarah M.'s eye gaze is away from her daughter and downward, yet her hand, in making the sign SEE, is directed precisely toward her daughter. In sign communication Sarah M.'s gaze would be expected to be in the same direction—toward her addressee. The daughter expressed surprise that Sarah M. was able to read signs from this odd angle of eye gaze. Sarah M. went on to explain that she really could perceive signing in this way and then explained aspects of her own inner sense of the effects of her stroke: She pointed in three different directions (figure 5.2c) and signed the ASL equivalent of, "Sometimes I feel like I have three eyes. One sees directly in front of me, one sees off to the left side, and one sees off to the right."

As we will indicate, this unusual eye gaze pattern, which Sarah M. consistently uses, results from deficits produced by her right-hemisphere lesion. One would certainly expect that such markedly deviant behavior might have profound consequences leading to serious disturbances in the perception, processing, and comprehension of a visuospatial language.

5.1.1   Neurological Findings

A neurological examination of Sarah M. revealed paralysis of the left arm and leg and moderate increased reflexes in the entire left side. There was also a gross deficit of identification of tactile stimulation in the entire left side. Sarah M. showed a deficiency of saccadic eye movements toward her left. Right-left orientation, finger sense, and simple arithmetic ability were intact. She did not have any visual field deficits. Sarah M. appeared alert, attentive, and cooperative. A CT scan at the time of testing (figure 5.3) showed a large lesion occupying most of the territory of the middle cerebral artery:

CT Findings
The lesion extends from the frontal operculum, the homologous area of the right hemisphere to Broca's area, involves premotor,

Sarah M.

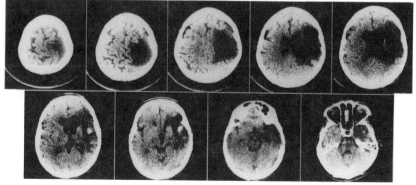

Figure 5.3
Lateral reconstruction of lesion and CT scan for right-lesioned patient Sarah M.

motor, and somatosensory areas, to include the inferior parietal lobule (supramarginal gyrus and partially the angular gyrus). The inferior portion of the superior parietal lobule is involved as well. Inferiorly, the lesion extends into the temporal lobe, involving the superior and middle temporal gyri. The most posterior portion of the superior temporal gyrus seems spared, as well as is area 37. The lesion not only involves these cortical areas, but also the underlying subcortical areas. In fact, it extends all the way to the frontal horn of the lateral ventricle anteriorly, involves all of the insula and probably the more lateral portion of the lenticular nucleus (sparing most of the caudate nucleus), and posteriorly, goes deep towards the trigone but leaves the tapetum intact; this may explain the intactness of Sarah M.'s visual fields. Sarah M.'s lesion is a massive one, with large, critical areas of the right hemisphere damaged.

5.1.2 *Preservation of Written English*

Sarah M.'s written English was good before her stroke (and her penmanship was beautiful). As evidence, she and her family provided letters and notes from her personal diary of a trip. Names have, of course, been changed to conceal identities. Even though the following sample includes many abbreviations, the English is good:

> In the eve., John and I went to their house for a while and then we all went to Juarez, Mexico. They invited us to eat out at Alfred's cafeteria. . . . Arrived in S.F. China Town. Golden Gate. It rained there and went back to S.F. . . . Saw the Capitol. Very pretty. Visited inside of the Capitol. Left for Reno. . . . Stopped at several antique shops and looked around. . . . Very pretty day but very cold.

Excerpts from a letter show Sarah M.'s good command of written English before her stroke:

> . . . to several antique shows and art and craft shows. The last art and craft show we went was two Sundays ago and we saw so many pretty pictures with wind mills and that made us think of you, and also saw a display of decorated egg shells. So plain and tacky. The price was from $8.00 to $25.00. I almost fainted. . . . Susan said that if I sold all of my perfume bottles and egg shells I'd be a millionaire.

After her stroke, when Sarah M. sent us excerpts from the diary, she enclosed a note in her own hand, in perfect English: "The notes I am sending you are all we could find." During testing, when given sentences in ASL and asked to write a translation of them in English, her writing was as good as that before the stroke. For example, she wrote: "A woman has not seen her children. A boy stole some cookies or biscuits. If a boy isn't careful, he will fall down."

The only clear irregularity in the English is in her use of the indefinite rather than the definite article, as in "If a boy isn't careful . . ." (assuming that this mention of "boy" refers to the same individual introduced in the preceding sentence). But this is a nicety of English usage that trips up many nonnative writers of English, stroke or no stroke.

We also have excerpts from a letter that Sarah M. wrote after her stroke; it shows the preservation of her written English:

> . . . Just to let you know I'm very happy at home. . . . I think of you everyday and wish to see you. . . . I'm so happy I'll not go to a nursing home any more and I hate the nursing home. We are looking forward to your coming to visit us on 28th.

5.1.3   Preservation of Signing

During the interview Sarah M. used only her dominant right hand. We present a portion of a transcript of Sarah M.'s signed description of the Cookie Theft picture (figure 2.1). As is typical of her poststroke signing, Sarah M.'s description is perfectly grammatical, without error at any level of structure. Therefore a translation into English is provided here. The remarks of the examiner are also translated into English.

> SARAH M.: It makes me think of Niagara Falls. [Pointing to the water sweeping down to the floor from the sink.] The water is overflowing from the sink. Accidentally, the boy almost slipped on the stool. He is taking the cookies and the stool almost slipped from under him.
> EXAMINER: Okay, now tell me the whole story.
> SARAH M.: The woman is washing the dishes. The boy walked over to the cupboard. He climbed up the stool and tried to reach the cookies. Accidentally, the stool slipped. . . . The woman is washing the dishes while the water is overflowing. She's stupid.
> EXAMINER: Do you see anything else? [An effort to draw her attention to the girl on the left.]
> SARAH M.: There is a window to the outside. That's all I can see.
> EXAMINER: [Points at the girl on the left.] There.
> SARAH M.: [Looks puzzled and surprised.] Oh, she has bare legs

and no socks. The girl is looking at the boy taking down the cookies.

EXAMINER: Okay, now tell the story in order again, please.

SARAH M.: There is a woman washing the dishes. It seems that the mother saw her boy climb up and take down the cookies. The girl is looking up at him. It seems to be his sister; I'm not sure. She is looking up at him. He is helping himself to cookies. Accidentally, the boy is slipping on the stool.

EXAMINER: What happened to the mother?

SARAH M.: The mother ignored them. She is still busy washing. Accidentally, the water was overflowing from the sink. Maybe she can't hear. That's strange.

EXAMINER: You're right. Maybe she's deaf. [Laughs.]

Sarah M. clearly is not aphasic. Indeed, in the language samples we analyzed, her signing is without error at any of the structural levels of ASL. Her signing has complex sentences, correct verb agreement, appropriate use of classifiers, correct morphology and syntax, and no sublexical errors. All these characteristics are in marked contrast to the aphasic signing we observed in the left-hemisphere-damaged patients.

Note that in describing the picture, Sarah M. described events from the right-hand side of the picture (the woman and the sink overflowing and the boy climbing on the stool) and then stopped as if her description were complete. In an effort to draw her attention to the girl on the extreme left-hand side of the picture, the examiner asked if she saw anything else, but Sarah M. still did not seem to notice. Finally, the examiner had to point to the girl on the left, and Sarah M. looked surprised.

This reaction, and some of Sarah M.'s other behavior, suggests that her stroke has produced a spatial disorder called left hemispatial neglect. (See Heilman (1979b) for a discussion of the disorder and its underlying mechanisms.) Discussed briefly in chapter 7, this disorder is not traceable to any elementary sensory or motor disorder. It causes some patients with right-hemisphere damage to ignore the left half of visual space—sometimes extending to the left half of their own bodies. Such a patient may, for example, fail to eat the food on the left side of the plate; when someone simply rotates the plate 180 degrees, the patient goes on to finish the entire meal with good appetite, as the food is now on the right side.

The test results presented in chapter 7 show that Sarah M. has left hemispatial neglect. The presence of this spatial disorder may explain the unusual eye gaze pattern during sign conversations. Throughout our testing of Sarah M., the examiner sat on her right side in order to mitigate the effects of any left hemispatial neglect. It appears that Sarah M.'s unusual gaze pattern is part of a strategy for coping with her neglect of left hemispace. With the examiner on her right side, Sarah M. is putting the examiner in her good right visual field by directing her gaze straight ahead instead of at the examiner. Sarah M. maintains this gaze pattern so long as there is signing addressed to her.

Additionally, while Sarah M. herself is signing and someone is at her side, as our examiner was throughout most of the videotaping, Sarah M. often looks straight ahead, not at the addressee. When she finishes signing, she looks partway in the direction of the addressee, as if to check if the addressee has understood the message. When she is not sure if the addressee is following, she looks partway in that direction (from the downward ahead gaze) and repeats her sentence or asks a question.

The phenomenon of hemispatial neglect has particular importance in the testing of signers with right-hemisphere damage. Some considerations are discussed later in this chapter.

5.2   Brenda I.: The Keypunch Operator

At the time of testing, Brenda I. was a 75-year-old woman who experienced a right-hemisphere stroke three years before our visits with her. She is congenitally deaf and attended a residential school for deaf children. Although she is now widowed, she had been married to a deaf man. When we visited her, she had been living in a nursing home for several years and has good friends there who sign with her. Throughout her life her primary mode of communication has been sign language. In fact, she herself evaluated her command of English as poor even before her stroke (such evaluations are not uncommon among deaf individuals). When she was younger, Brenda I. had worked as a keypunch operator.

5.2.1   Pronounced Spatial Disorientation

Aside from the visuospatial deficits revealed by the tests described in chapter 7, we were able to observe first-hand how pronounced Brenda I.'s spatial disorientation is. During a break in one of our testing sessions, the examiner was wheeling her in a wheelchair down the hall of the building she had lived in for a number of years. Brenda was to direct the examiner to the cafeteria, but she was disoriented and could not find her way. The examiner had to stop and ask someone else directions, even though the cafeteria was directly below them. Brenda I. shows strong evidence of topographical disorientation in a number of ways. In addition to giving inconsistent and incorrect instructions on how to get from one place to another within the building, she described the location of furniture and parts of her room in an almost helter-skelter fashion.

Brenda I. has a close friend living in the nursing home. The two have been friends since grammar school; they are the same age, grew up together, lived near each other, and now (both widows) live in the same nursing home and see each other almost every day. When Brenda explained where her friend lived in relation to herself, she pointed in entirely the wrong direction. Brenda I. indicated that she herself lives on the first floor and that her friend's room is on the floor above her. Both statements are incorrect. Indeed, there is no floor above Brenda I.'s. Thus, in both getting around in space and describing locations, Brenda I. shows severe spatial disorientation.

5.2.2   Neurological Findings

Brenda I. has a dense paralysis of her left arm. Her hospital records indicate that an infarction in the distribution of the right middle cerebral artery is suspected; however, a CT scan was not obtained. Because she was unable to move her left hand or arm, Brenda I. performed all tests using her dominant right hand.

5.2.3   Grammatical Signing with a Few Spatial Irregularities

On the whole, Brenda I.'s signing and written English are good, but as we will see, her impairment in nonlanguage visuospatial functions do affect some of her sign output in subtle ways. This is shown in the portion of Brenda I.'s signed description of the Cookie Theft picture, which is translated into English in our presentation. At first, Brenda I. described only the objects and people on the right-hand side of the picture. (The other two right-hemisphere-damaged patients are similar in this regard.) She did not mention items on the left until the examiner specifically turned the card around to emphasize the left-hand side of the picture and asked her, "What about the girl and the boy?" We pick up with Brenda I.'s Cookie Theft description at this point:

> EXAMINER: What is happening in the picture?
> BRENDA I.: The woman is telling the children to get the jar. . . .
> The woman looks outside through the window as she washes the dishes.

EXAMINER: What about the girl and the boy?

BRENDA I.: The girl asks for a cookie, and the boy picks one up and gives it to her. Oh, the stool is falling.

EXAMINER: [Asks her to retell the story.]

BRENDA I.: The woman is washing dishes. The boy asks the girl what she wants. The girl tells the boy to take some cookies.

EXAMINER: Good, tell me more.

BRENDA I.: The boy gets up and takes cookies. The girl takes one from him and starts to eat it. Accidentally, the stool starts to slide out from under him.

EXAMINER: What is happening to the woman?

BRENDA I.: The woman looks around the yard and then dries the dishes. The sink is full of water, and it overflowed because the drain was stuck.

Although, on the whole, Brenda I.'s signing is fluent and grammatical, a few interesting formational errors were noted. These errors all had something in common: They were sublexical errors with some spatial component. For example, in making the sign for SQUARE, Brenda I. repeatedly omitted the left side of the sign. (When made with one hand, the sign SQUARE is formed by moving the index finger in a squarelike path in a plane parallel to the front of the signer's torso; see figure 5.4.) Brenda I. was the only patient to leave off half of a sign. This omission is most likely a manifestation of hemispatial neglect; it raises questions about the nature of the internal representation of such concepts as a square. Her other errors involved incorrect orientation of the hand, not the configuration of the hand itself (a common type of error in left-hemisphere-damaged signers). Aside from these few obviously spatial errors, there were no grammatical errors, no incorrect selections of lexical items, and no morphological simplifications, substitutions, or overelaborations in

Correct form   Brenda I.'s error

SQUARE

Figure 5.4
Spatial error of Brenda I. Note the omission of the left-hand side of the square.

her signing, such as we found with the left-hemisphere-damaged patients.

5.3   Gilbert G.: The Airplane Mechanic

Gilbert G. impressed us as being both dignified and genial. He is actually loquacious in signing, eager to narrate a good story whenever he has a receptive audience. Even at age 81, after his stroke, he is quite able to care for himself and to take long trips. He is married to a deaf woman, whom he met at school, and both are active participants in the local deaf community. He is right-handed. Gilbert G. had become deaf during an attack of spinal meningitis at the age of 5. At first his parents did not send him to school because they did not know of any facilities nearby. Gilbert G. likes to tell the story about how his schooling began: One day, when he was riding in a carriage with his father to a nearby town, they picked up a hitchhiker. When the man turned to say a few words to the 9-year-old, Gilbert G.'s father explained that the boy was deaf, could not speak, and therefore could not attend school. Their companion informed them that there was, in fact, a special school for deaf children less than two miles from that very spot. It was this chance meeting that resulted in Gilbert G.'s entering a residential school for deaf children at the age of 9.

Gilbert G. was graduated from high school and went on to attend college but left after one year to return to his home state. He went to work first as a forest ranger and then as a laborer on a succession of jobs. He eventually found permanent work as a skilled technician and repairman in a company that manufactures airplanes, where he rose to the rank of supervisor. Gilbert G. read blueprints and was responsible for the plane assembly from plan to final product. He retired at age 65 but kept active in woodworking, home repair, and the like. He also spent time camping and mountain climbing. His right-hemisphere stroke at age 78 put an end to most of these pursuits.

5.3.1   Neurological Findings

Three and one-half years before we tested him, Gilbert G. experienced sudden weakness of the left side, fell down, and was diagnosed as having had a cerebrovascular infarct. By the time we tested him, he had recovered the use of his left side, but he continues to experience some awkwardness with his left hand; he nevertheless is able to sign with both hands without difficulty. He still walks with a slight limp, favoring the left leg. At the time of testing Gilbert G. had no visual field deficits. Neurological examination revealed lower fa-

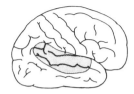

Gilbert G.

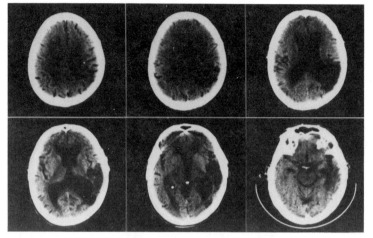

Figure 5.5
Lateral reconstruction of lesion and CT scan for right-lesioned patient Gilbert G.

cial weakness on the left side, abnormally high reflexes on the left side, and a deficit in recognizing objects felt with his left hand, but not with his right hand. These abnormalities provide indications of a damaged right hemisphere and, together with his CT scan, performed at the time of our testing, helped pinpoint the nature of his right-hemisphere lesion (see figure 5.5).

CT Findings
The scan shows a lesion in the temporal-parietal area of the right hemisphere. It involves the cortex and underlying white matter in the superior temporal gyrus, extending inferiorly to partially involve the middle temporal gyrus. Posteriorly, the lesion extends into the lower portion of the inferior parietal lobule, mainly involving the angular gyrus, and minimally, the supra-marginal gyrus.

5.3.2   *Preserved English Writing and ASL Signing*

Gilbert G.'s written English after his stroke seems unimpaired. Even without a written language sample from before his stroke, it is evident that there is no deficit. In describing the Cookie Theft picture, for example, Gilbert G. wrote in English:

> The mother was washing the dishes. Water was running in the sink. It ran over and wet the floor. The son saw a jar full of cookies. He climbed on a stool. While reaching for them, he lost his balance and fell off the stool.

Similarly, Gilbert G.'s poststroke signing is completely unimpaired, exhibiting full grammatical marking of morphology and excellent spatially organized syntax. Even immediately after his stroke, his wife reported that his signing was as before the stroke. A translation of his ASL description of the Cookie Theft picture into equivalent English is:

> The mother was washing the dishes, and the water was left running. The little girl and boy looked up at the cupboard where the cookie jar was resting. They looked at the mother to make sure that she was not looking at them. . . . The boy decided to push the stool and step up on the stool to reach for the cookie jar, but he lost his balance and started falling. . . . The girl turned and looked at her brother, saw what was going to happen to him. She was shocked to see her brother fall.

As this passage shows, Gilbert G.'s signing is impeccable, perfectly full and grammatical, and without error at any level of structure. Moreover, analysis of his free conversation, his storytelling, and elicited language samples show that after his stroke Gilbert G. had no deficits in signing whatsoever.

5.4   Comparison of Test Results across Right- and Left-lesioned Patients

An important aspect of our testing program is that we used the same range of tests across both the left- and right-lesioned signers; thus we can readily compare performance across the two groups. Here we compare the effects of left- and right-hemisphere lesions on the performance of our subjects on some of the tests, described in chapter 2 and briefly summarized here, that probe both comprehension and production of ASL.

5.4.1   A Special Issue in Testing Signers with Right-hemisphere Lesions

The phenomenon of hemispatial neglect has already been discussed with respect to two of the right-lesioned patients. In the case of Sarah M., hemispatial neglect affects her perception of others' signing, although she has managed to find a means of coping with this problem—making sure that people signing to her are in her good, right visual field.

But hemispatial neglect can impinge not only on the perception of signing but also on perception and response to items on a response-choice card; that is, hemispatial neglect can lead to a misinterpretation of test scores. For example, on one comprehension subtest of the BDAE (sign discrimination), subjects are asked to demonstrate understanding of single signs by pointing to the appropriate item from an array on cards. In the testing of deaf signers the subject or patient must attend visually to the examiner's signs before scanning the response array. Deaf, signing patients with right-hemisphere lesions demonstrate slightly lower scores than control subjects (figure 5.6a). To investigate whether these are errors of sign comprehension or are instead related to the visuospatial deficits of the right-hemisphere-damaged signers, namely, to neglect of items in the response array, we rescored responses excluding all items on the extreme left and right sides of the cards. If the patient shows neglect, one would expect this to affect responses to the side of the card contralateral to the lesion, that is, on the left-hand side of the card for the right-lesioned signers and on the right-hand side for the left-lesioned signers. The scores for the left-hemisphere-damaged patients were virtually unchanged by excluding both extreme sides of the card; however, the right-hemisphere-damaged patients had nearly perfect scores. In fact, as figure 5.6b shows, 75 percent of the errors of the right-lesioned signers were for signs whose responses appeared on the extreme left; no such effect was found for patients with left-hemisphere damage or for controls. In this instance the larger percentage increase, of course, is based on a relatively small increment in absolute scores. The errors by patients with right-hemisphere damage appear not to be errors in comprehension but rather errors resulting from hemispatial neglect.

As we show in chapter 7, left hemispatial neglect is only one type of spatial disorder that signers with right-hemisphere damage show. These impairments present special issues for the language testing of signers with right-hemisphere damage because spatial relations and linguistic structure are so intimately interwoven in sign language. In the discussion that follows, such special issues are mentioned where relevant.

5.4.2   Tests of American Sign Language Structure

Results of Sublexical Tests
In the phonology of ASL three parameters within which sublexical distinctions occur are Hand Configuration, Place of Articulation, and

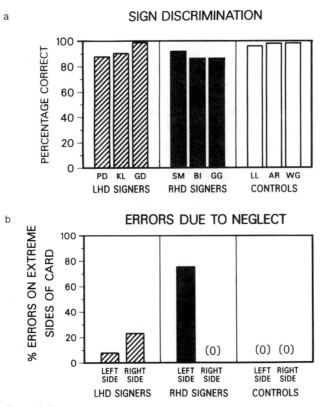

Figure 5.6
Errors related to neglect on the Sign Discrimination subtest of the Boston Diagnostic
Aphasia Examination. (a) Results of left-hemisphere-damaged (LHD) and right-
hemisphere-damaged (RHD) signers and controls for entire card. (b) Results for the
extreme sides of the card. Note that the right-lesioned signers showed some deficits
that are attributable to neglecting the extreme left-hand side of the card. (In this and
subsequent figures, the abbreviations are PD, Paul D.; KL, Karen L.; GD, Gail D.; SM,
Sarah M.; BI, Brenda I.; GG, Gilbert G.)

Movement. In one item of the test of decomposition of signs, for example, the experimenter signs DOLL (an /X/ handshape brushing downward) and the subject is asked to pick the one item of four pictured whose sign has the same handshape. In this particular test question the items pictured are a dog, a ball, an onion, and a fox. The correct response is the onion, because the ASL signs DOLL and ON-ION have the same handshape.

Another sublexical test uses the ASL functional equivalent of rhyme; the subject is asked to select the two pictures out of four whose signs in ASL are similar in all but one parameter. Figure 5.7 includes a sample item from the ASL Rhyming Test: A key, a violin, grapes, and an apple are pictured, and the correct choices for this item are key and apple, because the ASL signs KEY and APPLE are alike in all respects except one. The two signs share the same Hand Configuration and Movement, differing only in Place of Articulation; in this respect the pair are considered to be ASL equivalents of rhymes.

On these two tasks, which tap subjects' ability to decompose signs and show appreciation of sublexical structure, we find that patients with left-hemisphere lesions are impaired, whereas those with right-hemisphere lesions are not (see figure 5.7); right-lesioned Sarah M. scored 82 percent correct on one test and 100 percent correct on the other, and right-lesioned Gilbert G. scored 91 percent correct on the rhyming test and 82 percent correct on the test for decomposition.

Results of Morphological Tests
The formal marking of the distinction between noun-verb pairs in ASL is not a spatial one. When nouns and verbs that share the same root are derivationally related, the distinction between them is based on features of movement; in contrast to verbs, nouns are signed with restrained, repeated movement, which produces a more rapid and shorter trajectory. Figure 5.8 shows two sample pairs of derivationally related nouns and verbs: SIT and CHAIR, and SWEEP and BROOM. Note that the derivationally related signs in each pair share Handshape, Place of Articulation, and basic Movement shape. The two signs differ from one another only in features of movement (repetition and manner); the nouns always have movement that is restrained and repeated.

All the signers with right-hemisphere lesions performed better than any of those with left-hemisphere lesions on tests requiring processing of verbs and their derivationally related nouns in ASL; this superior performance was found on both the test of comprehension and the test of production described in chapter 2 (see figure 5.8).

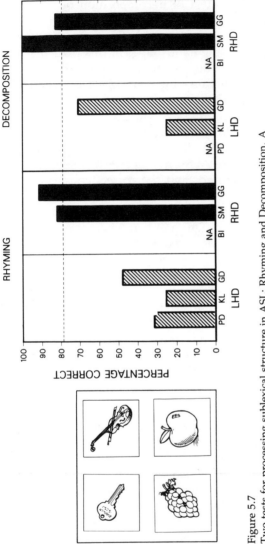

Figure 5.7
Two tests for processing sublexical structure in ASL: Rhyming and Decomposition. A sample item from the rhyming test is illustrated. The correct answers are the KEY and the APPLE, because the signs for these items share all major formational parameters but one. Right-hemisphere damaged (RHD) signers performed better than left-hemisphere-damaged (LHD) signers on both these tests.

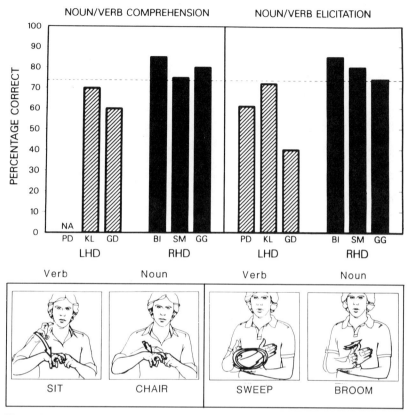

Figure 5.8
Two tests for processing ASL morphology: comprehension and elicitation of the formal distinction between nouns and related verbs. The illustration below the graph shows two pairs of derivationally related signs.

Sarah M. scored well on comprehension (75 percent correct) and production (80 percent) of this morphological distinction; Brenda I.'s
scores were even higher on both tests (85 percent correct on each
test), and Gilbert G. scored 80 percent correct on the comprehension
test and 73.7 percent correct on the elicitation test. These tests of ASL
grammatical morphology do not rely on spatial contrasts; all three
patients with right-hemisphere lesions performed well on these tests
and in a manner that is different from the impairment shown across
the board in both tests by the left-lesioned patients. Clearly, damage
to the right hemisphere does not impair the ability to control this
layered morphological distinction in a visual-gestural language.

Results of Tests of Spatialized Syntax
The tests of spatialized syntax, described in detail in chapter 2, probe
subjects' perception and memory for spatial loci. The test of nominal
establishment requires subjects to recall and specify where nominals
have been established and what nominal has been associated with
a particular locus. We have scores for two patients with right-
hemisphere damage: Gilbert G. scored 87.1 percent correct, which is
in the range of the control subjects, and Brenda I. scored 59.1 percent
correct, well below that range. Patients with left-hemisphere damage
also showed a range of scores on this test: Gail D. and Karen L. were
in the control range, but Paul D.'s score was only 40.9 percent correct.

On the two tests of verb agreement (Verb Agreement with Fixed
Framework and Verb Agreement with Shifting Reference), there are
some gaps in our data, but we have scores for most of the patients on
one or the other of the tests. Two left-lesioned patients showed poor
performance and one was exceptionally good: Gail D. scored 80 percent correct on the test of verb agreement with fixed framework and
100 percent correct on the other verb agreement test; Paul D. scored
57.1 percent on the fixed framework test and 43.35 percent on the
shifting framework test; and Karen L. scored 53.3 percent on the fixed
framework test and 42.9 percent on the shifting framework test. On
these tests the right-hemisphere-damaged patients performed worse
than the controls. On the Verb Agreement Test with Fixed Framework, Sarah M. scored 64.3 percent and Gilbert G., 42.9 percent. On
the Verb Agreement Test with Shifting Reference, Sarah M. scored
63.3 percent and Gilbert G. scored 60.0 percent. Unlike any of our
previous processing tests, on both tests of verb agreement, the right-
hemisphere-damaged patients, like the left-lesioned ones, were
impaired.

In view of the flawless signing of these right-lesioned signers, who
show normal processing on the tests of other components of ASL

structure, their performance on tests of spatialized syntax seems surprising. Let us consider the basis for the impaired performance on these tests. The nonlanguage spatial capacities of right-lesioned signers bear much on this issue and are presented in chapter 7. Recall that processing spatialized syntax in ASL requires complex underlying nonlanguage prerequisites: processing spatial relations (spatial loci), spatial memory (association of nominals with spatial loci, and perception and memory for direction of movement of the verb between spatial endpoints), and spatial transformations (changes in spatial referential framework). Thus a deficit in the ability to process any of the underlying spatial cognitive prerequisites for the spatialized syntax of ASL might result in impaired processing on these tests.

It appears that different functions may be crucial to the production of spatialized syntax and its comprehension. Although both linguistic and spatial functions are required, the fact that patients with right-hemisphere lesions *produce* errorless signing (including spatialized syntax and discourse) is evidence that the linguistic function is the more basic one here, requiring mostly left-hemisphere processing. It is our view that the perceptual processing involved in the *comprehension* of spatialized syntax critically involves both the left and the right hemispheres; certain crucial areas in each must be relatively intact for accurate performance. Because of the spatial nature of the units of perception, right-hemisphere processing would be required; but because of the linguistic nature of the underlying grammatical representations, left-hemisphere processing would also be required. In fact, the results of our tests show that (with one exception) neither left- nor right-lesioned patients perform perfectly across the range of these tests of spatialized syntax. It is particularly striking that the right-lesioned patients appear to be impaired on these tests, for they do quite well on perceptual processing of other grammatical constructs that do not involve spatial contrasts.

It would be reasonable to suppose that the basis for poor performance is different in the two groups. In left-lesioned patients the basis may be the grammatical nature of the constructs; in right-lesioned patients the basis may well be in the spatial nature of the perception.

There are several lines of evidence that indicate that sign language is intact in right-lesioned signers. The first (and most powerful) line of evidence lies in the fact that their signing is flawless and without aphasic symptoms and is in contrast to the signing of deaf patients after left-hemisphere damage where clear and marked disruption is found. The second line of evidence comes from the right-lesioned patients' excellent performance on all grammatical processing tasks that do not involve spatial perception; morphological and phonological processing is normal in these patients. The right-lesioned signers do not show comprehension deficits in any linguistic test, other than that of spatialized syntax. Finally, the right-lesioned signers do show profound deficits with respect to perceiving, manipulating, and transforming nonlanguage spatial relations. These lines of evidence are compelling in arguing for a specifically spatial-perceptual deficit, as opposed to a linguistic deficit, as the basis for the impaired performance of right-lesioned signers. An analysis that is restricted to the behavior exhibited on a test without analysis of other factors might miss the true underlying factors resulting in the deficit.

5.5   Profiles of Language Functions of Right-lesioned Patients

Given their obvious perceptual deficits and their impairment on nonlanguage visuospatial tasks, one might have expected a profound effect on language functions at all levels, such as that found in patients with left-hemisphere lesions. Figure 5.9a shows the rating-scale profiles for the three left-hemisphere-lesioned signers. Note that on each scale the scores are scattered; on most of them the scores span virtually the entire range of values, pointing to the different impairments of the left-lesioned patients. As shown in chapter 4, the individual profiles of the left-lesioned signers deviate from normal in different ways and represent different patterns of sign aphasia. Recall that one left-hemisphere-damaged patient was agrammatic, another was grammatical in her signing but made sublexical errors and failed to specify her pronominal indexes, and a third was paragrammatic and had failure in spatially organized syntax. Figure 5.9b presents the rating-scale profiles of three matched deaf control subjects. This part of the figure shows that normal performance falls at the extreme right-hand side of all scales except one, sign finding, where normal performance falls at the middle value of the scale.

   In contrast to the left-lesioned patients, no patient with right-hemisphere damage was aphasic. The signing of all three was fluent and varied, with conversational engagement and good understanding of everyday communication. All three right-lesioned patients, Sarah M., Brenda I., and Gilbert G., have well-formed grammatical sentences that exhibit a variety of grammatical forms. The rating-scale profiles of their sign characteristics, shown in figure 5.9c, reflect this grammatical (nonaphasic) signing; in fact, their scales are much like those of the control subjects.

5.6 Brain, Language, and Modality

Patterns of language breakdown and preservation in left- as opposed to right-lesioned signers led us to the following conclusions. Because the left-lesioned signers show frank sign language aphasias and the right-lesioned signers show preserved language function, it appears that it is, indeed, the left cerebral hemisphere that is specialized for sign language. This provides support for the proposition that the left cerebral hemisphere in humans has an innate predisposition for language. Thus there appear to be anatomical structures within the left hemisphere that emerge as special-purpose linguistic processors in persons who have profound and lifelong auditory deprivation and who communicate with a linguistic system that uses radically different channels of reception and transmission from that of speech. In this most crucial respect brain organization for language in deaf signers parallels that in hearing, speaking individuals.

On the other hand, our data suggest the possibility that those anatomical structures within the left hemisphere that subserve visual-gestural language differ from those that subserve auditory-vocal language. Recall that Karen L. has a lesion in the left inferior parietal lobule, an area known to function for higher-order spatial analysis (Mountcastle et al. 1984; Andersen, in press). She has both major spoken language mediating areas intact: Broca's area and Wernicke's area. Yet Karen L. has a marked and lasting sign comprehension loss, a language deficit that would not be predicted from her lesion if she were hearing.

There is other evidence that indicates that brain structures are not indelibly and unalterably wired for particular functions but rather that particular processing tasks are optimized by the brain. For example, Merzenich and his colleagues (Merzenich et al. 1984; Merzenich et al. 1983; Merzenich and Kaas 1982) have studied the cortical reorganization that occurs in the central representation of the body's skin surface after peripheral nerve injury. Experimenting with monkeys, these investigators cut the peripheral nerves that provide the brain with sensory input from skin surfaces. They found that the brain's map of these surfaces was dramatically reorganized. In that reorganization the representation of skin surfaces in cortical areas

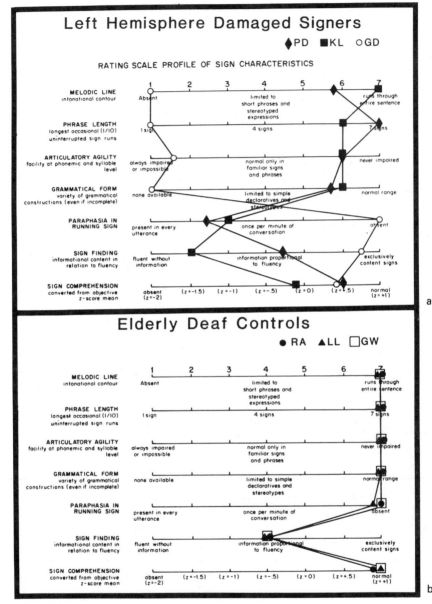

Figure 5.9
Rating-scale profiles of sign characteristics from the Boston Diagnostic Aphasia Examination for left- and right-lesioned signers and controls. Note that the right-lesioned signers are similar to the controls in performance.

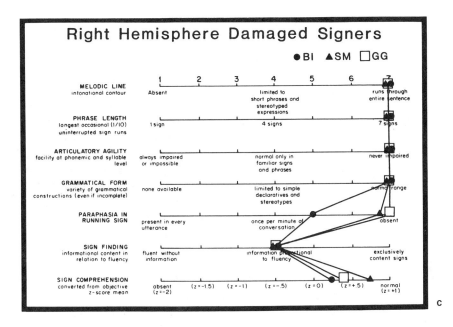

c

adjacent to deprived areas expanded to occupy the deprived cortical zones. Furthermore, this reorganization (and optimization) of brain function occurred after only relatively brief periods of altered somatosensory input to the brain. In a similar vein Neville and colleagues (Neville, Schmidt, and Kutas 1983; and Neville, in press) found that visually evoked brain potentials differ in deaf and hearing adults. Brain regions that subserve auditory processing in hearing subjects respond to visual stimulation in deaf subjects.

As we have said, the parietal lobes in humans function for higher-order spatial analysis, and we believe them to be more intimately involved with the processing of signed rather than with spoken language. With respect to processing the spatialized syntax of ASL, both the left and the right parietal lobes may be involved, although they play different roles. Let us review for a moment some of the differing spatial functions of the two parietal lobes in humans. It has been argued that the parietal lobes create a continually updated central neural image of the spatial surround and the body position within it (Mountcastle et al. 1984). In humans the right parietal lobe appears to mediate perception of spatial relations in extrapersonal space, that is, in the space beyond arm's reach from the body. This mediation includes perception of absolute location and of the spatial relations among objects in space. The left parietal lobe mediates processing of spatial relations in intrapersonal space; by intrapersonal space we mean the body and the space within arm's reach. The left parietal lobe seems to generate an internal representation of the body and of moving body parts and controls the accurate placement of the limbs without sensory feedback (Kimura 1979).

The CT scans for both Sarah M. and Gilbert G. show damage to the right parietal lobe. Although no brain scan was available for Brenda I., her specific spatial loss, as shown in chapter 7, is consistent with right parietal damage. Recall that the only deficits of language performance of the right-lesioned signers was in *comprehension* on our tests of spatialized syntax. Their production of these same grammatical processes was completely unimpaired. Comprehension, as opposed to production, of these spatial relations occurs in extrapersonal space. Perhaps initial preprocessing of this spatial signal is carried out preferentially by the right parietal lobe to extract spatial features. This initially processed information may then be transmitted to the left parietal lobe for linguistic decoding. Such linguistic decoding is precisely what Karen L. and Paul D., who have lesions in the left parietal lobe, could not perform. Also, of course, left-lesioned signers but not right-lesioned signers are impaired in the production of the spatialized syntax of ASL, providing strong evidence for the crucial role of the left hemisphere for the syntactic processing of ASL. It is our view, then, that not only is the left cerebral hemisphere innately predisposed for language but also anatomical structures mediating language may be linked to the modality in which language has developed.

It is important to note that we are not implying that sign language (or sign language processing) is localized in the left parietal lobe (or in a left anterior region). There are a number of cortical and subcortical brain regions that are intimately involved with spoken language processing (Damasio and Geschwind 1984), and there is undoubtedly a similarly large number of brain structures on whose integrated performance sign language functioning crucially depends.

The parietal (and frontal) lobes are heavily and reciprocally interconnected with many other cortical and subcortical structures, making them important nodes in a number of distributed systems (Mountcastle et al. 1984). It may well be that the brain's execution of the complex linguistic functions of sign language are carried out by neuronal processing mechanisms of those distributed systems. It is important to note that our data lead to the view that those distributed brain systems that underlie visual-gestural languages differ in part from those that subserve language in the vocal-auditory mode.

5.7   A Note on Hemispheric Specialization

As we have seen, the right-lesioned patients are not aphasic and do not exhibit linguistic deficits. An especially dramatic finding in our view is the case of Sarah M., who has a massive lesion to the right hemisphere that includes most of the territory fed by the right middle cerebral artery. The lesion includes areas that would be crucial to language if the lesion occurred in the left hemisphere of a hearing patient. In all likelihood, Sarah M. would have been globally aphasic if she had not been deaf and if the lesion had occurred in her *left* hemisphere. Thus there is more than ample possibility that aphasic symptomatology would have been manifested as a result of the particular lesion in this case because of the size and location of the lesion. Yet astonishingly, no aphasia for sign language resulted! Despite Sarah M.'s profound visuospatial impairment, her signing is absolutely impeccable. This underscores the complete separation in function that can occur between the specializations of the right and the left cerebral hemispheres in congenitally deaf signers. This result is particularly revealing because, in sign language, language and spatial relations participate in one and the same channel.

Chapter 6
Apraxia and Sign Aphasia

American Sign Language displays complex linguistic structure but does so by means of gestures (primarily of the arms and hands). Gesture and language are transmitted in the same modality. Is the breakdown of sign language dissociated from disorders of movement and gesture? That is, is sign language represented in the brain in a different way from that of learned movement in general? Investigators have raised much the same question with regard to speech, but there the issue is more difficult to address because most movements of the speech articulators are hidden from view. The movements of the hands and arms, however, are directly observable.

6.1 Apraxia: Motor Disorder or Symbolic Disorder?

In attempting to understand the principles of neural organization underlying language, some investigators have tried to root language in movement control and others have tried to base it in the human capacity to convey meaning through symbols. Both sets of investigators have linked the apraxias (neural disorders of purposive movement) with the aphasias.

Kimura (1976, 1979), for example, considers the left hemisphere to be specialized for positioning the oral and manual articulators rather than for symbolic functioning per se. The system of control in the left hemisphere apparently depends on the accurate representation of moving body parts, not on sensory feedback, and thus it is fundamental to the production of a series of self-generated movements (Kimura 1979). Kimura and her colleagues find that aphasics, unlike patients with damage to the right hemisphere, are unable to copy sequences of meaningless movements of the hands or mouth (Kimura 1976). In further support of a link between left-hemisphere dominance for language and left-hemisphere control of movement, Kimura notes that there is a close connection between brain lateralization for speech and hand dominance, that disorders in manual communication quite often result from left-hemisphere lesions in deaf people, and that persons with left-hemisphere dominance for speech show frequent occurrence of certain right-hand movements during speaking.

Other investigators have proposed a common basis for movement and speech disorders on quite different grounds: They attribute both apraxia and aphasia to an underlying inability to express or comprehend symbols (see Feyereisen and Seron (1982) for a review). The type of apraxia most pertinent to language is ideomotor apraxia, the inability to make purposive movements with either hand when the associated object is absent; for example, a patient able to use a hammer she is holding is unable to pretend to use a hammer. Here, the movement disorder is not explicable by weakness, lack of coordination, sensory loss, or incomprehension of commands (Geschwind 1975). Ideomotor apraxia unequivocally signals symbolic involvement resulting from a lesion in the left hemisphere, and it frequently co-occurs with aphasia. Also, impairments in the comprehension of meaningful gestures and pantomime occur almost exclusively in association with aphasia. These considerations have led to the proposal that aphasia is a disorder in conveying and comprehending symbols of any kind (Goldstein 1948).

Aphasia and ideomotor apraxia do not, however, invariably occur together, suggesting that they may be independent disorders, not manifestations of the same underlying defect in symbolization (Marshall 1980). Some investigators therefore postulate that aphasia and apraxia often occur together because of the anatomical proximity of the neural substrates responsible for language and gestural behavior (Goodglass and Kaplan 1979). Although the neural substrates of praxis are not well known, it does seem clear that both the left frontal and the left parietal lobes are particularly important for the control of learned motor activities. Geschwind (1965) proposed that (visual) imitation of gestures or the following of (auditory) verbal commands is first processed in their respective receptive areas; then messages are relayed to the motor association area of the left frontal lobe by means of the arcuate fasciculus. The left motor association area is connected to a similar area on the right by means of the corpus callosum, and each motor association area is connected to the primary motor area on the same side, which in turn affects the movement of the opposite limbs. Lesions that destroy the left motor association cortex or the anterior portion of the corpus callosum would "disconnect" the right premotor and motor areas from the left hemisphere, resulting in apraxia of the left hand. Apraxia may also result from a lesion in the left parietal lobe, a region that is thought to store visuokinesthetic motor learning and to program the motor association cortex of the left frontal lobe for the necessary movements (Heilman 1979a). Apraxia, then, may result from a parietal or a frontal lesion in the left hemisphere or from a lesion disconnecting the left parietal from the left frontal lobe or from a corpus callosum lesion disconnecting the right premotor and motor areas from the left hemisphere.

Breakdowns in sign language and in nonlinguistic gesture suggest several new ways to investigate apraxia and its relation to aphasia. Because gesture and linguistic symbol are transmitted in the same modality in sign, the breakdown of the two can be directly compared.[1] The breakdown of speech, by contrast, involves disruption of a different channel (the vocal tract) from that of gesture (the hands). Therefore sign language lends itself to a more direct determination of whether or not both aphasia and apraxia result from an underlying asymbolia.

The multilayered nature of ASL provides a second vehicle for assessing the relation between apraxia and aphasia. A pervasive principle in ASL is the concurrent (rather than linear) conveyance of information. For example, it is superimposed changes in movement and spatial contouring of a sign stem that convey inflectional and derivational processes in ASL. A sign and its inflection co-occur in time rather than follow each other in linear succession. Because grammatical and lexical structures are displayed concurrently, grammatical errors within inflected signs allow a unique test of the hypothesis that aphasia is the result of an inability to program complex movements in sequence.

A third way in which the study of sign language might clarify the relationship between aphasia and apraxia comes from the fact that the movements of the articulators in sign are open to view and thus make language production directly available for analysis. By relating impairments in sign language to patients' control of nonlanguage movement and comprehension of gestures, we shed new light on the relationship between aphasia and apraxia.

6.2   Deficits in Sign Language

Although the signing of the three patients with left-hemisphere damage is clearly aphasic, their linguistic disorders are quite different,

1. Deaf ASL signers can easily distinguish meaningful gestures that are ASL signs from those that are not. The signal made by a policeman holding his hand up, palm forward, to indicate "stop" is a symbolic gesture for hearing and for deaf people alike, but it is clearly not a sign of ASL. The ASL sign STOP is entirely different. Thus one can distinguish gesture and language within one and the same channel.

involving impairment at different structural layers of the language. Even though the patients with right-hemisphere damage show severe left-sided neglect or serious impairment in their visuospatial capacities, all three are fluent and normal in their sign production.

As we have seen, Paul D.'s aphasia is shown primarily in an abundance of semantic and grammatical paraphasias and errors in spatial syntax. He often uses semantically bizarre constructions. He tends to make inappropriate use of morphologically complex forms where simple ones are the norm. Sometimes he substitutes one inflectional form for another. Grammatical and semantic paraphasias abound. Furthermore, Paul D. tends to avoid using spatial indexes, and when he does use them, he does so inconsistently, disregarding the requirement of the system of verb agreement in ASL.

Karen L.'s signing output is also rich and fluent. Her deficits in expression are confined primarily to two domains: sublexical structure and nominal reference. We did not find any tendency to make semantic or grammatical errors in her ongoing conversation; in this respect she is different from Paul D. In many ways her signing appears to be the least impaired of the left-hemisphere-damaged patients. However, she frequently fails to specify who or what is the subject of her freely and correctly used indexical pronouns; that is, she establishes indexes at abstract points in space but often fails to specify the nominals associated with the spatial indexes. Furthermore, Karen L. has a marked comprehension impairment.

Gail D.'s expressive signing output is the most severely impaired of the patients we have studied; her utterances are often limited to single signs. Her output is effortful, and she often gropes for the sign. There is no trace of the grammatical apparatus of ASL in her signing; signs are made singly and in uninflected form, with selection almost exclusively from referential open-class signs. On a variety of sign language tests, we found marked differences in her skills: Her comprehension of sign language is nearly normal, as is her visuospatial nonlanguage processing. Yet her expression of sign language is grossly impaired, in fact, agrammatic.

6.3   Apraxia and Deaf Signers

We administered two tests of apraxia: For nonrepresentational movements we used Kimura's Movement Copying Test (Kimura and Archibald 1974; Kimura 1982); for symbolic movements we used the ideomotor apraxia tests of the BDAE adapted for deaf signers. These tests evaluate movements of the cheeks and mouth (buccofacial) and arm and hand movements; the arm and hand movements tested are both transitive (related to object manipulation) and intransitive (not involving objects, for example, waving goodbye). As before, all instructions came from a native ASL signer.

6.3.1 Nonrepresentational Movement

We used the slightly abbreviated form of Kimura's Movement Copying Test described in Kimura (1982). The task is to imitate movements of the hands and arms in unfamiliar and meaningless sequences (figure 6.1). These sequences are meaningless to signers as well as to nonsigners. The subject sees three movements to be imitated, all involving only one hand and arm. The first movement has an open hand with all fingers spread, positioned perpendicular to the body in front of the opposite arm. The hand is swept across the body from one side to the other. As the hand sweeps across the body, the extended fingers move from spaced apart to touching each other (figure 6.1a). This movement is scored for initial hand posture, initial hand orientation, lateral and straight movement, and proper hand closing. In the second movement the extended fingers and thumb of the hand

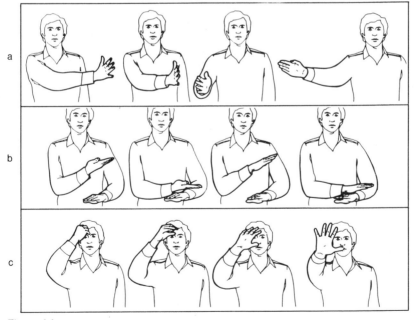

Figure 6.1
Nonrepresentational movements: Kimura Movement Copying Test.

are in contact, the back of the hand slaps the other forearm, rotates, and then the palm slaps the forearm (figure 6.1b). This movement is scored for hand posture, back slap, forearm rotation, and front slap. The final movement in the series starts with the fingertips and thumb together in a ring, all touching the forehead; then the hand moves out and away from the forehead, rotating and opening as it moves (figure 6.1c). This movement is scored for starting posture, forward and linear movement, forearm rotation, and hand opening. Two trials are given for each sequence. Each component of each sequence is given a score of two if performed correctly on the first trial, a score of one if performed correctly on the second trial, and a score of zero if not performed correctly on either trial. Each of the three sequences has four components that can be scored, so the maximum possible score is 24 points per hand.

Kimura (1982) reports data from 118 hearing patients with unilateral brain damage: 72 patients with left-hemisphere damage and 46 patients with right-hemisphere damage. Because many patients have one hand or arm paralyzed, we follow Kimura in reporting only scores for the hand on the same side as the lesion, where strength is typically unaffected. Table 6.1 presents the mean scores of the hearing patients from Kimura (1982) and the scores of our six deaf patients. The mean score of Kimura's hearing patients with left-hemisphere damage is 59 percent correct, whereas the mean score of the hearing patients with right-hemisphere damage is 78 percent correct, significantly higher. Kimura indicates that scores falling below a level of 90 percent of the mean score of the patients with right-

Table 6.1
Performance on the Kimura Movement Copying Test

Subject	Left-hemisphere-damaged patients' scores (percent correct)	Right-hemisphere-damaged patients' scores (percent correct)
Hearing patients (from Kimura (1982))	59 (mean)	78 (mean)[a]
Deaf patients		
Paul D.	92	
Karen L.	63	
Gail D.	71	
Brenda I.		83
Sarah M.		75
Gilbert G.		70.8

a. Ninety percent of this level is 70.2 percent; patients with scores below 70.2 percent are considered to be impaired.

hemisphere damage should be considered impaired. Table 6.1 shows that on the basis of this cutoff value only Karen L. is impaired; the other deaf patients are not.

The types of error that the deaf signing patients made are revealing. The left-hemisphere-damaged patients made errors on all components (hand configuration, movement, location, and orientation), but Brenda I., a right-hemisphere-damaged patient, made only spatial errors. For the first movement sequence (figure 6.1a), Brenda I. began the movement in the space near her midline rather than far to her left. Right-lesioned Sarah M. also made this error. Because both Brenda I. and Sarah M. manifest severe left hemispatial neglect in other situations, their spatial errors may be related to this condition. Brenda I.'s only other error was in the orientation of the hand with respect to the body, another spatial error.

6.3.2   Representational Movement

As in the BDAE, our adaptation of the tests of apraxia is divided into three sections: buccofacial movements, intransitive limb movements, and transitive limb movements. When subjects were unable to carry out a movement to command ("Show me how you would . . ."), the experimenter demonstrated the movement and asked the subject to copy it. We selected commands that would elicit gestures that differ markedly from corresponding signs, for example, "Show me how you would write your name." The gesture should involve configuration of the hand as if holding a pen or a pencil and movement characterizing writing. The ASL sign is radically different. When a subject was unable to copy a transitive limb movement, he or she was given the actual object and asked to show its use. Figure 6.2 presents the results of the ideomotor apraxia testing for each patient to each movement.

In making buccofacial movements, only left-lesioned patient Gail D. had difficulty. She failed to perform correctly four of the five movements to command and two of the movements to copy. When asked to demonstrate how to cough, she opened her mouth, signed VOMIT, then explosively mouthed "pop" as she moved her hand outward from her mouth. In trying to demonstrate a sneeze, she produced the sign SNEEZE (an opening and downward movement of the hand from the nose). For the movement for a kiss she mouthed "kiss," and in demonstrating chewing, she pursed her lips. The only gesture that she correctly performed to command was moving her eyes up; eye movement, however, forms a special category because it is represented primarily by the nonpyramidal motor system and is

	Left Hemisphere Damaged Patients									Right Hemisphere Damaged Patients									Controls								
	PD			KL			GD			BI			SM			GG			GW			RA			LL		
	Command	Imitation	W/Obj.	Command	Imitation	W/Obj.	Command	Imitation	W/Obj.	Command	Imitation	W/Obj.	Command	Imitation	W/Obj.	Command	Imitation	W/Obj.	Command	Imitation	W/Obj.	Command	Imitation	W/Obj.	Command	Imitation	W/Obj.
Buccofacial																											
cough	pass			pass			fail	fail		pass			pass			pass			pass			pass			pass		
sneeze	pass			pass			fail	fail		pass			pass			pass			pass			pass			pass		
kiss	pass			pass			fail	pass		pass			pass			pass			pass			pass			pass		
chew	pass			pass			fail	pass		pass			pass			pass			pass			pass			pass		
move eyes up	pass			pass			pass			pass			pass			pass			pass			pass			pass		
Intransitive Limb																											
wave goodbye	pass			pass			fail	pass		pass			pass			pass			pass			pass			pass		
signal "stop"	pass			fail	pass		pass			fail			pass			fail	pass		fail	pass		pass			pass		
call a dog	pass			pass			fail	pass		pass			fail	pass		pass			pass			pass			pass		
Transitive Limb																											
throw a ball	pass			pass			fail	fail	pass	pass			pass			pass			pass			pass			pass		
clean a bowl	pass			pass			pass			pass			pass			pass			pass			pass			pass		
write name	pass			fail	pass		fail	fail	pass	fail	pass		pass			pass			pass			pass			pass		
start a car	pass			fail	pass		fail	fail	pass	pass			pass			pass			pass			pass			pass		
cut meat	pass			pass			fail	fail	pass	fail			fail	pass		pass			pass			fail	pass		fail	pass	

pass ◪ fail ●

Figure 6.2
Results for left- and right-lesioned signers and controls for the ideomotor apraxia test, which evaluates representational movements.

often preserved in hearing apraxic patients (Geschwind 1975). The right-hemisphere-damaged patients and the controls had no difficulty with buccofacial movement.

For intransitive limb movements Gail D. again had some difficulty, whereas the other left-hemisphere-damaged patients, the right-hemisphere-damaged patients, and the controls did not. Gail D. failed to perform two of the four movements to command correctly, although she was able to imitate these gestures correctly. As for the other patients, Paul D. performed all the gestures correctly; Karen L. and right-lesioned Brenda I. and Gilbert G. failed to perform one gesture to command ("Signal to stop"), as did Sarah M. ("Call a dog") and one elderly control patient ("Signal to stop"). Finally, Gail D. had severe difficulty with transitive limb movements, whereas the other patients did not. She correctly gestured only one of the five movements to command ("Clean a bowl"). Furthermore, her errors to two of the items were the classic apraxic error of using a body part as an object. When asked to write her name and to cut meat in gestures, Gail D. extended her index finger from her fist, as if representing an implement: a pen for carrying out a writing motion, and a knife for demonstrating how to cut meat. Gail D. was also unable to make correct imitations of the movements that she had failed to produce to command. And even in her imitations of the movements, she produced body-part-as-object errors for the commands "Write your name" and "Cut meat." She was easily able to make the movements when given the actual objects, so it was clear that she had no elementary motor disorder; rather, she quite clearly exhibited ideomotor apraxia.

Karen L. was unable to produce two of the gestures to command ("Write your name" and "Start a car"). She repeatedly used the sign SIGNATURE rather than the gesture but correctly copied the gesture. Karen L. seemed to show great difficulty comprehending the item "Show me how you start a car." She repeatedly tried to relate a story about the time she first started driving at age 12. She was, however, able to copy the gesture correctly.

Finally, right-lesioned Brenda I. was unable to perform correctly two of the five movements to command ("Write your name" and "Cut meat"). For these two commands she gave tangential descriptions without producing the correct gestures. For one of them, however, "Write your name," she did gesture correctly when the examiner demonstrated the starting position of the hand. For the other gesture, "Cut meat," we note that two control subjects also failed to produce the gesture correctly to command. Right-lesioned Sarah M. was also unable to produce the latter gesture to command, but she easily imitated it. Right-lesioned Gilbert G. had no difficulty with performing any of the gestures to command.

6.3.3   Pantomime Recognition

Varney and Benton's (1978) Pantomime Recognition Test assesses the ability to understand meaningful, nonlinguistic gestural communication. The test consists of four practice items followed by a series of thirty videotaped pantomimes of a man miming the use of some common objects, such as a spoon, a pen, or a saw. From a test booklet containing four response choices per item, the patients are asked to point to the drawing depicting the object pantomimed. The four drawings for each test item include the correct choice (saw, for example), a semantic foil (an axe), a regular foil (an object whose use is pantomimed elsewhere on the test), and an odd foil (a train). Varney and Benton provide hearing patient norms for forty aphasic patients and for twenty control subjects without brain damage. Defective performance on the test is defined as performance below the level of the poorest control patient, which was 86.7 percent correct. By this criterion, 35 percent of the hearing aphasic patients had defective performance in pantomime recognition. The performance of all of our deaf patients fell in the normal range (figure 6.3): Paul D. scored 90 percent, Karen L. 86.7 percent, and Gail D. 100 percent correct. The two right-hemisphere-damaged patients who received the test, Brenda I. and Gilbert G., scored 93.3 percent and 100 percent correct, respectively.

6.4   The Separability of Apraxia and Sign Aphasia

In a long-standing controversy over the nature of aphasic disorders, certain investigators have proposed a common underlying basis for disorders of gesture and disorders of language. In this view disorders of language result from more basic disorders of movement control. The data we have obtained on apraxia and aphasia from six brain-damaged signers do not support either those who attribute the specialization of the left hemisphere specifically to the control of changes in the position of both oral and manual articulators (Kimura 1976, 1979) or those who claim that both apraxia and aphasia result from an underlying deficit in the capacity to express and comprehend symbols (Goldstein 1948). Instead, our findings suggest that sign language can break down along linguistic lines, independently of disorders of movement and gesture (both symbolic and meaningless).

In regard to representational gestures, the data clearly show that of

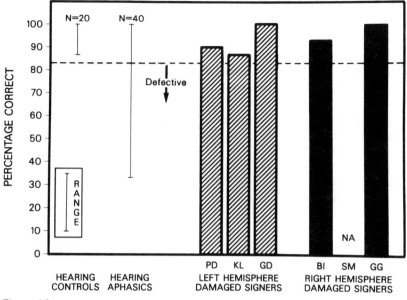

Figure 6.3
Performance of left- and right-lesioned signers on a test of Pantomime Recognition.
The range of hearing control scores and of scores of hearing aphasics are shown for
comparison. None of the deaf signers is impaired.

our six brain-damaged subjects only Gail D. has ideomotor apraxia.
Gail D. has severe difficulty in producing and imitating movements to
command. Furthermore, she produces the classic apraxic error of
using a body part as an object, both to command and in imitation. It is
interesting that her ideomotor apraxia can be predicted from her lesion, according to the Geschwind (1965) model. Her lesion affects the
left motor and premotor areas as well as the anterior portion of the
corpus callosum, resulting in right hemiplegia and apraxia on the left
side. The other deaf patients we studied are generally able to make
correct gestures to command, and all correctly imitate gestures presented to them. The few mistakes they did make in gesturing to
command actually result from difficulties in comprehension. In fact,
these patients make no errors in imitation, a task that does not require
intact language comprehension.

Because ideomotor apraxia occurs with sign aphasia only for Gail
D. (but not for the other two left-lesioned patients, Paul D. and Karen
L.), we can dissociate the capacity for using the linguistic gestures of
sign language from the capacity to produce and to imitate communicative but nonlinguistic gestures. In a similar vein, all the patients performed normally on a test of pantomime recognition; yet
some showed impairment in the comprehension of ASL (as shown by

performance on the BDAE and on other sign language tests). Hence the deficits in sign comprehension are unlikely to be explained by a general loss in the comprehension of communicative gestures.

With regard to nonrepresentational movements, only Karen L. was impaired on Kimura's movement copying test (with a score less than 90 percent of the mean score of the right-hemisphere-damaged hearing patients). Gail D. scored within the 90-percent level of hearing subjects with right-hemisphere damage, and right-lesioned Brenda I., Sarah M., and Gilbert G. were unimpaired, as was expected. It is significant that Gail D., who is extremely impaired on tests of ideomotor apraxia, performed well on copying nonrepresentational movements. Clearly, her apraxia is based on a motor-symbolic deficit rather than on a motor-sequencing one.

It is interesting that Paul D. showed no impairment when we administered Kimura's Movement Copying Test, whereas four years after his stroke he was tested and reported to be impaired in copying these movement sequences (Kimura, Battison, and Lubert 1976). Because he has recovered his ability to imitate nonrepresentational movements, his remaining aphasia for sign language cannot be due to a more basic incapacity to make nonrepresentational movements of the hands and arms.

Both Karen L. and Paul D. have fluent sign output; yet they show a double dissociation of sign language components. It seems highly unlikely that a movement-sequencing deficit could account for their double dissociation of linguistic structures. Furthermore, Paul D.'s semantic paraphasias and Karen L.'s comprehension deficits are clearly not attributable to a movement disorder. Nor are Karen L.'s sublexical errors and Paul D.'s paragrammatisms in sign the product of a disorder in the sequencing of movements, because the components of a sign (Handshape, Place of Articulation, Movement) co-occur throughout the sign and because grammatical morphemes also occur simultaneously with it; that is, lexical stem and inflection co-occur in time. This is not to say that capacities for movement sequencing are not an important function of the left hemisphere (Kimura and Archibald 1974; Kimura 1979, 1982). Clearly, more cases are needed for a fuller understanding of the relationship between apraxia and aphasia for sign language. The language deficits of the three aphasic signers with left-hemisphere damage, however, are related to specific linguistic components of ASL, rather than to an underlying motor disorder or to an underlying disorder in the capacity to express and comprehend symbols of any kind. This *separation between linguistic and nonlinguistic functioning* is all the more striking because for sign language gesture and linguistic symbol are transmitted in the same modality.

Chapter 7
Visuospatial Nonlanguage Capacity

In hearing people the right cerebral hemisphere has its own specialized abilities. The right hemisphere is clearly dominant for perception and processing of spatial patterns, spatial relations, and spatial transformations. Our investigation of language capacity in six brain-damaged signers shows that brain organization for a language in the visuospatial mode is in many ways similar to that for a language based on hearing and speech. We have shown that it is the left hemisphere that is specialized for sign language—but do signers display cerebral specialization for nonlanguage visuospatial processing? Spatial relations, transformations, and linguistic structure are intimately intertwined in sign language. Does the acquisition of a language that makes intricate use of visuospatial relations change the organization of the brain for processing nonlanguage visuospatial relations?

When we began the research that forms the basis for this book, little was known about hemispheric specialization for spatial analysis in deaf signers (see Poizner and Battison (1980) for a review). Many studies indicate a greater role for the right hemisphere than for the left hemisphere in deaf as well as hearing subjects in processing visuospatial stimuli, although there has been considerable controversy and quite a number of conflicting results (Kelly and Tomlinson-Keasey 1977; Kettrick and Hatfield 1986; Manning et al. 1977; Neville 1977; Neville and Bellugi 1978; Phippard 1977; Poizner, Battison, and Lane 1979; Poizner and Lane 1979; Samar 1983; Virostek and Cutting 1979). In order to assess the visuospatial abilities of right- and left-lesioned deaf signers, we selected spatial tests that had independently been found to maximally distinguish performance of brain-damaged hearing patients; that is, on these tests, hearing patients with right-hemisphere lesions were impaired compared to those with left-hemisphere lesions. The battery of tests we administered to our six subjects allows us to draw some definitive conclusions about visuospatial capacities in deaf signers.

7.1   The Effects of Right-hemisphere Damage on a Deaf Artist

As we mentioned in her case study, Sarah M. had been an accomplished artist before her stroke; she was skilled in painting and the elaborate artwork required in decorating eggshells and ceramics with exquisite designs. We were fortunate enough to obtain photographs of some of her prestroke artwork. The top half of figure 7.1 shows two paintings that Sarah M. executed before her stroke: a tall Indian chief in full headdress, standing, looking out over a hillside and pointing toward something in the distance, and a detail from a field of mountain flowers clustered together. Both paintings utilize strong colors. These paintings provide evidence of Sarah M.'s superior visuospatial capacities before her stroke. The lower half of figure 7.1 shows Sarah M.'s attempts, one year after her stroke, to copy two drawings that are part of our battery of visuospatial tasks. The poststroke drawings, which are barely recognizable without the model present, show severe distortions and omissions. Note the omissions of the head and all but one leg of the elephant and of the left-hand side of the house, the bottoms of the windows, and most of the roof; note also the overwriting of lines in an attempt to reproduce the sidewalk in front of the house. It is as if Sarah M. were attempting to copy pieces of the drawings without an overall spatial organization. This severe loss of her ability to draw after her right-hemisphere stroke brings out in a pronounced way the spatial loss seen in right-lesioned signers across a variety of visuospatial nonlanguage tasks.

7.2   Nonlanguage Visuospatial Functions

We have carefully selected tests that in hearing individuals discriminate maximally between the performance of right-hemisphere-damaged patients and that of left-hemisphere-damaged patients. Damage to either hemisphere in hearing patients can produce spatial impairment (DeRenzi 1982; Goodglass and Kaplan 1979; Warrington, James, and Kinsbourne 1966). What often differentiates the performance of left-brain-damaged patients from that of right-lesioned subjects is not only the degree of absolute impairment exhibited but also the different types of error made and the different processes used in performing the tasks (Kaplan 1983; Goodglass and Kaplan 1979).

We begin with an analysis of the performance of the six patients on the block designs from the WAIS-R Block Design subtest of the Wechsler Adult Intelligence Scale. We then turn to an analysis of drawings from the parietal lobe battery of the BDAE, performance in copying the Rey-Osterreith complex figure, and tests of unilateral

Sarah M.'s prestroke oil paintings.

Sarah M.'s copying of models after her stroke.

MODEL   MODEL

Figure 7.1
Comparison of Sarah M.'s prestroke paintings and poststroke drawings. The spatial deficits shown in Sarah M.'s drawings stand in marked contrast to her good artistic abilities before her stroke, as revealed by her paintings.

neglect. We finally turn to performance on visuospatial tests of facial recognition and line orientation. These tasks tap into the specialized capacities of the right hemisphere, and hence right-hemisphere damage often leads to marked impairment. It is certainly true that spatial analysis does not involve only the right hemisphere; the left hemisphere is also involved, but lesions to the left hemisphere produce qualitatively different and quantitatively less severe impairment. No single performance is taken as definitive; rather, converging evidence from the array of tasks provides the necessary test as to whether or not brain organization for processing nonlanguage visuospatial relations is modified in deaf signers.

7.2.1 Visuoconstructive Tasks

For all tasks a native signer instructed the patients in ASL. We recorded their responses on videotape, except in tests requiring them to point to a response-choice card or to sign a response-choice number; these responses were recorded at the time of testing.

Block Design
For hearing patients the WAIS-R block design (Wechsler 1981) has proved to be a sensitive instrument in distinguishing left- from right-brain damage. In this test the subject assembles either four or nine three-dimensional blocks, the surfaces of which are colored red or white or half-red and half-white, to match a two-dimensional model of the top surface. Hearing patients with right-hemisphere damage consistently demonstrate greater impairment than patients with left-hemisphere damage (DeRenzi 1982). Right-hemisphere damage impairs the maintenance of the overall configuration (Ben-Yishay et al. 1971) and increases the likelihood of a piecemeal approach to the problem (Patterson and Zangwill 1944). In contrast, damage to the left hemisphere produces little change in patients' treatment of the overall configuration of the design. Left-lesioned patients do, however, often err on the internal features of the design and tend to make more errors on the right-hand side of the design.

The performance of commissurotomized patients working on block designs with the right hand (reflecting the activity of the left hemisphere in isolation) is comparable to patients with lesions lateralized to the right hemisphere. The constructions of these patients using the left hand (reflecting the capacity of the isolated right hemisphere) is comparable to patients with lesions lateralized to the left hemisphere (Geschwind 1979). Adequate performance on block design, therefore, requires the integrity of both cerebral hemispheres, and a lesion in

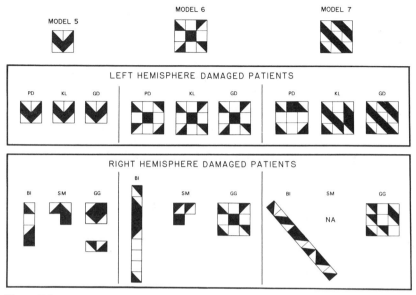

Figure 7.2
Performance on the WAIS-R Block Design Test. Note the broken configurations and severe spatial disorganization of the right-lesioned signers.

either hemisphere produces a distinctive performance that reflects the contribution of the nondamaged hemisphere.

Figure 7.2 presents sample designs produced by six deaf patients we studied. We see that the right-lesioned patients perform differently from the left-lesioned ones; the nature of their designs and the differences between them closely resemble the performances of hearing subjects with lateralized lesions. Each of the three patients with right-hemisphere damage, Brenda I., Sarah M., and Gilbert G., broke the external configuration of the designs. Gilbert G., who had been an airline mechanic before his stroke and therefore was especially skilled in the assembly of complex machine parts from blueprints, did not reproduce any of the designs correctly. Brenda I. broke the external configurations in all nine designs. On design 7 she appears to have attempted to capture the salient feature of the design—the diagonal stripes—by orienting the blocks on the diagonal. This kind of error is often seen in hearing patients with right-hemisphere lesions. Sarah M. produced incomplete, rudimentary constructions and would not even attempt the more difficult designs. Clearly, the performance of the patients with right-hemisphere lesions shows gross spatial disorganization (despite the fact that they were using their dominant right hands in constructing these designs).

The left-lesioned patients, in contrast, show no broken configurations on any of the designs. As figure 7.2 shows, the errors that they did make in the more complex designs deal with internal features of the design. Their performance closely resembles that of hearing patients with left-hemisphere lesions. Gail D., whose lesion is primarily anterior, had a flawless performance. Karen L., with left parietal involvement, performed well on design 6. The errors she made in design 7 were on the right-hand side of the design; the left-hand side is quite well reproduced. Paul D., who is more severely impaired, made errors on designs 6 and 7; however, on design 6, the major aspect of the figure is preserved, and on both designs the left half is better reproduced than the right.

Thus the impairments demonstrated by both the right- and left-lesioned signers on the revised WAIS-R Block Design test are characteristic ones, similar to those made by hearing patients with comparable lesions.

Drawing Tasks
Hearing patients with left-hemisphere damage characteristically draw a general contour or configuration but leave out internal details and features. Their drawings generally display correct spatial relationships but appear simplified. In contrast, the drawings of hearing patients with right-hemisphere damage are usually replete with details but lacking in overall spatial organization (Goodglass and Kaplan 1979; Warrington, James, and Kinsbourne 1966; Delis, Robertson, and Efron 1986). Also, some people with right-hemisphere lesions characteristically leave the left-hand parts of a drawing unfinished because of hemispatial neglect. Aside from the classic phenomenon of neglect, however, difficulty in the hemiattentional space contralateral to their lesion is common to both left- and right-lesioned patients (Kaplan 1980). The drawings of left-lesioned patients, for example, often contain distortions on the right half of the figure, and the converse is true for right-lesioned patients.

All six patients were asked to draw figures with and without a model; the figures were adapted from the parietal lobe battery of the BDAE. One right-hemisphere-lesioned patient, Gilbert G., did not show dramatic distortions in these drawings, although he did show marked visuospatial impairment on other tasks. Thus we compare the drawings of the three left-lesioned patients and of two right-lesioned patients; we present Gilbert G.'s drawings separately.

In the task without models the patients were asked to draw a clock (showing numbers, with two hands), a daisy, an elephant, a box (showing three sides), and a house (front and sides), as shown in figure 7.3. The left-lesioned patients drew simplified two-dimensional representations. In many of the drawings the contours are executed in essentially one continuous line, a technique seen most dramatically in the drawings of the elephants and in Gail D.'s daisy. Most distortions appear in the right hemiattentional field. Note, for example, the difference between the right- and left-hand sides of Karen L.'s daisy; the leaves do not join the stem on the right-hand side but do on the left. Similarly, the contour of Karen L.'s elephant is generally correct but distorted on the right-hand side. The characteristics of Karen L.'s and Gail D.'s drawings are consistent with those of hearing patients with damaged left hemispheres. Paul D.'s drawings are the most severely impaired. They are grossly oversimplified and unusually small (note the daisy and the elephant). His box and house

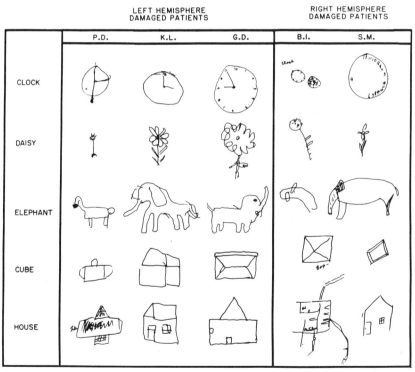

Figure 7.3
Drawing without a model from left- and right-lesioned signers. Note that the right-lesioned signers show severe spatial distortions.

lack perspective. He wrote the words "side" and "front" in response to the examiner's request to indicate these parts. His drawings, however, are equally impaired on each side. Because aging has a greater impact on visuospatial functioning than on language functioning (Hochanadel and Kaplan, in press), Paul D.'s visuospatial impairment may reflect his age more than his left-hemisphere lesion.

The drawings (without models) of the right-lesioned patients Brenda I. and Sarah M. show severe spatial disorganization, with Brenda I.'s the more impaired. There is a focus on component parts at the expense of contour (see Brenda I.'s elephant and house), and the parts are not related well spatially to each other or to the whole (as in both clocks). Left hemispatial neglect quite clearly appears in Brenda I.'s daisy, which has petals and leaves only on the right-hand side, and in Sarah M.'s clock, nearly all of whose numbers appear on the right-hand side. Several of the drawings feature unprompted words written by the patient (Brenda I.'s "clock" and "box"). Brenda I.'s drawing of a house is remarkable because of its profound lack of perspective; it fuses into one plane the component parts, such as the roof, the chimney, the path, the side of house, and the floor plan ("Bd" means 'bedroom'). In addition, there is neglect for the left-hand side of the house. All of Brenda I.'s drawings are consistent with the classic description of drawings produced by hearing patients with posterior right-hemisphere lesions. Sarah M.'s drawing, although less impaired than Brenda I.'s, shows severe visuospatial loss in light of Sarah M.'s accomplished artistry before her stroke.

Drawing With a Model

Figure 7.4 reproduces patients' drawings when they were asked to copy the models shown in the left-hand column. As in the preceding test, the drawings by the right-lesioned patients differ considerably from those of the left-lesioned patients. Although these drawings are generally better than those produced without a model, the right-lesioned patients' copies continue to show spatial disorganization, whereas those of the left-lesioned patients do not. Right-lesioned Sarah M. showed only minimal improvement when she had a model to copy (note the elephant and the box). None of the drawings of the left-lesioned patients show evidence of neglect, whereas those of two right-lesioned patients do; for both Sarah M. and Brenda I. significant features on the left-hand side of space (for example, the trunk of the elephant, the arm of the cross, the features on the far left-hand side of Brenda I.'s house) are deleted or distorted. Left hemispatial neglect is especially pronounced in the copies made by Sarah M. All her drawings omit significant features on the left-hand side of space, leaving

Figure 7.4
Drawing from a model by left- and right-lesioned signers. Note that, even when copying from a model, the right-lesioned signers show spatial distortion, left hemispatial neglect, and failure to indicate perspective.

broken contours (note the elephant, the cross, the box, and the house).

The left-lesioned patients, in contrast, produced fairly good drawings. The distortions in the cross occur only on the right-hand side of space (Paul D. and Karen L.), with the left-hand side of the cross remarkably well preserved. Even Paul D., who had the poorest performance on drawing without a model, does much better with a model to copy. It is interesting that Paul D.'s drawings reveal distortions on the right-hand side (for example, three hind legs on the elephant and the right arm of the cross). The drawings of all three left-lesioned patients now show perspective (the only exception being Gail D.'s box).

The severe spatial disorganization and neglect of the left hemiattentional field of two right-lesioned patients and Brenda I.'s continued tendency to add unprompted verbal information (for example, "car" to the right of the house) are all features characteristic of hearing patients with posterior lesions to the right hemisphere. The marked superiority of the copied drawings produced by the left-lesioned patients over those of the right-lesioned patients and the fairly well-preserved contours on the drawings by the left-lesioned patients with distortions more prominent in the right hemiattentional field are again consistent with the performance of hearing patients with lesions to the left hemisphere.

Gilbert G.'s drawings are much less distorted than those of the other two right-lesioned patients, as shown in figure 7.5; they are not without distortion, however. In the copy of the cross the arms are elongated and nonsymmetric, and the house shows complete lack of perspective. Despite his reasonably good performance on these drawing tests relative to the other two patients with right-hemisphere damage, we know that Gilbert G.'s ability to do tasks involving visuoconstructive activities was greatly impaired by his stroke. Before his stroke he had been a repair specialist for airplane engines; he also had been a carpenter and had designed and built a patio for his house. As a hobby, he built models and repaired furniture. After his stroke, not only was he unable to continue working in his former capacity, but he also could no longer continue his hobbies or even carry out simple repairs on his home.

Rey-Osterreith Complex Figure
The final drawing task required the patients to copy the Rey-Osterreith complex figure (Osterreith 1944). The model was presented in an upright orientation to four patients (Paul D., Karen L., Sarah M., and Gilbert G.) and in an inverted orientation to the other two patients (Gail D. and Brenda I.). Because the figure is quite complex (figure 7.6), normal subjects usually adopt a number of effective organizational strategies. By far, the most efficient is the drawing of the base rectangle first, then the vertical and horizontal bisectors, followed by the major diagonals. With the figure thus divided into smaller subunits, it is easier to place the internal features in correct relationship to each other. An alternative strategy is simply to divide the base rectangle into four units and then to treat each of the four quadrants separately. The strategies of patients with lateralized lesions not only differ from normal strategies but also show characteristic differences depending on the side of the lesion. In general, hearing patients with damage to the left hemisphere start at the upper left of the figure and draw the contour before filling in (or omitting) internal details. They do not typically draw the base rectangle but tend to

GG's DRAWING
WITHOUT MODEL

MODEL

GG's DRAWING
WITH MODEL

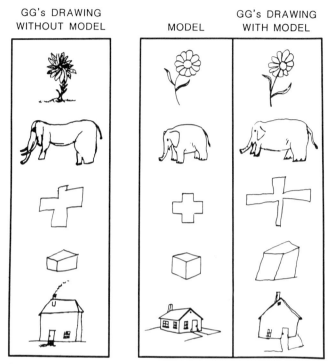

Figure 7.5
Right-lesioned Gilbert G.'s drawings with and without a model. Gilbert G.'s drawings do not show the same degree of impairment as those of the other right-lesioned signers.

track long continuous lines. Their distortions are more prominent on the right-hand side of the figure. Hearing patients with right-hemisphere damage, however, tend to start on the right-hand side of the figure; they typically do not delineate the contour before drawing internal features, and they place component parts in poor spatial relation to each other. Their distortions are more prominent in the left half of the figure (Goodglass and Kaplan 1979).

Of our six patients the three with left lesions produced recognizable copies, whereas two of those with right lesions produced grossly distorted ones. Gilbert G.'s drawing is again much less distorted than those of the other two right-lesioned patients; its overall contour is appropriate, and it shows no neglect. In common with most right-lesioned patients, however, Gilbert G. shows overdrawing of lines, and he extends a series of four parallel lines from the upper left quadrant into the upper right quadrant. Sarah M.'s copy shows massive neglect of left hemispace, with complete omission of the lower

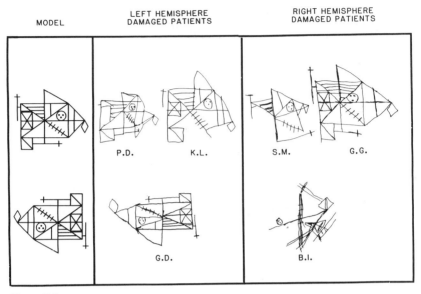

Figure 7.6
Performance in copying the Rey-Osterreith complex figure by left- and right-lesioned signers. The three left-lesioned signers (Paul D., Karen L., and Gail D.) produce recognizable copies, whereas the copies of right-lesioned signers Sarah M. and Brenda I. are grossly distorted.

left quadrant. The broken contour, with parts in incorrect spatial relations, reflects a piecemeal approach without any coherent spatial organization. Brenda I.'s copy is grossly distorted and hardly resembles the model at all. It lacks the overall contour and shows massive left hemispatial neglect and profuse repetition of the same few lines. The few isolated features are drawn in a profoundly segmented fashion. The features that are retained in Brenda I.'s drawing are in poor spatial relationship to one another and are collectively rotated 45 degrees to the right. We scored the copies of the Rey-Osterreith figure according to the criteria set forth by Lezak (1976). Out of a maximum 36 points, the left-lesioned patients scored as follows: Gail D., 31; Karen L., 18; and Paul D., 15. Of the patients with right lesions, Gilbert G. scored 27, and Brenda I. and Sarah M. had extremely low scores of 2 and 8, respectively.

The drawings of the three left-lesioned patients have relatively complete contours, and the features drawn are in relatively good relation to each other. Both left-lesioned Paul D. and Karen L. produced the left-hand side of the rectangle and drew the left-most line of the base rectangle and external square in one continuous line. Left-lesioned Gail D. started at the left-hand side and worked from left to right. In addition, she tended to organize her drawing into smaller units and then fleshed out the features in each subunit.

Our left-lesioned patients' productions of this complex figure are remarkably similar to the productions of left-lesioned hearing patients. And the contrasting characteristics of the drawings by right-lesioned signers Sarah M. and Brenda I.—the massive left hemispatial neglect and profound spatial disorganization—are virtually indistinguishable from the characteristics of productions by hearing patients with significant large frontoparietal lesions to the right hemisphere.

7.2.2 Visuoperceptual Task: Facial Recognition

In hearing individuals it is the right hemisphere that predominantly mediates the recognition of faces (Benton 1980; Rizzolati, Umilta, and Berlucchi 1971). To assess this capacity in our patients, we administered the Benton et al. (1978) test of facial recognition, which has been standardized by testing a large number of left- and right-lesioned patients and controls. In the first part of the test the patient matches identical front-view photographs. The patient is shown a front-view photograph of a face and is then asked to pick out the identical face from a display of six front-view photographs appearing below it. The patient may identify the target face by pointing to it or by calling out its number. In the second part the patient matches a front-view photograph with three-quarter-view photographs of the same face. The person shown in front-view in the target photograph appears three times in the three-quarter-views in the display of six (figure 7.7). The patient picks out the three faces that match the target one. In the third part a single front-view photograph must be located three times in a display of six front-view photographs taken under different lighting conditions.

Benton et al. (1983) provide normative data on control subjects and on brain-damaged patients, with corrections for age and educational level. They found that hearing patients with right-hemisphere damage performed substantially worse than patients with left-hemisphere damage. Scores ranging from 41 to 54 are considered normal; 39 and 40, borderline; 37 and 38, defective; and 0 to 36, severely defective. The left-lesioned patients in our study scored as follows: Paul D., 47; Karen L., 41; and Gail D., 47. Of the right-lesioned patients, Brenda I. scored 38, and both Gilbert G. and Sarah M. scored 43. The three left-lesioned patients and two of the right-lesioned patients performed well within the normal range; one right-lesioned patient, Brenda I., showed defective performance.

1

2

3

4

5

6

FACIAL RECOGNITION

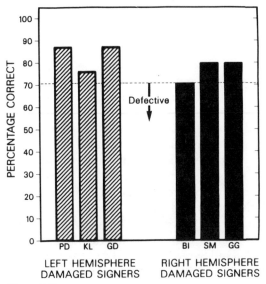

Figure 7.7
Performance on the Benton et al. Test of Facial Recognition by left- and right-lesioned
signers.

7.2.3 Visuospatial Tasks

Unilateral Neglect

We administered two tests for unilateral visual neglect. The left-lesioned patients Paul D. and Karen L. were asked to mark the mid-points of a series of horizontal lines of different lengths. Patients with unilateral neglect tend to put the mark off center, away from the neglected side, as if they were bisecting only the portion of the line that they do not neglect (Benton 1979). Patients with unilateral lesions who do not show neglect tend to show slight displacements toward the side of their lesion. Neither Paul D. nor Karen L. substantially displaced their marks from center; their bisections were, however, all displaced slightly to the left of center (averaging 3.1 percent and 5.3 percent, respectively). There was no evidence of neglect in these left-lesioned signers, which is consistent with their performance on the visuospatial tests previously discussed.

All the patients except Paul D. also took a test of unilateral visual neglect (see Albert 1973). In this test patients cross out forty lines that are arranged pseudorandomly on a page (figure 7.8). Albert (1973) reports that control subjects (subjects with no brain damage) cross out every line but that patients with neglect cross out fewer lines in the neglected half of the page than in the other half. The performance of the five signers, two left-lesioned and three right-lesioned, are shown

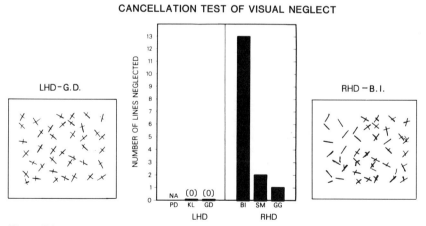

Figure 7.8
Performance on a test of unilateral visual neglect by left- and right-lesioned signers. The contrast between performance of a left- and a right-lesioned signer is presented. All right-lesioned signers showed evidence of neglect.

in figure 7.8. The two left-lesioned patients, Gail D. and Karen L., showed absolutely no evidence of neglect; they crossed out every line. In contrast, all of the right-lesioned signers showed left hemispatial neglect. Sarah M. and Gilbert G. showed mild neglect, failing to cross out two and one lines, respectively, all on the left-hand side. Brenda I. showed massive left neglect. She failed to cross out one line on the right, missed none in the center, but failed to cross out *thirteen* lines on the left. Although Sarah M. showed only mild left neglect on this test, she exhibited strong left neglect in her drawings. These results are also consistent with the performance of hearing patients with lateralized lesions.

Judgment of Line Orientation
In hearing persons it is primarily the right hemisphere that mediates the perceptual capacity to judge the spatial orientation of lines. As with facial recognition, the superiority of the right hemisphere for this processing has been demonstrated in experimental studies of normal subjects and in studies of brain-damaged patients (Fontenot and Benton 1972; Benton, Hannay, and Varney 1975). To assess this capacity in our patients, we used the Benton, Varney, and deS Hamsher (1977) test of judgment of line orientation. This test has been standardized by testing a large number of brain-damaged and control subjects (Benton et al. 1983). The subject is required to match the angular orientation of two simultaneously presented lines to a response-choice display of eleven lines. Each of the five practice items consists of a pair of lines from the response-choice display that are shown in full length. Each of the thirty test items consists of a pair of lines of partial length. Each partial line corresponds to the orientation of one of the lines appearing in the response-choice display below it. The partial lines represent the upper, middle, or lower segments of the response-choice lines. The subject responds by pointing to or giving the numbers of the appropriate response-choice lines. Score corrections are provided for age level and sex of the subject.

Benton et al. (1983) classify scores based on percentile rankings of control subjects. Scores from 21 to 30 range from average to superior; scores from zero to 20 range from severely defective to borderline. It is interesting that left-lesioned Paul D. obtained a score of 13 (and on a retest a score of 12). These scores fall in the severely defective range. Karen L. obtained a score of 17, which is classified as moderately defective. Gail D. scored 24, which is classified as average. With respect to the right-lesioned patients, Brenda I. obtained a score of 5, which is classified as severely defective, and Sarah M. scored 20, which is borderline. It is also interesting that Gilbert G. was severely impaired on this task, receiving a score of only 12, thus showing severe impairment on this spatial task of matching and extrapolating the angular orientation of lines. In general, the right-lesioned patients performed worse on this task than the left-lesioned patients (although Paul D., left-lesioned, is defective). This task taps certain spatial cognitive capacities that may also serve as prerequisites to ASL grammar, because the task depends heavily on spatial distinction and spatial location (for example, in the pronominal and verb agreement systems).

7.3   Capacities across Right- and Left-lesioned Signers

The data presented here suggest that the effects of lesions in the left or right hemisphere of deaf signers are similar to the effects in hearing individuals for the processing of visuospatial information. In fact, the behavior of a patient with damage to one hemisphere may be viewed not as the impaired performance of a damaged hemisphere but rather as a manifestation of the functioning of the relatively intact hemisphere (Goodglass and Kaplan 1979). The three deaf patients with left-hemisphere damage tended, in general, to process spatial relationships appropriately; this reflects the functioning of their intact right hemisphere. The deaf patients with damage to the right hemisphere, however, showed, in general, the classic visuospatial impairments seen in hearing patients with right-hemisphere damage.

The WAIS-R Block Design Test provides an important assessment of visuospatial capacity. The deaf patients generally performed in a manner similar to hearing patients. The left-lesioned deaf patients had difficulty with the right-hand side of the designs and did not break the external configurations of the designs. In contrast, all three right-lesioned patients broke the external configurations of designs.

In drawing with and without a model, the left-lesioned patients generally drew the contour or configuration but tended to simplify and omit details. In sharp contrast, two of the right-lesioned patients grossly distorted the spatial relations of component parts but nonetheless included many internal details. (The third right-lesioned patient, Gilbert G., was less impaired in these drawing tasks.) Furthermore, consistent with the results from hearing patients, left-lesioned patients' copies of a model were much improved over their drawings without a model; indeed, perspective was indicated as well. The right-lesioned patients, however, were unable to indicate perspective, and the addition of the model did not substantially improve the performance of one right-lesioned patient (Sarah M.). In addition,

Sarah M.'s poor performance is remarkable, because she was an accomplished painter before her stroke. Clearly, her right-hemisphere damage produced a serious spatial loss.

One of the left-lesioned patients, Paul D., performed somewhat differently from the other two. His drawings from memory were extremely simplified and showed some bilateral distortion. Indeed, Paul D.'s performance across the array of tests was the most severely impaired of the three left-lesioned patients. A generalized visuospatial loss often occurs in elderly subjects, brain damaged or not. Paul D. is 81; thus in his case the effects of age and of brain damage may be confounded. (In fact, we plan to pursue the possibility that loss of visuospatial capacities with age might impair certain aspects of sign comprehension and production.) The performance of the six patients in copying the Rey-Osterreith complex figure also parallels that of hearing patients with unilateral brain damage. Again, the right-lesioned patients distorted spatial relations, showing massive left hemispatial neglect and overwriting of lines. On the other hand, the three left-lesioned patients drew fairly accurate configurations and proceeded with the task in a manner similar to hearing patients with left-hemisphere damage.

Another parallel between the performances of deaf and hearing patients comes from an evaluation of unilateral visual neglect. As is generally true of hearing patients, the left-lesioned signers showed no unilateral neglect, whereas the right-lesioned signers did. We also note that, clinically, the only deaf patient unable to find her way about a familiar environment was the right-lesioned patient Brenda I. She had difficulty locating her own room and that of a deaf friend in a nursing home where they both had lived for several years. Again, consistent with hearing patients, none of the left-lesioned patients showed this topographic disorientation.

Concerning the recognition of unfamiliar faces, the left-lesioned patients performed normally, whereas one right-lesioned patient (Brenda I.) was defective and the other two scored within the normal range. On another test of right-hemisphere ability, judgment of line orientation, the right-lesioned signers performed poorly. Two of the three right-lesioned signers were severely defective, consistent with the performance of hearing patients with right-hemisphere damage. It is interesting to note that right-lesioned Gilbert G., who showed less impairment in drawing than the other right-lesioned patients, was severely defective in the perception of this spatial task.

In summary, the overwhelming weight of evidence from this study indicates that deaf signers show hemispheric specialization for non-language visuospatial processing that is similar in almost all respects to that of hearing speakers. We confirmed this with tests that have been shown to differentiate clearly between the performances of left-lesioned and right-lesioned hearing subjects. What are the implications of these data for hemispheric specialization? First, it seems clear that auditory experience is not necessary for the development of hemispheric specialization. Three of our patients were congenitally deaf (Gail D., Brenda I., and Sarah M.); one has been deaf since the age of 6 months (Karen L.). Only two became deaf postlingually (Paul D. and Gilbert G.); only they could have developed hemispheric specialization based on hearing and speech before deafness. Yet all the deaf patients clearly show hemispheric specialization. Indeed, the congenitally deaf patients are exactly the ones whose performance most clearly mirrors the classic differences in visuospatial functioning that have been found between hearing left-lesioned and right-lesioned patients.

Chapter 8

Spatialized Syntax, Spatial Mapping, and Modality

The reports of our intensive analysis of the six deaf, brain-damaged signers are part of a larger ongoing program of study in which we continue to test patients with unilateral brain damage. In this chapter we first provide converging evidence on nonlanguage spatial capacities from additional deaf signers with unilateral brain damage. We then examine syntactic capacity across left- and right-hemisphere-lesioned signers. Finally, we turn to a unique issue in sign language: comparison of two uses of space in ASL, one for syntax and the other for mapping.

As we have discussed, ASL incorporates both complex language structure and complex spatial relations, thereby exhibiting properties for which the hemispheres of hearing people have shown different predominant functioning. Space has more than just a syntactic function in ASL, however; it also functions in a topographic way in ASL. The space within which signs are articulated can be used to describe the layout of objects in space. In such a mapping spatial relations among signs correspond in a topographic manner to actual spatial relations among the objects described. In this concluding chapter we investigate in deaf signers the nature of cerebral specialization of the use of space for the representation of syntactic relations and that of spatial relations.

8.1 Nonlanguage Visuospatial Capacity

In trying to understand the language deficits of brain-lesioned signers, it is important to assess subjects' capacity for nonlanguage spatial cognition. The following discussion includes evidence from not only the six cases we have detailed but also our larger program of study investigating the effects of brain lesions on spatial cognition. Let us look first at the drawing performance of eight brain-lesioned signers on a simple but telling task, the copying of a complex three-dimensional model (figure 8.1). The figure shows eight drawings,

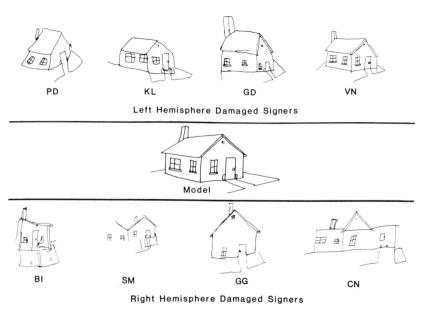

Figure 8.1
Drawings of a house from a model by four left- and four right-lesioned signers. Drawings of the right-lesioned signers show spatial disorganization, left hemispatial neglect,
and lack of perspective. (PD, Paul D.; KL, Karen L.; GD, Gail D.; VN, Violet N.; BI,
Brenda I.; SM, Sarah M.; GG, Gilbert G.; and CN, Christina N. in this and subsequent
figures.)

four by signers with damage to the right hemisphere and four by
those with damage to the left. The additional two subjects, one left-
lesioned and the other right-lesioned, were selected according to the
same criteria as the others—sign language environment, right-
handedness, and unilateral brain lesion.

The drawings of the left-lesioned signers (Paul D., Karen L., Gail
D., and Violet N.) are recognizable copies, with overall spatial contours and maintenance of perspective. In contrast, the signers with
right-hemisphere damage exhibit severe spatial disorganization, left
hemispatial neglect, and marked lack of perspective. Severe spatial
disorganization is shown, for example, in Christina N.'s house,
which has the chimney attached to a dislocated upper wall and the
door floating in the middle of the wall. Brenda I.'s house is a distorted
rendition of a series of rectangles. The clear left hemispatial neglect
can be seen in Sarah M.'s failure to complete lines on the left-hand
side of the house; in fact, she failed to indicate most aspects of the
left-hand portions of the model. In Gilbert G.'s drawing the left-hand
side of the model (wall and roof) are omitted, except for the chimney.
Finally, none of the right-lesioned signers is able to indicate perspec-

tive. Gilbert G. shows only the front surface of the house, without any indication of the sides or top of the model from which he was copying. (His drawing might be construed as a representation of the house under the condition of a rotation to a head-on view, but even with this interpretation the drawing completely lacks perspective.) Brenda I. shows a similar inability to represent the three-dimensional nature of the model. Christina N.'s drawing also shows profound loss of perspective; she draws the individual components of the house, including the front and side surfaces and roof, but lays them out linearly without any clue to their three-dimensional relationships.

Thus the spatial distortions, the evident left hemispatial neglect, and the lack of perspective in the drawings of the right-lesioned patients are immediately apparent and reflect their dysfunctioning right hemispheres. In contrast, the drawings of the left-lesioned signers, although simplified, have coherent spatial organization.

Figure 8.2 presents the performance of five brain-lesioned signers who took a test of perceptual closure, the Mooney faces test. Unfortunately, the other three patients were not available for this test. The results must be considered as merely suggestive. In this test subjects must discriminate photographs of human faces (top) from photographs of nonfaces (bottom); the photographs have highly exaggerated shadows and highlights. To identify the photographs accurately, the subject must achieve a configurational percept from fragmentary information, an ability that has been associated with intact right-hemisphere functioning (Newcombe and Russell 1969). Figure 8.2 shows that the three right-hemisphere-lesioned signers performed poorly in this task, none above 65 percent correct, and that the two left-hemisphere-lesioned signers were superior to them in performance.

A visuospatial task, the line orientation test, was discussed in chapter 7. In this task patients are asked to match the spatial orientation of partial lines to that of the full-length lines presented in an array (figure 8.3). This task, which taps the orientation aspects of spatial perception, is different from the Mooney faces task, which is more closely linked with figural aspects (shape and form). In this respect, right-lesioned patient Brenda I. shows an interesting contrast. Although she appears able to perceive figural aspects better than the other two right-lesioned patients (as shown by her performance on the Mooney faces test), her ability to perceive orientation aspects (as shown by her performance on the line orientation test) is the most severely impaired and, in fact, grossly impoverished if not nearly nonexistent. With the converging evidence from eight patients on this test, four with left-hemisphere lesions and four with right-

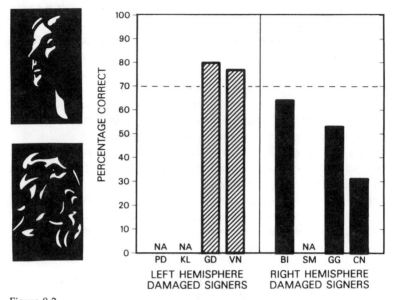

Figure 8.2
Performance on a test of perceptual closure, the Mooney faces test, by left- and right-
lesioned signers. Subjects must discriminate photographs of faces from nonfaces, given
fragmentary information. Note impairment in right-lesioned signers.

hemisphere lesions, the pattern of relative impairment in deaf signers
is now becoming clear, as shown in figure 8.3. In general, left-
lesioned signing patients are not impaired, whereas right-lesioned
signing patients are severely defective. Scores on the orientation task
that are below the dashed line in figure 8.3 are scores exceeded by
98.5 percent of normal hearing controls, after corrections for age and
sex to accommodate for the possibility of undiagnosed defects among
the population used as controls (Benton et al. 1983).

The data presented here and in chapter 7 demonstrate marked
differences in spatial capacity following lesions to the right or the left
hemisphere in deaf signers; it seems clear that right-hemisphere lesions (but not left-hemisphere lesions) lead to pronounced spatial
disruption. These results are brought out even more strongly by the
results of additional tests to more right- and left-brain-lesioned signers. These nonlanguage data show that the right hemisphere in deaf
signers develops cerebral specialization for nonlanguage visuospatial
functions. A stark contrast helps make the point: Gail D., the left-
hemisphere-damaged patient whose language functioning is the

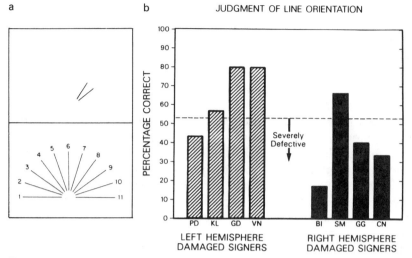

Figure 8.3

Performance on a spatial task, Judgment of Line Orientation, by four left- and four right-lesioned signers. (a) Sample test item. Note depressed performance of most right-lesioned signers (b).

most severely impaired of our subjects, shows highly accurate performance on every one of the visuospatial tests given. These data already strongly suggest that the two cerebral hemispheres in deaf people can show a principled separation between language and nonlanguage functioning, even when both involve visuospatial processing.

8.2 Specialization for Spatial Language Functions

The three left-hemisphere-damaged patients discussed in the preceding chapters are clearly aphasic for sign language; yet their linguistic disorders are different. Their impairments show different patterns, involving disabilities at different structural layers of the language. One left-hemisphere-lesioned patient (Gail D.) is grossly impaired. In sharp contrast to her prestroke signing, her poststroke signing is dysfluent and limited to single sign utterances. Her output is effortful, and she often gropes for the sign. Her difficulties are clearly not due to peripheral motor problems, because she produces the same signs normally in some contexts. There is no trace of the grammatical apparatus of ASL in her signing; signs are made singly and in uninflected form, with selection almost exclusively from referential open-class signs. She produces primarily nouns and some verbs, but with no grammatical inflection, no grammatical use of space, hardly any closed-class items, and none of the spatial apparatus that links signs in sentences. Her language profile is identical with that of markedly impaired hearing Broca's aphasics.

Another left-hemisphere-lesioned patient (Karen L.) has motorically fluent signing and communicates well and freely. She can carry on a conversation with normal rate and flow and can exhibit a full range of grammatical structure. Her deficits in expression are confined primarily to impairment at the *sublexical* level, involving Handshape, Movement, and Place of Articulation substitutions (the equivalent of phonemic errors in spoken language). She shows no tendency to make semantic or grammatical errors in her conversation; indeed, she has relatively preserved grammar (but impaired comprehension). In many ways her signing appears to be the least impaired of the left-hemisphere-lesioned patients; however, she frequently fails to specify the referents of her freely and correctly used indexical pronouns and indexed verbs.

The third left-hemisphere-lesioned signer, Paul D., also retained his motoric fluency after his stroke. He carries on conversations smoothly and with nearly normal rate and flow and does not appear frustrated, although he has occasional sign-finding difficulties. The content of the conversation, however, is revealing. His expressive language deficit is shown primarily in an abundance of paragrammatisms, including semantically bizarre constructions and neologisms. Furthermore, he has a tendency to use morphologically complex forms where simple ones would be appropriate, adding an inflection for temporal aspect or a derivationally complex form. And yet, at the same time, he fails to use the spatialized syntax of ASL (pronominal index and verb agreement markers). His signing is marked by an overabundance of nominals, few pronominal indexes, and failure to mark verb agreement correctly or at all. This appears to be an impairment of spatially organized syntax and discourse.

Thus two left-hemisphere-lesioned patients have primary impairment at the *grammatical* level, the one agrammatic and the other *paragrammatic*. Figure 8.4 shows errors characteristic of each of the three left-hemisphere-damaged patients: articulatory difficulties for the Broca-like patient, Gail D. (figure 8.4a shows articulatory difficulties in making the sign GIRL), errors at the sublexical level for Karen L. (figure 8.4b shows a Handshape substitution and a Movement substitution), and paragrammatisms for Paul D. (figure 8.4c shows the use of a morphologically complex form where a simple one would have been appropriate and the substitution of one morphological form for another).

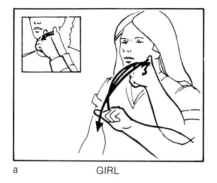

a   GIRL

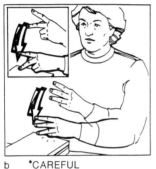

b   *CAREFUL
     (Handshape substitution:
     /W/ for /K/)

*ENJOY
(Movement substitution:
/N/ for /ᴑ/)

c   *CARELESS[Predispositional]
         (addition of Inflected Form)

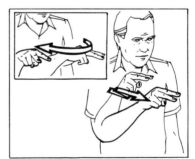

*LOOK[Habitual]
(Substitution of Habitual
Inflection for Multiple)

Figure 8.4
Typical errors of left-hemisphere-damaged signers. Correct signs are shown in insets.
Note different levels of linguistic deficit across left-lesioned signers. (a) Articulatory
difficulty typical of Gail D. (b) Sublexical substitutions of Karen L. (c) Paragrammatisms
of Paul D.

In direct contrast, the signers with damage to the right hemisphere are not aphasic for sign language; they exhibit fluent, error-free signing, a good range of grammatical forms, and no signing deficits. Whereas the left-hemisphere-lesioned patients are generally impaired in our tests of ASL structure at different linguistic levels, those with right-hemisphere damage are not. We have focused in this book on the grammatical capacity of these brain-damaged signers because of the central role grammar plays in the human capacity for language. Such an analysis has not been possible in previous studies of deaf signers because the grammatical structure of sign language has only recently been understood. Our results demonstrate that a visuospatial language breaks down as a result of left-hemisphere lesions in deaf signers and that sign language can break down at different structural levels. Our results also demonstrate that signers with lesions in the right hemisphere are, on the whole, not impaired linguistically. To highlight these differing language capacities, we now turn to a linguistic analysis of spatial syntax of left- and right-lesioned signers.

8.3   Syntactic Capacity across Left- and Right-lesioned Signers

The most important feature of sign language for revealing the organization of the brain for sign language is the unique role that space plays. Spatial contrast and spatial manipulation figure structurally at all linguistic levels in sign. The spatially realized framework for the syntax and discourse of ASL therefore provides a testing ground for our explanation of the specialization of the two hemispheres.

In ASL the distinction between nouns and pronouns is one between certain content signs and certain function signs. (See our discussion of this measure in chapter 3.) Figure 8.5 shows the ratio of nouns to pronouns for three elderly control signers, for our three signers with left-hemisphere damage, and for our three signers with right-hemisphere damage. These measures are taken from 10-minute samples of free conversation and expository signing from each person.

One might well expect damage to the right hemisphere to impair the spatially realized grammar of sign, but it does not. Remarkably, the three patients with right-hemisphere damage (Brenda I., Sarah M., and Gilbert G.) fall within the range of the controls; they have the normal noun/pronoun ratio of about 2 to 1. In contrast, the three patients with left-hemisphere damage deviate dramatically from this pattern. Gail D., the Broca-like patient, has almost ten times as many nouns as pronouns; this ratio is not surprising in light of her extreme

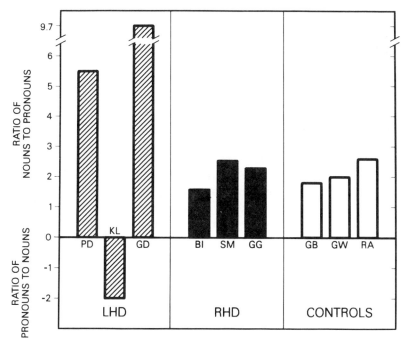

Figure 8.5
Spatialized syntax: ratio of nouns to pronouns in signing. Recall that pronouns in ASL are spatially realized indexes. Ratios greater than zero indicate greater use of nouns than pronouns, whereas ratios less than zero indicate greater use of pronouns than nouns. Note that right-lesioned signers are indistinguishable from controls, whereas all left-lesioned signers are deviant.

dysfluency and almost exclusive use of referential open-class nouns. Far more surprising is the contrast between the two fluent signers with left-hemisphere damage, Paul D. and Karen L. Although both remained fluent, even garrulous, conversationalists after their strokes, they are not only strikingly deviant from the normal pattern but also dramatically different from each other. Karen L. uses only half as many nouns as pronouns, a highly unusual pattern. Her tendency to make free use of pronominal indexes without specifying the associated nominals makes her signing seem vague; this vagueness is associated with the low information content of her signing. Paul D.'s pattern is the reverse of Karen L.'s, with more than five times as many nouns as pronouns, but, unlike Gail D., his fluent signing exploits the full range of grammatical categories. His overuse of nouns indeed appears to be a means to avoid using pronouns, which are spatially realized in ASL. All three patients with left-hemisphere damage show deviant patterns in this respect, whereas none of the patients with right-hemisphere damage is at all deviant.

In ASL the pronominal indexes are just one element of the framework on which spatialized syntax is realized. Another essential element is the system of verb agreement—the network of grammatical relations specifying the movements of verbs between spatial points. We examined every mutable verb in the same 10-minute videotaped samples of discourse for each patient and control subject. Each verb was analyzed to determine whether it had been indexed with respect to space and if such indexing was necessary. Then we computed the percentage of errors, whether failures of omission (verbs without an index in a linguistic context that required it) or errors of commission (verbs indexed incorrectly). The verb agreement errors for patients with left-hemisphere damage and for those with right-hemisphere damage are shown in figure 8.6.

The massive left hemispatial neglect and severe overall distortions shown by the signers with right-hemisphere lesions might lead one to expect that their signing would be noticeably affected, especially because syntax in ASL is highly dependent on spatial relations. Therefore we examined their signing closely to observe its spatialized syntax and discourse (the various reflections of pronouns, indexed verbs, and their spatial arrangements). First, because both Sarah M. and Brenda I. have immobile left arms and consequently right-

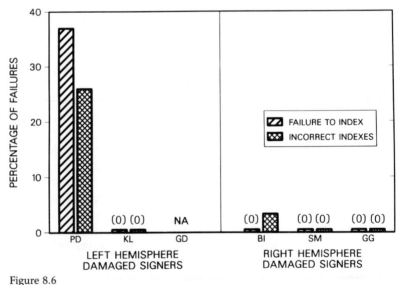

Figure 8.6
Spatialized syntax: errors in verb agreement.

handed signing and because both women exhibit neglect of left hemispace, one might expect that each would produce signs only in the right half of signing space. This was not the case, however. Brenda I.'s signs extended beyond the right-hand side of the signing space, as she often set up indexes on the left and, furthermore, maintained them consistently where required throughout a stretch of signing. In one sample she indexed half of the twenty-four pronouns and thirty-four verbs on her left. Not only did she index on her left-hand side as well as on her right, she also had a noun/pronoun ratio in the normal range (1.58). Thus, despite her severe visuospatial disorganization, Brenda I. made correct use of the system of verb agreement in ASL, a system central to the spatially organized syntax of ASL. We found no instances of verbs that should have been indexed but were not. Brenda I. did index a large number of verbs correctly. The lone error in verb agreement was the form SEE$_{a(to\ left)}$ (this sign was indexed on her left even though no indexing was appropriate for the context). In addition to making correct use of verb agreement, Brenda I. maintained the same locus point for coreference across a stretch of discourse.

The signing of right-lesioned Sarah M. was virtually impeccable. Her sentences were grammatical, and her signs were without error (except for occasional errors in fingerspelling and in hand orientation while signing numbers). Her noun/pronoun ratio was in the normal range (2.54). In the 10-minute sample of free conversation, she used many verbs that could be indexed, with no errors of omission or commission. In light of her severe visuospatial deficit for nonlanguage tasks, Sarah M.'s correct use of spatial mechanisms for sign syntax highlights the abstract nature of these mechanisms in ASL.

The signing of right-lesioned Gilbert G. was also completely correct, without error in aspects of spatialized syntax. In his signing there were fifty-two verbs that could be indexed, all of which were correctly handled. Thus his signing is entirely error free, and his use of spatialized syntax is perfect.

The patients with left-hemisphere damage use spatialized syntax differently from the patients with right-hemisphere damage. Beginning with the left-hemisphere-damaged patient Gail D., we noted that she produced few verbs and no indexes of verb agreement. Her utterances were mostly single signs, too sparse to allow scoring of this grammatical feature of ASL. The left-hemisphere-damaged patient Karen L. had a perfect score on both aspects of verb agreement, and her frequent use of verb indexing was uniformly grammatical. With left-lesioned Paul D., however, we see failure to index nearly 40 percent of the verbs that require indexing; in addition, when he did index a verb, he tended to do so incorrectly for the context (see figure 8.6). This omission of syntactically based verb agreement is quite unlike his overelaboration and augmentation of other aspects of his ASL morphology (such as inflections for temporal aspect and derivationally related forms). His omissions and simplifications were primarily restricted to inflections specifying the arguments of the verb (subject and object relations), that is, to syntactically based morphology.

Thus the left-hemisphere-damaged patients were all deviant on our measures of spatially organized syntax, although the deviations differed from one patient to another. In these spatial underpinnings of sentences and discourse in ASL, however, the right-hemisphere-lesioned patients, despite their severe visuospatial deficits, showed no impairment.[1]

8.4   Dissociation of Language and Nonlanguage Visuospatial Functions

We have found two double dissociations of function among left-lesioned and right-lesioned signers. These are particularly telling with regard to how sign language and nonlanguage visuospatial functions are represented and interact in the brains of deaf signers. Thus these findings have important implications for an understanding of cerebral specialization in humans. In double dissociations one component function is intact and another impaired in one individual, and in another person the pattern is reversed. The first double dissociation we found is at the level of brain mechanisms for language and nonlanguage functions. Left-lesioned Gail D. and right-lesioned Sarah M. present a remarkable set of dissociations of function.

All six of our patients before their strokes were skilled signers who had used ASL as their primary mode of communication throughout their lives. Although the left-lesioned patients are able to process visuospatial relations well and although the right-lesioned patients are extremely impaired, the language behavior of these patients, as we have shown, is quite the opposite. All three left-hemisphere-damaged patients are clearly aphasic for sign language. The most severely aphasic patient is Gail D., who suffered massive damage to

1. We have recently obtained some remarkable converging evidence from the study of a hearing signer who underwent chemical anesthesia of her left hemisphere and subsequently had portions of her right hemisphere surgically removed. This patient was globally aphasic for both sign and speech following anesthetization of her left hemisphere and was aphasic for neither following removal of portions of her right temporal lobe (Damasio et al. 1986).

the left frontal lobe. It is important to note that her capacity for non-language visuospatial processing is the most intact of any of the six patients. She had excellent performance on the WAIS-R Block Design test, in drawing, and in copying the Rey-Osterreith complex figure, and she scored in the normal range on tests of facial recognition and line orientation. Gail D.'s case is striking because it shows the separation that can occur in brain organization for linguistic and for visuospatial capacity, even for a visuospatial language.

The case of Sarah M., one of the right-hemisphere-lesioned patients, is in marked contrast. Sarah M. suffered massive damage to the right hemisphere, involving most of the territory of the right middle cerebral artery. Her case is a dramatic one, because she had been an accomplished artist before her stroke, with superior nonlanguage visuospatial capacities. After her stroke Sarah M.'s visuospatial nonlanguage functioning showed profound impairment. Her drawings were spatially disorganized, and they showed massive left hemispatial neglect. Her performance on the block design test was extremely impoverished. Her few eforts to resume her artwork after her stroke reflect this profound effect of right-hemisphere damage. Her spatial disorder also affects other aspects of her communication in sign language; Sarah M. no longer looks directly at her addressee but receives signing with an averted gaze. These profound deficits might lead one to expect an equally profound effect on Sarah M.'s signing and on her comprehension of a visuospatial language. Thus it was astonishing to us to find that Sarah M.'s signing is flawless, without a trace of impairment, and furthermore that her comprehension of sign and her performance on tests for processing the structural levels of ASL is good.

These two cases—one with massive damage to the left hemisphere and the other with massive damage to the right hemisphere—bring into focus the central questions addressed in this book, namely, the nature of the principles underlying the specialization of the cerebral hemispheres. The left-hemisphere-lesioned patient Gail D. is the most severely aphasic, with extremely impoverished sign language functions; yet she is normal in other visuospatial capacities. Her pattern of abilities shows that left-hemisphere specialization is also operative for language in a visuospatial mode. The right-hemisphere-lesioned patient Sarah M. shows extreme impairment of nonlanguage visuospatial functions, and yet her signing (including spatially expressed syntax) is completely unimpaired. This pattern shows how little of an effect right-hemisphere damage can have on language function, even though the language is expressed in a visuospatial mode. It seems clear that the differing functions of the two cerebral hemispheres emerge for spatial cognition and for language, even for deaf signers whose language is visuospatial. We now turn to the second dissociation of function between left- and right-lesioned signers, one that occurred between two aspects of sign language that depend on the use of space.

8.5   Spatialized Syntax versus Spatial Mapping

In the last part of our battery of tests for language, we asked patients to give a sign language description of their living quarters. Such verbal descriptions in spoken language have been studied from a number of viewpoints (for example, Jarvella and Klein (1982)). In ASL such descriptions are of particular interest. They involve the use of a variety of special signs (called classifiers, or size-and-shape specifiers, and verbs of motion or location). In signed descriptions of spatial arrangements space is used to represent space, and, unlike the use of space in syntax, actual spatial relations among points are significant. Figure 8.7 shows such a simple spatial description of the arrangement of three pieces of furniture in a room. The signer indicates the furniture (chair, TV, table) using lexical nouns and shows their spatial location with respect to one another using classifier signs to indicate the size, shape, and relative locations of the referents. Such spatial descriptions involve spatial mapping. In these descriptions the spatial relations among the locations established by the classifier signs (for example, for chair, TV, and table) represent topologically the spatial relationships among the actual items.

We first saw this mapping aspect of signing in its full form when a visiting deaf friend was telling us about his recent move to new quarters. For five minutes or so, he described the garden cottage in which he now lived—rooms, layout, furniture, windows, landscaping, and so forth. He described it in exquisite detail, with such explicit signing that we felt he had sculpted the entire cottage, garden, hills, trees, and all in front of us. Since then we have systematically studied layout descriptions in ASL (Corina 1984). In ASL such descriptions of spatial array and layout use the same horizontal plane of signing space as do ASL nominal and pronominal reference and ASL verb agreement devices. But in spatial description the relations among spatial loci become significant because they represent actual spatial relations topologically. This significance of relations among loci for mapping stands in contrast to the arbitrary, abstract nature of loci established for the syntax and discourse of ASL. This duality of func-

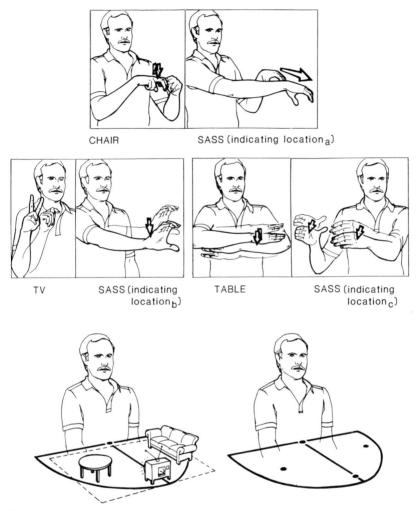

CHAIR   SASS (indicating location $_a$)

TV   SASS (indicating   TABLE   SASS (indicating
               location $_b$)   location $_c$)

Figure 8.7
Spatial description in ASL showing topological relations established for signed description. Instead of illustrating the signs used, we have substituted objects in appropriate locations for the description. We use the abbreviation SASS for classifiers called size and shape specifiers.

tion of spatial loci in a plane of signing space permits a unique investigation of brain organization for differing linguistic uses of space.

We asked four deaf patients—two with left-hemisphere lesions (Paul D. and Karen L.) and two with right-hemisphere lesions (Sarah M. and Brenda I.)—to describe their living quarters from memory. We asked them to specify both the items in the room and their arrangement within the spatial layout. In this task signing space is used to describe space, and actual spatial relationships are thus significant. The patients' spatial impairments varied according to whether the points in space were used for syntactic function or for giving relative position in space. As we will show, we found a striking double dissociation among the patients, even within the signing itself.

Right-lesioned Sarah M. was asked to draw her bedroom from memory and also to describe it in sign. In both her description and her drawing she indicated all the major items of furniture in the room correctly, and she specified correctly the locations of all but one item. Her description and her drawing matched. Both contained the major pieces of furniture arranged correctly throughout, except for the leftmost wall, which was left blank. A large white dresser, which is actually located on the left wall (from the point of view of the entrance, which Sarah M. was using for reference), was displaced to the far wall, more toward the right. Furthermore, there is a hallway to the left of the bedroom, which Sarah M. displaced in her signed description from the left to the lower right. Thus it appears that Sarah M.'s drawing and description show the effects of her left hemispatial neglect. The items are appropriately named but displaced in topographic relationship.

Right-lesioned Brenda I. also described her room in sign but with far greater spatial distortion. Again, the major pieces of furniture were correctly enumerated, but their spatial locations were greatly distorted: The entire left-hand side of the room was left bare, and the furniture was piled in helter-skelter fashion on the right. Even a bathroom that is actually to the left of the entrance was displaced to the right (figure 8.8).

In contrast, when left-lesioned Paul D. described his apartment, he showed omission of spatial detail (walls were not always indicated, for example), and his signing was linguistically bizarre—replete with grammatical paraphasias; however, there was no evident spatial distortion. Thus Paul D. tends to omit detail and to simplify in his description.

Karen L.'s description of her bedroom is indicative of the way left-lesioned signers can correctly use spatial mapping mechanisms in ASL despite their linguistic impairments. We first asked Karen L. to

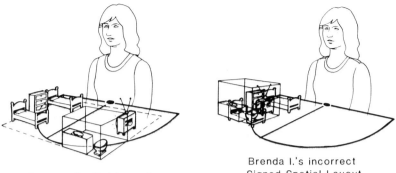

Correct Spatial Layout

Brenda I.'s incorrect
Signed Spatial Layout

Figure 8.8
Brenda I.'s incorrect signed spatial mapping of her room. Instead of illustrating the
signs used, we have substituted objects in the appropriate locations for the description.
Notice the severe distortion in Brenda I.'s use of signing space, including neglect of the
left side and incorrect arrangement.

describe her bedroom and the arrangement of furniture in it, without
having seen the room ourselves. From her description we could not
reconstruct the arrangement of the items in her room, and the examiner stopped her many times to ask for clarification ("You mean the
closet is here?"). Then we asked her to draw the layout of furniture in
the room, giving her a frame on a piece of paper and having her first
indicate the location of the door. Her drawing was clear and, in fact,
matched in every detail the correct spatial arrangement of furniture,
windows, closets, etc. in her room, as we later ascertained. An analysis of the videotape of the signed interview afterward revealed the
problem in her signed description. Karen L. used classifiers and size-
and-shape specifiers in a generally appropriate way (but with a sublexical error or two), and she correctly indicated their spatial locus
with respect to one another in the signing space she had designated.
What made her communication unclear was her failure to specify the
nominals, that is, her failure to enumerate the referents of the
classifiers. In fact, in ASL the classifiers and their use with verbs of
motion and location require the prior specification of the nominal
referents; this is what Karen L.'s spatially correct description failed to
communicate clearly. Karen L. correctly indicated the spatial placement and orientation of the classifier but often failed to specify its
nominal referent. Thus her description in ASL was spatially correct
and was appropriate in terms of spatial mapping but showed the
same kind of linguistic deficit that characterized her signing, failure to
specify nominals and some sublexical errors.
    It appears that the spatial descriptions of the left- and right-

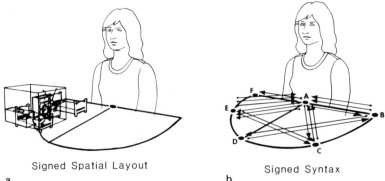

Signed Spatial Layout

a

Signed Syntax

b

Figure 8.9
Brenda I.'s spatial mapping versus spatialized syntax. (a) Schematized representation of Brenda I.'s signed room description. (b) Schematized representation of Brenda. I.'s spatialized syntax, showing correct nominal establishment and verb agreement. Notice the dramatic difference between spatial mapping (highly distorted) and spatialized syntax (virtually error free).

hemisphere-damaged signers are not unlike their nonlanguage visuospatial functions: Generally, left-lesioned Paul D. omits and simplifies, whereas the signers with right-hemisphere damage include many features but make errors of spatial organization.

When space is used in the language to represent syntactic relations, however, the pattern is reversed. Paul D. showed impaired spatialized syntax; he had a disproportionately high ratio of nouns to pronouns and tended to omit verb agreement. (Both pronouns and verb agreement involve spatial indexing.) Furthermore, when Paul D. did use spatial syntactic mechanisms, he sometimes failed to maintain the correct agreement. For all three right-hemisphere-lesioned signers, spatially organized syntax is correct and appropriate; indeed, all three even used the left-hand side of signing space in syntax. Figure 8.9 presents the contrast between spatial mapping and spatialized syntax in Brenda I.'s signing. For example, in her mapping everything is piled on the right in a disorganized fashion, whereas the left part of the spatial framework is unused. In her use of the spatial framework for syntax in ASL, she establishes spatial loci freely throughout the signing space (including on the left); furthermore, she even maintains consistent coreference to spatial loci.

There is evidence that left hemispatial neglect can affect both the internal representation of space and the exploration of space. In an intriguing report Bisiach and Luzzatti (1978) found neglect in descriptions from memory of familiar surroundings by hearing patients. Two patients with left hemispatial neglect were asked to name the buildings on the two long sides of the main square of Milan. The patients were asked to make the descriptions in two ways: as if they were facing the square and as if their backs were turned to it. In both descriptions the patients failed to recall buildings on the left-hand side, given the particular perspective taken. Thus the *same* buildings were omitted when they were on the left-hand side of the imagined square but were recalled when they were imagined on the right. Patients with hemispatial neglect, then, can show specific deficits in dealing with the mental representation of the left half of space, either in terms of mental scanning or in terms of the representation of space itself (see also Bisiach, Luzzatti, and Perani (1979) and DeRenzi (1982)).

The dissociation between mapping and syntax in sign language is all the more remarkable because both involve arm movements that cross the body's midline to the left-hand side of space. Nonetheless, we found left hemispatial neglect for mapping but not for syntax in signing. This dissociation strongly suggests that the internal representations for the two uses of space in signing—spatial mapping and spatialized syntax—are basically different. Clearly, the internal representation for mapping relies heavily on the inherent spatial relationships among objects described in the real world, whereas the internal representation for syntax is based on abstract linguistic syntactic properties, despite their realization in a spatial medium.

Thus within signing the use of space to represent *syntactic* relations and the use of space to represent *spatial* relations may be differentially affected by brain damage, with the syntactic relations disrupted by left-hemisphere damage and spatial relations disrupted by right-hemisphere damage.

Analysis of the patterns of breakdown of a visuospatial language in deaf signers allows new perspectives on the nature and determinants of cerebral specialization for language. First, these data show that hearing and speech are not necessary for the development of hemispheric specialization: Sound is *not* crucial. Second, the data show that in these deaf signers, it is the left hemisphere that is dominant for sign language. The patients with damage to the left hemisphere show marked sign language deficits but relatively intact capacity for processing nonlanguage visuospatial relations. The patients with damage to the right hemisphere show much the reverse pattern. Thus not only is there left-hemisphere specialization for language functioning but there is also a complementary right-hemisphere specialization for visuospatial functioning. The fact that much of the grammatical information is conveyed by means of spatial manipulation appears not to alter this complementary specialization. Furthermore, the fact that components of sign language (for example, lexicon and grammar) can be selectively impaired suggests that the functional organization of the brain for sign language may turn out to be *modular*. Finally, patients with left- and right-hemisphere damage show dissociations between two uses of space in ASL: the representation of spatial relations and the representation of syntactic relations. Right-hemisphere damage disrupts spatial relations but spares syntactic ones; left-hemisphere damage disrupts the use of space for syntactic relations but spares its use for spatial relations.

Taken together these data suggest that the left cerebral hemisphere in humans may have an innate predisposition for the central components of language, independent of language modality. Studies of the effects of brain damage on signing make it clear that accounts of hemispheric specialization are oversimplified if stated simply in terms of a dichotomy between language and visuospatial functioning. Such studies may also permit us to come closer to the real principles underlying the specializations of the two cerebral hemispheres, because in sign language there is interplay between visuospatial and linguistic relations within one and the same system.

Appendix
Notation

In this book we have not notated all aspects of patients' signing; we have designated only those notations that are relevant to the discussions and figures. Otherwise, we present English translations of the signing.

SIGN	Words in capital letters represent English glosses for ASL signs. A gloss is chosen on the basis of common usage among deaf researchers and informants in giving an English translation for the sign. The gloss represents the meaning of the unmarked, unmodulated, basic form of a sign out of context.
SIGN-SIGN	Multiword glosses connected by hyphens are used when more than one English word is required to translate a single sign, for example, LOOK-AT.
W-O-R-D	Fingerspelled words are represented by hyphenated capital letters. Fingerspelling is one of the many special subsystems of ASL (see Battison 1978).
'meaning'	Words within single quotation marks indicate the meaning or referent of the signs.
"word"	Double quotes for words or signs indicate direct quotations, nonliteral meanings, etc.
/W/	For specifying sublexical parameters of signs, for example, specific Hand Configurations, Places of Articulation, or Movements, we use notation

within slashes, using symbols from Stokoe, Casterline, and Croneberg (1965). Slashes are also used for specifying phonemic components in spoken languages, for example, /r/.

ASL Morphology

SIGN^SIGN

Sign glosses joined by a circumflex indicate compound signs in ASL.

SIGN[Modulation]

A superscript bracketed word following a sign gloss indicates that the sign is made with some change in form associated with a change in meaning from its basic, uninflected form. Thus the sign has undergone a morphological process. The particular specifications of grammatical processes in ASL (for example, Reciprocal, Iterative, Continuative, Apportionative External, Allocative Indeterminate) are spelled out in Klima and Bellugi (1979).

SIGN[D], SIGN[iD]

Derivational processes can also be specified in ASL (for example, SIGN[D:Nominalization]). Some derivational processes are called Idiomatic Derivatives ([iD]), such as CHURCH[iD] meaning 'narrow-minded.'

SIGN['regularly']

Morphological processes can be indicated by the specification of grammatical category of change or by the meaning of the inflected form. The sign GIVE under the Exhaustive inflection may be indicated as either GIVE[Exhaustive] or GIVE['to each'].

SIGN[+]

A plus indicates that a sign has not been made in its uninflected form but does not specify what change the sign has undergone.

SIGN[[X]X]

Inflectional forms embedded within other inflections are indicated by nested brackets.

PERSON-classifier-GO-BY; CL:/G/

Classifier verbs in ASL are indicated either semantically (PERSON-classifier, VEHICLE-classifier) or by the particular Hand Configuration used to mark the class (CL:/G/, CL:/3/), using the notation from Stokoe, Casterline, and

Croneberg (1965). More information on classifiers as verbs of location and motion can be found in Supalla (1982, 1986).

ASL Spatialized Syntax

As part of the spatialized syntax of ASL, a horizontal plane in signing space is used for abstract spatial loci. Nouns, verbs that can be indexed, pronouns, classifiers, and size and shape specifiers can be associated with abstract spatial loci, and these are indicated by subscripts. Description of notation for this system is as follows.

INDEX or (SHE)	Pronominal forms made with a pointing hand may be specified either as INDEX or as a sign gloss within parentheses. The form within parenthesis ((ME), (HE), (IT), (THERE)) is interpreted from context.
$_a$SIGN$_b$; SIGN$_a$; SIGN$_{b-c}$	Subscripts from the beginning of the alphabet are used to indicate spatial loci. Nouns, pronouns, and verbs of location are marked with a subscript to indicate the loci at which they are signed (INDEX$_a$, BOY$_a$, AT-X$_a$) in planes of signing space. Inflected verbs are marked with an initial subscript to mark origin location; a final subscript indicates the endpoint location ($_a$GIVE$_b$). Subscripts with a hyphen indicate a plural index (SIGN$_{b-d}$).
$_i$SIGN$_j$	Subscripts from the middle of the alphabet are used to indicate abstract indexes, reference as well as coreference.
$\overline{\text{neg}}$ SIGN	A line over a sign or signs indicates a particular facial expression occurring simultaneously with the sign(s). The facial expression may be part of the grammatical meaning. The particular meaning of the facial expression indicated by the gloss, is written above the line.
*SIGN	An asterisk preceding a sign or sentence indicates that the sign or word is inappropriate for the context and/or ungrammatical. Asterisks are also used for paraphasias at different levels (phonemic, morphological, syntactic) as well as neologisms in aphasic signing or writing.

References

Albert, M. L. 1973. "A simple test of visual neglect." *Neurology* 23:658–664.

Andersen, R. A. In press. "The anatomy and physiology of the posterior parietal lobe," in *Spatial Cognition: Brain Bases and Development*, J. Stiles-Davis, M. Kritchevsky, and U. Bellugi, eds. Hillsdale, N.J.: Erlbaum Associates.

Arbib, M. A., D. Caplan, and J. C. Marshall, eds. 1982. *Neural Models of Language Processes*, New York: Academic Press.

Battison, R. 1978. *Lexical Borrowing in American Sign Language*. Silver Spring, Md.: Linstock Press.

Battison, R. 1979. "Linguistic aspects of aphasia in deaf signers." Psychology Department, Northeastern University. Unpublished.

Battison, R., and C. Padden. 1974. "Sign language aphasia: A case study." Paper presented at the 49th Annual Meeting of the Linguistics Society of America, New York, December.

Bellugi, U. 1980. "The structuring of language: Clues from the similarities between signed and spoken language," in *Signed and Spoken Language: Biological Constraints on Linguistic Form*, U. Bellugi and M. Studdert-Kennedy, eds. Weinheim and Deerfield Beach, Fla.: Verlag Chemie, 115–140.

Bellugi, U. 1983. "Language structure and language breakdown in American Sign Language," in *Psychobiology of Language*, M. Studdert-Kennedy, ed. Cambridge, Mass.: MIT Press, 152–176.

Bellugi, U. In press. "The acquisition of a spatial language," in *The Development of Language and Language Researchers: Essays in Honor of Roger Brown*, F. Kessel, ed. Hillsdale, N.J.: Erlbaum Associates.

Bellugi, U., and E. S. Klima. 1982a. "The acquisition of three morphological systems in American Sign Language," in *Papers and Reports on Child Language Development*. 21:K1–35.

Bellugi, U., and E. S. Klima. 1982b. "From gesture to sign: Deixis in a visual-gestural language," in *Speech, Place, and Action: Studies of Language in Context*, R. J. Jarvella and W. Klein, eds. New York: Wiley, 297–313.

Bellugi, U., E. S. Klima, and P. Siple. 1975. "Remembering in signs." *Cognition* 3(2):93–125.

Bellugi, U., and D. Newkirk. 1980. "Formal devices for creating new signs in American Sign Language," in *Proceedings of the National Symposium on Sign Language Research and Teaching*, W. C. Stokoe, ed. Silver Spring, Md.: National Association of the Deaf, 39–80.

Bellugi, U., H. Poizner, and E. S. Klima. 1983. "Brain organization for language: Clues from sign aphasia." *Human Neurobiology* 2:155–170.

Bellugi, U., H. Poizner, and E. Zurif. 1982. "Prospects for the study of aphasia in a visual-gestural language," in *Neural Models of Language Processes,* M. A. Arbib, D. Caplan, and J. C. Marshall, eds. New York: Academic Press, 271–292.

Bellugi, U., and P. Siple. 1974. "Remembering with and without words," in *Current Problems in Psycholinguistics,* F. Bresson, ed. Paris: Centre National de la Recherche Scientifique, 215–236.

Bellugi, U., and M. Studdert-Kennedy, eds. 1980. *Signed and Spoken Language: Biological Constraints on Linguistic Form.* Weinheim and Deerfield Beach, Fla.: Verlag Chemie.

Benton, A. L. 1979. "Visuoperceptive, visuospatial, and visuoconstructive disorders," in *Clinical Neuropsychology,* K. Heilman and E. Valenstein, eds. New York: Oxford University Press.

Benton, A. L. 1980. "The neuropsychology of facial recognition." *American Psychologist* 35:176–186.

Benton, A. L., K. deS Hamsher, N. R. Varney, and O. Spreen. 1983. *Contributions to Neuropsychological Assessment.* New York: Oxford University Press.

Benton, A. L., J. Hannay, and N. R. Varney. 1975. "Visual perception of line direction in patients with unilateral brain disease." *Neurology* 25:907–910.

Benton, A. L., M. V. Van Allen, K. deS Hamsher, and H. S. Levine. 1978. "Test of facial recognition." Iowa City: Benton Laboratory of Neuropsychology, University of Iowa.

Benton, A. L., N. R. Varney, and K. deS Hamsher. 1977. "Test of judgement of line orientation." Iowa City: Benton Laboratory of Neuropsychology, University of Iowa.

Ben-Yishay, Y., L. Diller, I. Mendleberg, D. Gordon, and L. Gerstman. 1971. "Similarities and differences in block design performance between older normal and brain injured persons: A task analysis." *Journal of Abnormal Psychology* 78:17–25.

Berman, R. A. 1978. *Modern Hebrew Structure.* Tel Aviv: University Publishing Projects.

Bisiach, E., E. Capitani, L. Claudio, and D. Perani. 1981. "Brain and conscious representation of outside reality." *Neuropsychologia* 19:543–551.

Bisiach, E., and C. Luzzatti. 1978. "Unilateral neglect of representational space." *Cortex* 14:129–133.

Bisiach, E., C. Luzzatti, and D. Perani. 1979. "Unilateral neglect, representational schema and consciousness." *Brain* 102:609–618.

Boyes-Braem, P. 1981. "Features of the handshape in American Sign Language." La Jolla, Calif.: The Salk Institute. Unpublished.

Bradshaw, J. L., and N. C. Nettleton. 1981. "The nature of hemispheric specialization in man." *The Behavioral and Brain Sciences* 4:51–91.

Brown, R., C. Fraser, and U. Bellugi. 1962. "Control of grammar in imitation, comprehension, and production." *Journal of Verbal Learning and Verbal Behavior* 2(2):121–135.

Burr, C. W. 1905. "Loss of the sign language in a deaf mute from cerebral tumor and softening." *New York Medical Journal* 81:1106–1108.

Caplan, D., ed. 1980. *Biological Studies of Mental Processes.* Cambridge, Mass.: MIT Press.

Caplan, D., A. R. Lecours, and A. Smith, eds. 1984. *Biological Perspectives on Language,* Cambridge, Mass.: MIT Press.

Caramazza, A., and E. B. Zurif, eds. 1978. *Language Acquisition and Language Breakdown.* Baltimore, Md.: Johns Hopkins University Press.

Chiarello, C., R. Knight, and M. Mandel. 1982. "Aphasia in a prelingually deaf woman." *Brain* 105:29–51.

Churchland, P. S. 1986. *Neurophilosophy.* Cambridge, Mass.: MIT Press. A Bradford Book.

Corina, D. 1984. "Linguistic mapping strategies of deaf signers." La Jolla, Calif.: The Salk Institute. Unpublished.

Critchley, M. D. 1938. "Aphasia in a partial deaf mute." *Brain* 61:163–169.

Damasio, A. 1983a. "The frontal lobes," in *Clinical Neuropsychology,* K. M. Heilman and E. Valenstein, eds. New York: Oxford University Press, 360–412.

Damasio, A. 1983b. "Language and the basal ganglia." *Trends in Neuroscience* 6:442–444.

Damasio, A., U. Bellugi, H. Damasio, H. Poizner, and J. VanGilder. 1986. "Sign language aphasia during left hemisphere amytal injection." *Nature* 332:363–365.

Damasio, A., and N. Geschwind. 1984. "The neural basis of language." *Annual Review of Neuroscience* 7:127–147.

Damasio, H. 1981. "Cerebral localization of the aphasias," in *Acquired Aphasia,* M. T. Sarnow, ed. New York: Academic Press, 27–65.

Delis, D. C., L. C. Robertson, and R. Efron. 1986. "Hemispheric specialization of memory for visual hierarchical stimuli." *Neuropsychologia* 24:205–214.

DeRenzi, E. 1982. *Disorders of Space Exploration and Cognition.* New York: Wiley.

Douglass, E., and J. C. Richardson. 1959. "Aphasia in a congenital deaf mute." *Brain* 82:68–80.

Entus, A. K. 1977. "Hemispheric asymmetry in processing of dichotically presented speech and nonspeech stimuli by infants," in *Language Development and Neurological Theory,* S. J. Segalowitz and F. A. Gruber, eds. New York: Academic Press, 63–73.

Feyereisen, P., and X. Seron. 1982. "Nonverbal communication and aphasia: A review, I, II. *Brain and Language* 16:191–212, 213–236.

Fok, Y. Y. A., U. Bellugi, and D. Lillo-Martin. 1986. "Remembering in Chinese signs and characters," in *Linguistics, Psychology and the Chinese Language,* H. Kao and R. Hoosain, eds. Hong Kong: University of Hong Kong Press, 336–362.

Fontenot, D., and A. Benton. 1972. "Perception of direction in the right and left visual fields." *Neuropsychologia* 10:447–452.

Frishberg, N. C. 1975. "Arbitrariness and iconicity: Historical change in American Sign Language." *Language* 51:696–719.

Fromkin, V. 1971. "The non-anomalous nature of anomalous utterances." *Language* 47:27–52.

Fromkin, V. A. 1973. "Slips of the tongue." *Scientific American* 229:109–117.

Gardner, H., H. H. Brownell, W. Wapner, and D. Michelow. 1983. "Missing the point: the role of right hemisphere in the processing of complex linguistic material," in *Cognitive Processing in the Right Hemisphere,* E. Perecman ed. New York: Academic Press, 169–191.

Geschwind, N. 1965. "Disconnexion syndromes in animals and man I, II." *Brain* 88:237–294, 585–644.

Geschwind, N. 1975. "The apraxias: Neural mechanisms of disorders of learned movement." *American Scientist* 63:188–195.

Geschwind, N. 1979. "Specialization of the human brain." *Scientific American* 241:180–199.

Geschwind, N., and A. M. Galaburda, eds. 1984. *Cerebral Dominance.* Cambridge, Mass.: Harvard University Press.

Geschwind, N., and W. Levitsky. 1968. "Human brain: Left-right asymmetries in temporal speech region." *Science* 161:186–187.

Goldstein, K. 1948. *Language and Language Disturbance.* New York: Grune and Stratton.

Goodglass, H., and E. Kaplan. 1963. "Disturbance of gesture and pantomime in aphasia." *Brain* 86:703–720.

Goodglass, H., and E. Kaplan. 1972. Revised edition, 1983. *The Assessment of Aphasia and Related Disorders.* Philadelphia: Lea and Febiger.

Goodglass, H., and E. Kaplan. 1979. "Assessment of cognitive deficit in the brain-injured patient," in *Handbook of Behavioral Neurobiology*, M. Gazzaniga, ed. New York: Plenum Press, vol. 2, 3–22.

Grasset, J. 1896. "Aphasie de la main droite chez un soud muet." *Le Progres Medical,* ser. 3, 4:44, 281.

Hannay, H. J., N. R. Varney, and A. L. Benton. 1976. "Visual localization in patients with unilateral brain disease." *Journal of Neurology, Neurosurgery, and Psychiatry* 39:307–313.

Hanson, V. L. 1982. "When a word is not the sum of its letters: Fingerspelling and spelling," in *Teaching American Sign Language as a Second Language*, F. Caccamise, M. Garretson, and U. Bellugi, eds. Silver Spring, Md.: National Association of the Deaf, 176–185.

Heilman, K. M. 1979a. "Apraxia," in *Clinical Neuropsychology*, K. M. Heilman and E. Valenstein, eds. New York: Oxford University Press, 159–185.

Heilman, K. M. 1979b. "Neglect and related disorders," in *Clinical Neuropsychology*, K. M. Heilman and E. Valenstein, eds. New York: Oxford University Press, 268–307.

Heilman, K. M., and E. Valenstein. 1979. *Clinical Neuropsychology.* New York: Oxford University Press.

Hochanadel, G., and E. Kaplan. 1986. "Neuropsychology of normal aging," in *The Clinical Neurology of Aging*, M. Albert, ed. New York: Oxford University Press, 231–244.

Hoemann, H. W., C. E. Andrews, V. A. Florian, S. A. Hoemann, and C. J. Jensema. 1976. "The spelling proficiency of deaf children." *American Annals of the Deaf* 121:489–493.

Hoffmeister, R., and R. B. Wilbur. 1980. "Developmental: The acquisition of sign language," in *Recent Perspectives on American Sign Language*, H. Lane and F. Grosjean, eds. Hillsdale, N.J.: Erlbaum Associates, 61–78.

Jarvella, R. J., and W. Klein. 1982. *Speech, Place and Action: Studies of Language in Context.* New York: Wiley.

Jennings, P., and H. Poizner. 1986. "Computer graphic modeling and analysis II: Three-dimensional reconstruction and interactive analysis." La Jolla, Calif.: The Salk Institute. Unpublished.

Johansson, G. 1973. "Visual perception of biological motion and a model for its analysis." *Perception and Psychophysics* 14:201–211.

Kantor, R. 1982. "Communicative interaction in American Sign Language between deaf mothers and their deaf children: A psycholinguistic analysis." Ph.D. dissertation, School of Education, Boston University.

Kaplan, E. 1980. "A qualitative approach to clinical neuropsychological assessment." Paper presented at American Psychological Association, Montreal.

Kaplan, E. 1983. "Process and achievement revisited," in *Toward a Holistic Developmental Psychology*, S. Wapner and B. Kaplan, eds. Hillsdale, N.J.: Erlbaum Associates, 143–156.

Kaplan, E., E. P. Palmer, C. Weinstein, and E. Baker. 1981. "Block design: A brain-behavior based analysis." Paper presented at the International Neuropsychological Society, Bergen, Norway, June.

Kean, M. L. 1985. *Agrammatism.* Orlando, Fla.: Academic Press.

Kelly, R. R., and C. Tomlinson-Keasey. 1977. "Hemispheric laterality of deaf children for processing words and pictures visually presented to the hemifields." *American Annals of the Deaf* 122:525–533.

Kettrick, C., and N. Hatfield. 1986. "Bilingualism in a visuo-gestural mode," in *Processing in Bilinguals: Psycholinguistic and Neuropsychological Perspectives,* J. Vaid, ed. Hillsdale, N.J.: Erlbaum Associates, 253–274.

Kimura, D. 1976. "The neural basis of language qua gesture," in *Studies in Neurolinguistics,* H. Whitaker and H. A. Whitaker, eds. New York: Academic Press, vol. 2, 145–156.

Kimura, D. 1979. "Neuromotor mechanisms in the evolution of human communication," in *Studies in Neurolinguistics,* H. D. Steklis and M. J. Raleigh, eds. New York: Academic Press, vol. 2, 197–219.

Kimura, D. 1981. "Neural mechanisms in manual signing." *Sign Language Studies* 33:291–312.

Kimura, D. 1982. "Left-hemisphere control of oral and brachial movements and their relation to communication." *Philosophical Transactions of the Royal Society of London,* ser. B, 298:135–149.

Kimura, D., and Y. Archibald. 1974. "Motor functions of the left hemisphere." *Brain* 97:337–350.

Kimura, D., R. Battison, and B. Lubert. 1976. "Impairment of non-linguistic hand movements in a deaf aphasic." *Brain and Language* 3:566–571.

Kimura, D., W. Davidson, and C. W. McCormick. 1982. "No impairment in sign language after right-hemisphere stroke." *Brain and Cognition* 17:359–362.

Klima, E. S., and U. Bellugi. 1978. "Poetry without sound." *Human Nature* 1(10):74–83.

Klima, E. S., and U. Bellugi. 1979. *The Signs of Language.* Cambridge, Mass.: Harvard University Press.

Lane, H., P. Boyes-Braem, and U. Bellugi. 1976. "Preliminaries to a distinctive feature analysis of handshapes in American Sign Language." *Cognitive Psychology* 8:263–289.

Launer, P. 1982. "Acquiring the distinction between related nouns and verbs in ASL." Ph.D. dissertation, Department of Speech and Hearing Sciences, City University of New York.

Leischner, A. 1943. "Die "Aphasie" der Taubstummen." *Archiv für Psychiatrie und Nervenkrankheiten* 115:469–548.

Levy, J. 1982. "Mental processes in the nonverbal hemisphere," in *Animal Mind—Human Mind,* D. R. Griffin, ed. New York: Springer-Verlag, 57–75.

Lezak, M. D. 1976. *Neuropsychological Assessment.* New York: Oxford University Press.

Liberman, A. M. 1982. "On finding that speech is special." *American Psychologist* 37(2):148–167.

Liddell, S. 1984. "THINK and BELIEVE: Sequentiality in ASL." *Language* 60:372–399.

Liddell, S., and R. Johnson. 1985. "American Sign Language: The phonological base." Washington, D.C.: Gallaudet College. Unpublished.

Lillo-Martin, D. 1986. "Parameter setting: Evidence from use, acquisition, and breakdown in American Sign Language." Ph.D. dissertation, Linguistics Department, University of California at San Diego.

Lillo-Martin, D., U. Bellugi, L. O'Grady, D. Schemenauer, and M. O'Grady. 1986. "What and where in language: The acquisition of spatial linguistic structures in ASL." La Jolla, Calif.: The Salk Institute. Unpublished.

Lillo-Martin, D., U. Bellugi, D. Schemenauer, M. O'Grady, and H. Poizner. 1985. "Processing of spatial organized syntax in ASL." La Jolla, Calif.: The Salk Institute. Unpublished.

Lillo-Martin, D., U. Bellugi, L. Struxness, and M. O'Grady. 1985. "The acquisition of spatially organized syntax." *Papers and Reports on Child Language Development* 24:70–78.

Lillo-Martin, D., and E. S. Klima. 1986. "Pointing out differences: ASL pronouns in syntactic theory." Paper presented at conference on Theoretical Issues in Sign Language Research, Rochester, N.Y.

Loew, R. C. 1982. "Roles and reference," in *Teaching American Sign Language as a Second/ Foreign Language*, F. Caccamise, M. Garretson, and U. Bellugi, eds. Silver Spring, Md.: National Association of the Deaf, 40–58.

Loew, R. C. 1983. "Roles and reference in American Sign Language: A developmental perspective." Ph.D. dissertation, Psychology Department, University of Minnesota.

Loomis, J., H. Poizner, U. Bellugi, A. Blakemore, and J. Hollerbach. 1983. "Computer graphic modeling of American Sign Language." *Computer Graphics* 17:105–114.

Manning, A. A., W. Goble, R. Markman, and T. LaBreche. 1977. "Lateral cerebral differences in the deaf in response to linguistic and nonlinguistic stimuli." *Brain and Language* 4:309–321.

Marshall, J. C. 1980. "Clues from neurological deficits," in *Signed and Spoken Language: Biological Constraints on Linguistic Form*, U. Bellugi and M. Studdert-Kennedy, eds. Weinheim and Deerfield Beach, Fla.: Verlag Chemie, 275–290.

Marshall, J. C. 1982. "What is a symptom-complex?" in *Neural Models of Language Processes*, M. A. Arbib, D. Caplan, and J. C. Marshall, eds. New York: Academic Press, 389–409.

Maxwell, M. 1980. "Language acquisition in a deaf child: The interaction of sign variations, speech, and print variations." Ph.D. dissertation, Linguistics Department, University of Arizona.

McClelland, J. L., D. E. Rumelhart, and the PDP Research Group. 1986. *Parallel Distributed Processing*. Vol. 2. *Psychological and Biological Models*. Cambridge, Mass.: MIT Press. A Bradford Book.

McKeever, W. F., H. W. Hoemann, V. A. Florian, and A. D. VanDeventer. 1976. "Evidence of miminal cerebral asymmetries for the processing of English words and American Sign Language stimuli in the congenitally deaf." *Neuropsychologia* 14:413–423.

Meckler, R., J. Mack, and R. Bennett. 1979. "Sign language aphasia in a non-deaf mute." *Neurology* 29:1037–1040.

Meier, R. 1981. "Icons and morphemes: Models of the acquisition of verb agreement in American Sign Language." *Papers and Reports on Child Language Development* 20:92–99.

Meier, R. 1982. "Icons, analogues, and morphemes: The acquisition of verb agreement in American Sign Language." Ph.D. dissertation, Linguistics Department, University of California, San Diego.

Merzenich, M. M., and J. H. Kaas. 1982. "Reorganization of mammalian somatosensory cortex following peripheral nerve injury." *Trends in Neuroscience* 5(12):434–436.

Merzenich, M. M., J. H. Kaas, J. T. Wall, M. Sur, R. J. Nelson, and D. J. Felleman. 1983. "Progression of change following median nerve section in the cortical representation of the hand in Areas 3b and 1 in adult owl and squirrel monkeys." *Neuroscience* 10:639–665.

Merzenich, M. M., R. J. Nelson, M. P. Stryker, M. S. Cynader, A. Schoppmann, and J. M. Zook. 1984. "Somatosensory cortical map changes following digit amputation in adult monkeys." *The Journal of Comparative Neurology* 224:591–605.

Miyawaki, K., W. Strange, R. R. Verbrugge, A. M. Liberman, J. J. Jenkins, and O.

Fujimura. 1975. "An effect of linguistic experience: The discrimination of /r/ and /l/ by native speakers of Japanese and English." *Perception & Psychophysics* 18:331–340.

Molfese, D. L., R. B. Freeman, and D. S. Palermo. 1975. "The ontogeny of brain lateralization for speech and nonspeech stimuli." *Brain and Language* 2:365–368.

Mooney, C. M. 1957. "Age in the development of closure ability in children." *Canadian Journal of Psychology* 11:219–226.

Mountcastle, V. B., B. C. Motter, M. A. Steinmetz, and C. J. Duffy. 1984. "Looking and seeing: Visual functions of the parietal lobe," in *Dynamic Aspects of Neocortical Function*, G. Edelman, W. Gall, and W. Cowan, eds. New York: Wiley, 159–193.

Neville, H. J. 1977. "Electroencephalographic testing of cerebral specialization in normal and congenitally deaf children: A preliminary report," in *Language Development and Neurological Theory*, S. J. Segalowitz and F. A. Gruber, eds. New York: Academic Press, 121–131.

Neville, H. In press. "Brain organization for spatial attention," in *Spatial Cognition: Brain Bases and Development*, J. Stiles-Davis, M. Kritchevsky, and U. Bellugi, eds. Hillsdale, N.J.: Erlbaum Press.

Neville, H. J., and U. Bellugi. 1978. "Patterns of cerebral specialization in congenitally deaf adults: A preliminary report," in *Understanding Language Through Sign Language Research*, P. Siple, ed. New York: Academic Press, 239–257.

Neville, H. J., A. Schmidt, and M. Kutas. 1983. "Altered visual evoked potentials in congenitally deaf adults." *Brain Research* 266:127–132.

Newcombe F., and W. R. Russell. 1969. "Dissociated visual perceptual and spatial deficits in focal lesions of the right hemisphere." *Journal of Neurology, Neurosurgery and Psychiatry* 32:73–80.

Newkirk, D., E. S. Klima, C. C. Pedersen, and U. Bellugi. 1980. "Linguistic evidence from slips of the hand," in *Errors in Linguistic Performance*, V. A. Fromkin, ed. New York: Academic Press, 165–197.

Newport, E. L., and E. F. Ashbrook. 1977. "The emergence of semantic relations in ASL." *Papers and Reports on Child Language Development* 13:16–21.

Newport, E. L., and R. Meier. 1986. "Acquisition of American Sign Language," in *The Cross-Linguistic Study of Language Acquisition*, D. I. Slobin, ed. Hillsdale, N.J.: Erlbaum Associates.

Newport, E. L., and T. Supalla. 1980. "The structuring of language: Clues from the acquisition of signed and spoken language," in *Signed and Spoken Language: Biological Constraints on Linguistic Form*, U. Bellugi and M. Studdert-Kennedy, eds. Weinheim and Deerfield Beach, Fla.: Verlag Chemie, 187–211.

Obler, L. K., and L. Menn. 1982. *Exceptional Language and Linguistics*. New York: Academic Press.

Osterreith, P. A. 1944. "Le test de copie d'une figure complexe." *Archives de Psychologie* 30:206–356.

Padden, C. 1983. "Interaction of morphology and syntax in American Sign Language." Ph.D. dissertation, Linguistics Department, University of California, San Diego.

Padden, C. In press. "Grammatical theory and signed languages," in *Linguistics: The Cambridge Survey*, F. Newmeyer, ed. Cambridge, England: Cambridge University Press.

Patterson, A., and O. L. Zangwill. 1944. "Disorders of visual space perception associated with lesions of the right cerebral hemisphere." *Brain* 67:331–358.

Petitto, L. A. 1983. "From gesture to symbol: The relationship between form and meaning in the acquisition of personal pronouns in American Sign Language." Ph.D. dissertation, Psychology Department, Harvard University.

Petitto, L. A. In press. "Language in the pre-linguistic child," in *The Development of Language and Language Researchers*, F. Kessel, ed. Hillsdale, N.J.: Erlbaum Associates.

Petitto, L. A., and U. Bellugi. In press. "Spatial cognition and brain organization: Clues from the acquisition of a language in space," in *Spatial Cognition: Brain Bases and Development*, J. Stiles-Davis, M. Kritchevsky, and U. Bellugi, eds. Hillsdale, N.J.: Erlbaum Associates.

Phippard, D. 1977. "Hemifield differences in visual perception in deaf and hearing subjects." *Neuropsychologia* 15:555–561.

Poizner, H. 1981. "Visual and 'phonetic' encoding of movement: Evidence from American Sign Language." *Science* 212:691–693.

Poizner, H. 1983. "Perception of movement in American Sign Language: Effects of linguistic structure and linguistic experience." *Perception and Psychophysics* 33:215–231.

Poizner, H. 1985. "Visual-gestural languages and the functional organization of the brain." Language and language processing, ten year outlook on research opportunities. Washington, D.C.: National Academy of Sciences.

Poizner, H. In press. "Sign language processing," in *Gallaudet Encyclopedia of Deaf People and Deafness*, J. VanCleve, ed. New York: McGraw-Hill.

Poizner, H., and R. Battison. 1980. "Cerebral asymmetry for sign language: Clinical and experimental evidence," in *Recent Perspectives on American Sign Language*, H. Lane and F. Grosjean, eds. Hillsdale, N.J.: Erlbaum Associates, 79–101.

Poizner, H., R. Battison, and H. Lane. 1979. "Cerebral asymmetry for perception of American Sign Language: The effects of moving stimuli." *Brain and Language* 7:351–362.

Poizner, H., and U. Bellugi. 1984. "Hemispheric specialization for a visual-gestural langauge." Paper presented at International Neuropsychology Society, Houston, Texas.

Poizner, H., U. Bellugi, and V. Iragui. 1984. "Apraxia and aphasia in a visual-gestural language." *American Journal of Physiology* 246:R868–R883.

Poizner, H., U. Bellugi, and V. Lutes-Driscoll. 1981. "Perception of American Sign Language in dynamic point-light displays." *Journal of Experimental Psychology: Human Perception and Performance* 7:430–440.

Poizner, H., U. Bellugi, and R. Tweney. 1981. "Processing of formational, semantic, and iconic information in American Sign Language." *Journal of Experimental Psychology: Human Perception and Performance* 7:1146–1159.

Poizner, H., E. Kaplan, U. Bellugi, and C. Padden. 1984. "Hemispheric specialization for nonlanguage visual-spatial processing in brain damaged deaf signers." *Brain and Cognition* 3:281–306.

Poizner, H., and H. Lane. 1978. "Discrimination of location in American Sign Language," in *Understanding Language through Sign Language Research*, P. Siple, ed. New York: Academic Press, 271–287.

Poizner, H., and H. Lane. 1979. "Cerebral asymmetry in the perception of American Sign Language." *Brain and Language* 7:210–222.

Poizner, H., E. Wooten, and D. Salot. 1986. "Computergraphic modeling and analysis: A portable three-dimensional movement monitoring system." *Behavior Research Methods, Instruments and Computers*, special issue on computers and vision.

Ratcliff, G. 1982. "Disturbances of spatial orientation associated with cerebral lesions," in *Spatial Abilities, Development and Physiological Foundations*, M. Potegal, ed. New York: Academic Press, 301–331.

Ratcliff, G., and F. Newcombe. 1973. "Spatial orientation in man: Effects of left, right, and bilateral posterior cerebral lesions." *Journal of Neurology, Neurosurgery and Psychiatry* 36:448–454.

Reider, N. 1941. "A note on the influence of early training on the development of aphasic manifestations." *Bulletin of the Menninger Clinic* 5:1–4.

Rizzolati, G., C. Umilta, and G. Berlucchi. 1971. "Opposite superiorities of the right and left cerebral hemispheres in discriminative reaction time to physiognomic and alphabetical material." *Brain* 94:431–442.

Samar, V. J. 1983. "Evoked potential and visual half-field evidence for task-dependent cerebral asymmetries in congenitally deaf adults." *Brain and Cognition* 2:383–403.

Sarno, J., L. Swisher, and M. Sarno. 1969. "Aphasia in a congenitally deaf man." *Cortex* 5:398–414.

Sperry, R. W. 1974. "Lateral specialization in the surgically separated hemispheres," in *The Neurosciences: Third Study Program*, F. O. Schmitt and F. G. Worder, eds. Cambridge, Mass.: MIT Press, 5–19.

Stiles-Davis, J., M. Kritchevsky, and U. Bellugi, eds. In press. *Spatial Cognition: Brain Bases and Development*. Hillsdale, N.J.: Erlbaum Press.

Stokoe, W., D. Casterline, and C. Croneberg. 1965. *A Dictionary of American Sign Language*. Silver Spring, Md.: Linstok Press.

Studdert-Kennedy, M., and H. Lane. 1980. "Clues from the differences between signed and spoken language," in *Signed and Spoken Language: Biological Constraints on Linguistic Form*, U. Bellugi and M. Studdert-Kennedy, eds. Weinham and Deerfield Beach, Fla.: Verlag Chemie, 29–39.

Stungis, J. 1981. "Identification and discrimination of handshape in American Sign Language." *Perception & Psychophysics* 29(3):261–276.

Supalla, T. 1982. "Structure and acquisition of verbs of motion and location in American Sign Language." Ph.D. dissertation, Psychology Department, University of California, San Diego.

Supalla, T. 1985. "The classifier system in ASL," in *Noun Classification and Categorization*, C. Craig ed. Philadelphia, Penn.: Benjamin North America.

Supalla, T., and E. Newport. 1978. "How many seats in a chair? The derivation of nouns and verbs in American Sign Language," in *Understanding Language through Sign Language Research*, P. Siple, ed. New York: Academic Press, 91–132.

Tureen, L., E. Smolik, and J. Tritt. 1951. "Aphasia in a deaf mute." *Neurology* 1:237–244.

Underwood, J., and C. Paulson. 1981. "Aphasia and congenital deafness: A case study." *Brain and Language* 12:285–291.

Vaid, J., U. Bellugi, and H. Poizner. 1985. "Hand dominance in a visual-gestural language." La Jolla, Calif.: The Salk Institute. Unpublished.

Varney, N., and A. L. Benton. 1978. *Pantomime Recognition Test*. Iowa City: Benton Laboratory of Neuropsychology, University of Iowa Hospitals.

Virostek, S., and J. Cutting. 1979. "Asymmetries for Ameslan handshapes and other forms in signs and nonsigners." *Perception & Psychophysics* 26:505–508.

Warrington, E., M. James, and M. Kinsbourne. 1966. "Drawing disability in relation to laterality of cerebral lesion." *Brain* 89:53–82.

Wechsler, D. 1981. *Wechsler Adult Intelligence Scale—Revised*. New York: Psychological Corporation.

Wilbur, R., E. S. Klima, and U. Bellugi. 1983. "Roots: The search for origins of signs in ASL," in *The Parasession on the Interplay of Phonology, Morphology and Syntax*, J. Richardson, M. Marks, and A. Chukerman, eds. Chicago: Chicago Linguistics Society, 314–336.

Zaidel, E. 1977. "Lexical organization of the right hemisphere," in *Cerebral Correlates of Conscious Experience*, P. Buser and A. Rougeul-Busser, eds. Amsterdam: Elsevier, 177–197.

Zurif, E. B. 1980. "Language mechanisms: A neuropsychological perspective." *American Scientist* 68:305–311.

Index